CORAL

AND

BRASS

GENERAL HOLLAND M. SMITH, U.S.M.C.

From a painting by Commander Albert K. Murray, U.S.N.R.

CORAL

AND

BRASS

BY

HOLLAND M. SMITH
General, U. S. Marine Corps (Ret.)
AND
PERCY FINCH

NEW YORK
CHARLES SCRIBNER'S SONS
1949

To the Men and Women of the
United States Marine Corps,
both Living and Dead,
And to Those Who are to Come

FOREWORD

THE AIM OF THIS BOOK is twofold: first, that due credit be given to a gallant body of men, the United States Marine Corps, who in their path across the Pacific were faithful to their traditions and to their country; second, to point out the errors that were committed in World War II in such a manner that they will not be repeated in World War III—God forbid.

This is a personalized account of over forty years in the service of my country, culminating in the greatest war in our history. I never kept a diary. I had no official historian at my elbow recording in detail the battles I fought. I was too busy fighting those battles to set down anything in chronological form. Therefore, I find myself largely relying on my memory to compile the story of those forty years. If I have erred in facts, it is due to the momentous times through which I have lived and served.

I bear no malice toward any man or any Service. Any criticism in this book is made only for constructive purposes in the light of national defense needs. I am sure that a grateful country will not forget the magnificent efforts made by the Marines in the Pacific for the successful prosecution of the war against Japan.

I fully realize that all branches of the Marine Corps and the other Services that helped us are not mentioned in the brief compass of this book. But I wish here to pay tribute to those I may have omitted—the Marine Women Reserves, the commanders of the small craft in the Pacific who got us ashore and supplied us, the Medical Service who cared for our wounded, the Seabees who never let us down, and those units of the Army who fought alongside of us.

I am grateful to the many friends, in and out of the Service, who inspired and helped me write this book. Lieutenant Colonel C. Robert Payne, USMCR, who served on my staff, suggested the title. Among those who helped to fill it were Andrew Higgins, Robert Sherrod, Mac Asbill, Jr., my former aide, Vice Admiral Charles A. Lockwood, Jr., who assisted me in the preparation of the submarine chapter, and my faithful orderly, Platoon Sergeant William L. Bradley.

I also had the assistance of Percy Finch as my collaborator. Finch, a veteran war correspondent, came to the Pacific with a long record from other wars, and by accompanying me on my major operations, he followed the Central Pacific drive which I had the honor to command.

HOLLAND M. SMITH.

INTRODUCTION

THIS IS A STORY ABOUT A MAN, a Corps, and a war. The accomplishments of the man and his Corps profoundly influenced the outcome of the war.

The man, of course, is Holland Smith, who, although he was in the public eye continuously throughout the late war, is actually little known to the average reader of this book. I say little known because to most of them he is the nickname "Howlin' Mad" or a tough General who got results at the expense of human life, or perhaps just a typical Marine. None of these newspaper characterizations portray the man. Nor am I so presumptuous as to claim either the knowledge or the ability to transmit to those who do not know him the essence of Holland Smith. For over two years, however, I was privileged, as his aide, to know him as intimately as any man ever did. Perhaps I can explain some of the aspects of the man which would otherwise be lost in the turmoil of this book.

On the surface, of course, he is a famous Marine whose successes against the Japanese enemy are legendary. Recipient of four Distinguished Service Medals, he initiated and supervised the training of our soldiers and Marines in the art of amphibious warfare and then led them across the Pacific in one of the most phenomenal military advances of all times. On many occasions, as the reader will see, he was forced to fight in order to be allowed to fight.

Beneath the surface a different pattern appears. Like that of most men General Smith's personality is complicated. Its many facets are presented in this book, but some of them may be overlooked by the reader whose attention is drawn from the man to the many conflicts in which he was embroiled. Perhaps few who lay down this book will realize that it was written by a man whose tenderness was scarcely exceeded by his courage. Few will know that he spent hours during this war in hospital wards imparting to the wounded and often the dying some of the courage with which he was possessed. I have seen him reprimand a Marine officer as severely for failing to demonstrate warmth, understanding and appreciation to a wounded veteran on whom he was bestowing the Purple Heart as he often did a Naval officer for attempting to usurp the functions of the landing force commander.

On the eve of every Pacific battle in which he participated I have heard him say with unutterable sadness but unflinching courage, and with profound regret that the objective required the sacrifice, "There will be a lot of dead Marines on that beach tomorrow." Much of his greatness lay in his ability to lead so courageously when he felt so deeply.

Few will know that he often threw the protective cloak of his authority and position around an erring subordinate whom he knew to be capable of rising above his mistakes. Yet he always tempered justice with mercy in dealing with his subordinates, even when reason alone indicated that the sword of justice should fall. Small wonder that every enlisted man and officer who was ever closely associated with Holland Smith felt the most profound admiration, loyalty and devotion toward his General.

Perhaps none who did not see the drama enacted will realize that the vehemence with which he fought his equals and superiors in the chain of command was manufactured by a man who sought to protect his corps and vindicate his convictions at the expense of his own reputation and position. Often during the hectic months in the Pacific I have heard him say, "No one can cast strictures upon my Marines and get away with it." No one ever did. Herein lies the genesis of the inter-service conflicts for which he has become famous. Always his battle was directed toward securing for a small and oft neglected Corps the dignity and recognition which it so richly deserves. Often a fight was necessary, and when it was, Holland Smith was ever available.

First, last and always he is a Marine. His love for and loyalty to his Corps are born of a conviction that the Marine Corps is the finest body of fighting men on earth. His conviction is shared by every other Marine, but few have fought for it as he did. This book is, in part, a continuation of that fight. The glorification which the reader will find herein is a glorification of the Marine Corps, not of Holland Smith.

The other purpose of the book, and perhaps the principal one, is to criticize constructively many of the things which were done during the war and which the writer thinks could have been done better or should have been left undone. This criticism is as frank as the man from which it comes. Many, perhaps, who feel its sting will grow bitter and resentful. It was not written for them. It is directed at those who some day may profit from lessons learned the hard way. If the reader would read this book in the spirit in which it was written, let him scrutinize carefully the facts which support the contentions herein advanced and decide for himself whether those contentions have merit. Let the mothers who learn that their sons were lost through some fault of preparation or organization or planning glean strength from the knowledge that someone has the courage to expose these faults in the hope that those to whom future decisions will be intrusted shall not fall prey to them again.

MAC ASBILL, JR.

SMITH, HOLLAND MCTYEIRE, and FINCH, PERCY. Coral and brass. 289p $3 Scribner

940.542 World war, 1939-1945—Pacific ocean. World war, 1939-1945—Personal narratives, American. U.S. Marine corps   49-7218

Memoirs of the part played by the Marines in the Pacific as set down by their commanding officer along with his side of several controversial questions concerning the conduct of the war. Index.

Booklist 45:169; 190   Ja 15 '49; F 1 '49
Canadian Forum 29:96 Jl '49 90w
Reviewed by Keith Wheeler
Chicago Sun Ja 18 '49 600w

'Swashbuckling, tender, rollicking, reverent, acrimonious, sentimental—its shifting moods come crashing through virile, colorful, stormy

+ Library J 74:57 Ja 1 '49 130w
Nation 168:137 Ja 29 '49 90w

"The celebrated General Holland M. ('Howlin' Mad') Smith returned from the Pacific in mid-1945 conscious, as he tells us, of duty well done. Whether he has done his duty, alike by his country and his own reputation, equally well in contributing this rambunctious, explosive memoir to the history of the Pacific war and the flames of inter-service jealousy is, perhaps, another question." Walter Millis
  N Y Herald Tribune Wkly Bk R p3 Ja 16 '49 1300w

"It will probably be a surprise to most people to learn that Holland M. Smith is a quiet-mannered, long-headed man, who was placed in charge of Marine forces during the Central Pacific drive because of his long study of amphibious war and his capacity for intricate strategic planning. He is forthright, but not notably more so than other officers of a service whose tradition is hard-hitting—whether with verbs or violence. It is accordingly somewhat unfortunate that, as a literary amanuensis Mr. Finch has chosen to emphasize the extrovert, even the controversial, features of a career that really included more thinking than action." Fletcher Pratt
  N Y Times p5 Ja 16 '49 800w
  New Yorker 24:94 F 5 '49 160w
Reviewed by Mike Capraro
  San Francisco Chronicle p20 Ja 30 '49 650w

"This book is one man's story, and that man tells it in his own way. His literary weapon bears no resemblance to that favorite of the Marines, the high-precision rifle. General Smith uses a shotgun, and with fine impartiality; no sooner has he let go a blast at the Army than he gives the Navy the other barrel. Yet it would be inaccurate to say that he is anti-anything; Holland Smith is simply pro-Marine. . . Rambling, repetition, and sloppy editing mar the literary performance; yet the general's collaborator, Percy Finch, has succeeded in conveying the flavor and personality of the man." F. O. Hough
  + — Sat R of Lit 32:19 Ja 22 '49 750w

CHAPTER I

~~~~~~

S AN FRANCISCO fog smelled good when I stepped off the plane at Hamilton Field early on that gray morning of July 5, 1945, after almost two years of blistering heat and blinding sun in the Pacific: two years of corroding, soul-destroying war. The first thing I did when the crewmen swung open the cabin door was to take a deep gulp of cold, moist air. Only twelve hours before I had left behind the roaring surf of Waikiki Beach and the fragrant green valleys of Hawaii. Beyond this deceptive peace lay the road to Tokyo—the chain of blasted coral islands won from Japan at such bitter cost in young American lives.

The City not only smelled good but looked good that morning. I knew that under the fog lay the Golden Gate, the symbol of home to every American in the Pacific, the Bay Bridges, the Ferry Building, Market Street, the cable cars, Nob Hill, smart women wearing fur coats in July as they bought nosegays at corner stands; all the rich panorama of a warm-hearted city typifying the America we were fighting for.

During the war, I had passed through San Francisco several times on my way to Washington to confer with General Alexander A. Vandegrift, Commandant of the United States Marine Corps, but this time I was back to stay. I felt that for me, a Marine, the war was over and, perhaps alone in this conviction, I also felt that the war was over in the Pacific.

The Fleet Marine Force, Pacific, of which I had been Commanding General until two days before, had carried the Stars and Stripes from Pearl Harbor to Iwo Jima and Okinawa and was kicking open Japan's front door. I had come home with the consciousness of duty well done: the only worth while reward to a man who serves his country.

San Francisco was a triumphant homecoming in my mind only. Wartime security still veiled all military movements and not even my wife knew I was arriving. As the pilot set down my converted B-24 Liberator on the field and taxied up the runway among hundreds of other planes, my arrival was merely a detail of daily routine at this busy Army terminal.

Reluctantly, I had discarded the faded Marine green utility suit I had worn all over the Pacific in favor of tropical worsteds. My "dungarees" had been through the wash half a dozen times and weren't presentable. As the Japanese (and the baffled war correspondents) discovered, you can't tell a Pfc from a General in this working outfit, and that's exactly why it was adopted. No amount of pressing will transform our utility clothing into any semblance of a well-tailored uniform. But that morning I was particularly proud of my "dungarees" and regretted I wasn't wearing them. What was good enough for Iwo Jima was good enough for San Francisco.

Major General Julian C. Smith, of the Department of the Pacific, was waiting at the terminal, surprised by our quick trip of 12 hours and 20 minutes from Honolulu. I had known Julian Smith for many years. He was my chief of staff in the Caribbean, my second in command in the Pacific, and he commanded the Second Marine Division at Tarawa. Captain Mac Asbill, Jr., my aide, and Platoon Sergeant William L. Bradley, who had been with me all through the Pacific campaign, were with me on the plane. Outside of General Smith, the "welcome committee" was made up of a ground crew and they weren't too impressed.

Bradley told me later he heard one of the men remark, "A Marine? That old buzzard looks pretty ancient for a Marine. He'd sure have to hit the beach in a wheel chair!"

He was correct in one respect. I was getting pretty ancient. After forty years in the Marine Corps, I was within a year of the retirement age, sixty-four. At my own request, I had been relieved as Commanding General of the Fleet Marine Force and my successor, Lieutenant General Roy S. Geiger, had been named. I was ordered to take charge of the Marine Training and Replacement Command at Camp Pendleton, California.

My reasons for seeking relief were twofold. The difference between success and failure in the Marine Corps is the opportunity to show ability and since opportunity is so often linked with higher command, I felt I should not stand in the way of promotion. Furthermore, I knew that future amphibious operations in the Pacific, due to the size of command, would be directed by Army officers. It never has been the policy of the War Department to permit a Marine to command an American army and I had no desire to settle down as an administrative officer at a desk in Pearl Harbor.

At his headquarters in Manila, General Douglas MacArthur, Supreme Commander-in-Chief, was working on plans for the grand assault on the home islands of Japan. These plans involved two landings at intervals of several months. OLYMPIC, the code name given the first phase of the operation, provided for a landing on the southern coast of Kyushu, Japan's southernmost island, in November, 1945. Nagasaki, target of the second atomic bomb, is the principal city on Kyushu. CORONET, the second phase, involved a landing on Honshu, the main island, in February, 1946.

These landings would be joint Army, Navy and Marine operations under General MacArthur. The Fleet Marine Force, Pacific, which I had trained and commanded, was to spearhead both assaults, and plans entailed employment of the largest force of Marines ever used. From two divisions at the time of the attack on Pearl Harbor, the Corps had expanded to six divisions with all ancillary troops, organized into two amphibious corps, the V and the III, and sizable contingents of these two corps had proved their mettle all over the Pacific. Marine Corps aviation had also expanded and by August, 1945, the Fleet Marine Force Air had reached a top total of 78 tactical squadrons.

The V Amphibious Corps, consisting of the Second, Third and Fifth Divisions and including veterans of Tarawa, Bougainville, Kwajalein, Guam, Saipan, Tinian and Iwo Jima, was earmarked for Kyushu. The III, consisting of the First, Fourth and

3

Sixth Divisions of Guadalcanal, Saipan, Iwo Jima and Okinawa fame, was to land on Honshu at the nearest point to Tokyo.

General MacArthur insisted that a large scale invasion approximating the magnitude of the European invasion was necessary to reduce Japan. The Joint Chiefs of Staff in Washington and our Allies were of the same opinion and all plans were based upon this strategical assumption. But despite these grandiose preparations I refused to believe that we would have to fight our way into the country. Japan was licked and it was only a matter of a very short time before the enemy would throw in the sponge. In fact, I was so sure that I told San Francisco newspapermen the war would be over by September 1, 1945.

I met reporters at a press conference at the St. Francis Hotel on the day of my arrival and I set that date in answer to a direct question. I don't claim any gift of prophecy and I never gazed into a crystal ball but I did know the war was due to end soon. My knowledge was founded on the cold facts as I saw them.

Some of the reporters at the conference smiled respectfully. Several looked dubious and one intimated that he had heard the same line from the big brass before, including Admiral William F. Halsey's assertion in 1942 that we would be in Tokyo by the end of 1943. Looking over the newspapers the morning after the conference, I noted one skeptical journal ignored my prediction completely.

The interview was given national prominence and from New York one of my war correspondent friends, a man of exceptional discernment and shrewdness, telegraphed expressing profound disagreement. His telegram offered:

THREE BETS OF FIVE DOLLARS EACH: FIRST, JAPAN WILL NOT QUIT FIGHTING UNTIL WE HAVE KILLED AT LEAST FIVE MILLION OF THEIR SOLDIERS: SECOND, NO AMOUNT OF BOMBING WILL INDUCE JAPAN TO SURRENDER: THIRD, JAPAN CANNOT BE BEATEN WITHOUT INVASION.

He lost all three bets and paid up. Six weeks after the press conference in San Francisco my prediction was borne out. The war ended on August 14, when Japan surrendered uncondition-

4

ally, and so far as the Marine invasion was concerned the Second Division did land at Nagasaki and the Fifth Division at Sasebo but only as temporary occupation forces until Army garrison troops could be organized.

Since that interview I've been asked the same questions dozens of times: How did you know the war would be over so soon? Why did you differ with military experts who predicted another year of fighting and a costly landing against a fanatical enemy resisting every yard and dying to the last man? Was it because you knew about the atomic bomb that was to be dropped on Hiroshima and Nagasaki?

Everyone inferred that as Commanding General of the Fleet Marine Force I must have been informed about the bomb, that I must have known the secret of the Manhattan Engineering project and the terrible weapon it was evolving for use against Japan.

To such questions I can reply quite honestly: No. The atom bomb was kept a complete secret from me. I never heard of it until I read in the papers here in the United States that the first bomb had been dropped on Japan at Hiroshima.

Then how did I know? The question persists. I knew because the back of Japan's resistance had been broken. Japan was licked when the Marines captured Saipan. Iwo Jima and Okinawa were the knockout blows. The atom bomb did not win the war; it only completed the job already done and hastened surrender. From conversations with Japanese officers taken prisoner at Saipan and Iwo, I was convinced that Japan was exhausted. The losses suffered during our amphibious offensive and the pressure we were able to bring to bear on her from naval and air bases captured in the Marine drive across the Pacific had knocked Japan to her knees.

Surface, submarine and air action had destroyed the Japanese Combined Fleet, wrecked her air force and sunk her merchant marine. She was crippled by a grave shortage of war materials and was denied by the U. S. Navy the use of rubber, oil and rice from the Netherlands East Indies, Borneo, Burma and other parts of her looted empire. Raids by vast fleets of B-29's and

5

other craft had smashed her war potential and razed entire industrial areas. It was impossible for her to hold out any longer.

The United States Marine Corps played a major part in the victory over Japan. Before the tumult and the shouting dies among a complacent, short-memoried people, who take so much for granted, let me have the honor of describing the Marine contribution to victory.

When I commanded the landing forces at the sixth of our prewar amphibious exercises on the island of Culebra, off Puerto Rico, in the spring of 1940, the strength of the Marine Corps was 1,410 officers and 25,070 enlisted men; equipment included five tanks you could kick your foot through. The total Marine strength during World War II was 599,693, of which 528,479, or nearly 90 percent, served abroad. Extensive and diversified armament included all the latest weapons, amphibious tanks and tractors and thousands of landing craft, all types of mechanized equipment, improved artillery, rockets and flame throwers, as well as carrier-based and shore-based air units that made the Marines the best equipped troops in the world.

The Corps mounted two separate offensives, distinctive in character and objective, and fought on different terrain. The first, launched in the South Pacific with landings in the Solomons Islands in August, 1942, pointed north toward the Philippines. The second started in the Gilbert Islands in the Central Pacific in November, 1943, and struck west.

In the South Pacific, the operation was at first a holding move to check the Japanese advance through the Solomons and South Pacific islands to Australia. It involved treacherous jungle fighting, in which large forces could not be employed. Here was a case of individual survival, that brought out the best qualities of the Marine. Once the long Japanese flank was turned at Guadalcanal and the southern march halted, the operation in that theater became offensive. One by one, Japan's bases in those tropical, mountainous and densely vegetated islands were captured or bypassed, and American forces advanced 3,000 miles up the New Guinea-Netherlands East Indies axis for the reconquest of the Philippines.

In the Central Pacific, where I commanded the V Amphibious Corps and later the Fleet Marine Force, the operation was offensive from the very beginning. It was here that the amphibious doctrine I had preached for years, and had made the basis of Marine training since we realized the inevitability of the Pacific war, was fully justified.

The Central Pacific campaign had as its objective the capture of a number of fortified points in the Japanese mandated atolls and the home islands, stretching from the Gilberts to the Volcano and Ryukyu Islands, the outer and inner defenses of Japan. In such a campaign among small, low lying coral islands, there could be neither guile nor surprise and few tactical advantages could be exploited. The only type of warfare possible was plain and open assault on strongly fortified positions which, according to a theory propounded before World War II, enjoyed unassailable superiority because the strength of modern defensive weapons was considered too decisive to permit a successful assault from the sea.

The experience of the British in their ill-fated Dardanelles campaign in 1916 was quoted as textbook authority by supporters of this school. The Turks prevented the British seizure of Gallipoli Peninsula and, it was argued, the Japanese would be equally successful in resisting us.

But in the twenty-five years between Gallipoli and Guadalcanal, the Marines had developed amphibious warfare to a point where it became a primary offensive tactic, not only in the Pacific but in every other theater where a major force had to land on a hostile and defended shore. In the Central Pacific, the Marines landed where they were assigned and captured every objective, no matter how strongly it was held.

The relentless Marine drive across the Pacific from Tarawa to Iwo Jima and Okinawa was the greatest operation of its kind in recorded history. There is nothing to compare with it in magnitude, extent and distance covered.

Napoleon in 1812 marched his men to Moscow, 1,530 miles from Paris, but actually the staging base for the *Grande Armée* was the Niemen River in Poland, making his advance only 550 miles. Genghis Khan in the 13th Century more nearly approached the Marine performance in mobility. The Khan's horde advanced 4,000 miles from the shores of Lake Baikal in Mongolia on its conquest of Central Asia, North India and Eastern Europe, reaching the banks of the Dnieper River in Armenia and almost touching the shores of the Mediterranean.

Both these military movements collapsed through clearly discernible causes. Napoleon, like Hitler, was defeated by the Russian winter, a stubborn Russian army and what we today would call poor logistics. The Mongol conquest disintegrated when the organizing brain behind this vast enterprise disappeared with the death of Genghis Khan.

Consider the record of the Marines in the Central Pacific. First and foremost, the campaign was successful. In their advance from Tarawa to Okinawa, via Kwajalein, Saipan, Guam, the Palaus and Iwo Jima, they moved 8000 miles. This is more than twice the distance from New York to San Francisco. Taking it another way, if the Marines had started in Seattle and travelled south, they would have overshot Buenos Aires by a thousand miles.

Actually, the distance covered by the Marines was far greater. Each operation necessitated the assembly of an assault force at a base thousands of miles from the objective, its transport to the scene of the operation and its return to base. This factor of distance illustrates the fundamental difference between the war in Europe and the war in the Pacific. After the capture of each Central Pacific island the Marines had to return to bases like the Hawaiian Islands to rehabilitate and prepare for the next operation. Troops fighting in Europe did not have to come back to New York after each operation. The British Isles, the major staging area for the European invasion, was no farther from the French coast than 100 miles, the widest point in the English Channel.

As a result, the Marines became the most travelled troops the world has ever known. Take the Kwajalein operation as an example. This involved a 5,000-mile round trip between Pearl Harbor and the Marshall Islands. Iwo Jima, only a few hundred miles off the coast of Japan, necessitated a 7,000-mile round trip, an incredible distance considering the huge amount of equipment and supplies we had to transport to the black lava island.

At first we had no convenient nearby bases in the Pacific. As we advanced, we annexed bases nearer our objectives, but the Tarawa operation actually was staged on the other side of the world, in New Zealand. On D-Day in Normandy, Army troops had been in landing boats from 24 to 48 hours before they reached the beaches. Marines frequently travelled five or six weeks before they set eyes on their objective.

The closer you examine the Marine drive across the Pacific, the more magnificent it becomes as a military achievement. Between our first engagement at New Providence, in the Bahamas, in 1776, until the outbreak of World War II, the Marines made 180 landings in various parts of the world. During the war the Marine score in the Pacific was approximately one hundred successful landings. Never has there been such a succession of victories unmarred by a single defeat or even a setback—and God knows there were moments when the issue seemed in doubt, although never once did I lose confidence in our final success. By this string of victories, the Marines showed beyond question that they were capable of taking any objective assigned to them, however difficult, thus confounding all the defense-vs.-offense doctrines and upsetting military theory, especially among the Japanese, who believed their Pacific bases impregnable.

My Marines were the best fighting men in the world and I never hesitated to tell them so. I'm not going to hesitate now. They might die but they were unconquerable. The Japanese General Staff recognized this fact. Their own troops, made fanatical by semi-divine indoctrination and brutally trained, were taught to live and die like animals. They were tough. But my Marines were tougher.

One of the highest tributes ever paid to the Marines came from the enemy, from Major Yoshida, a Japanese staff officer captured at Saipan. Yoshida was the man who wrote the plan for the final desperate *banzai* attack on Saipan. He was handsome by Oriental standards, intellectual and a graduate of the

9

Army staff school. He surrendered to us because he admitted frankly Japan had lost the war and he wanted to go home when peace came and live with his family. Immortalization at Yasakuni Shrine had no appeal for him.

"The Japanese can never hope to defeat a nation that produces soldiers like your Marines," he told our intelligence officers. "In the Japanese army, we revere the spirit of *Yamato Damashii,* which means the Spirit of Old Japan, and our soldiers will die for it. We have learned that the American Marine also reveres the spirit of his country and is just as willing to die as the Japanese soldier. Moreover, the Marine is a better soldier than the Japanese. His individuality is stronger, his training and fighting technique better. He has arms, ammunition and engineering equipment far superior to ours. Had I not believed this, I would not have surrendered."

This unsolicited tribute to the American Marine stirred me because the author was no ordinary buck-toothed Japanese officer. He was personal representative at Saipan of the Supreme General Staff in Tokyo and belonged to a different military category than Lieutenant General Saito, commanding general of all the Japanese forces on the island.

Yoshida's name was mentioned frequently in Japanese dispatches we seized. His tribute to the Marine as a fighting man so moved me that I almost relented and told him something about his own affairs that he did not know. One intercepted dispatch announced that Tokyo had promoted him to Lieutenant Colonel but I finally decided to keep the news to myself since the war was over for him.

Coming from a representative of the Japanese high command, Yoshida's tribute carried weight. Who should know better the qualities of the Marine than the man fighting him? The Japanese General Staff had only to count their losses in men and bases to make the proper assessment of the Marines.

Unfortunately, the American high command occasionally allowed recognition of Marine efforts to get lost in headquarters files. Few Pacific battles were fought without Marine support. Marines participated in General MacArthur's recapture of the

Philippines. The bulk of the Corps Artillery of the V Amphibious Corps, commanded by Brigadier General Thomas E. Bourke, and the Air Liaison Sections of two Marine Assault Signal Companies were part of the assault force at Leyte. Later, four Marine fighter squadrons operating from Tacloban airfield helped provide close air support. A Marine night fighter squadron, urgently requested by General George C. Kenney, commanding the Far Eastern Army Air Force, to replace slower, outranged Army night fighters, also operated from Tacloban. Ultimately, two full Marine Air Groups provided support for the Army in this operation. All performed their duties with bravery and distinction, according to independent reports.

You can search MacArthur's communiques describing the Philippines fighting and you will be unable to find a single reference to the Marines. The average American can be excused for believing the Philippines exclusively an Army show. I wager that not one newspaper reader in a thousand knows there were Marines at Leyte and Luzon unless he had a Marine in the family who was there. Granted that Marine numbers were small in comparison with the Army, nevertheless, the Marines were there when the Philippines were recaptured. Seventeen squadrons of Marine planes were employed in the Philippines—and that's quite a few planes to cloak in anonymity.

I met one of our young Marines who was being flown back from Leyte. He was in great pain but it was not the physical suffering that worried him. "I don't mind losing a leg, sir," he told me bitterly, "but at least Doug might have mentioned that Marines were there!"

Being omitted from MacArthur's communiques was no new experience for Marines. In 1941 and 1942, during the heroic and tragic defense of Bataan and Corregidor, although MacArthur's command included the veteran 4th Marines, evacuated from China in the nick of time, the public was kept in ignorance of their presence. After a period of the MacArthur silent treatment, the Navy Department became somewhat nettled to read of the exploits and presence of virtually every Army and Philippine unit, while seeing nothing of the Marine regiment on Corregidor.

11

Finally, after tactful representations had fallen on deaf ears, the Navy in Washington began issuing its own communiques in simple justice to the Marines who were silently sharing the perils and privations of Bataan and Corregidor beside much-publicized Army comrades.

Even after this inter-Service brush—which never should have happened—MacArthur had his innings again: the Marine regiment was absent from the General's list of units awarded the Army's Distinguished Unit Citation. Since this list was otherwise as inclusive as God's forgiveness, it came as a relief to me and to most Marines that General Jonathan M. ("Skinny") Wainwright, noted for his fairness and generosity, rectified this omission after MacArthur departed for Australia and left him to continue the forlorn defense of the Philippines.

A strange sidelight on the amorphous American command in the Pacific during World War II was the fact that MacArthur and I never met. By fate or circumstance, our paths never crossed during the war or before the war. We both were leaders of victorious troops moving toward the same goal but we were total strangers. My superior was Fleet Admiral Chester W. Nimitz, CINCPAC (Commander-in-Chief, Pacific) and CINCPOA (Commander-in-Chief, Pacific Ocean Areas). Our commands never overlapped and the first time more than two Army divisions were employed jointly with Marines, command went to the Army. This was at Okinawa.

There have been widespread charges that the Marines resented serving under Army leadership. Nothing is farther from the truth. As Lieutenant General Roy S. Geiger told the Senate Military Affairs Committee on December 7, 1945:

In our 170 years we [the Marine Corps] have never acquired the view that to support another arm or branch in the performance of a service to the country was to suffer either an indignity or a loss of prestige.

I was not invited to attend the surrender ceremony on the deck of the USS Missouri in Tokyo Bay on September 1, 1945. This was a great personal disappointment after fighting all those weary miles from Tarawa. However, the Marines are a team, not a collection of individuals, and our team was ably represented by General Geiger, who succeeded me as Commanding General of the Fleet Marine Force.

From our entry into the war until the Japanese surrender, nearly every major offensive launched by the United States was initiated by an amphibious assault. This specialized form of operation put Army troops ashore in North Africa, Sicily, Normandy, the Philippines and the Aleutians, and penetrated Japan's powerful defense perimeter running from the Aleutians almost to Australia. This type of warfare represented a unique achievement of the Marine Corps, although it later was adopted by the Army. Perfected amphibious warfare was a gift of the Marines to the Army and was essential in solving the new problems World War II brought in its train.

The success of its modern application dates back to the early 1920's. While most of the world's military leaders were studying and analyzing World War I, just ended, and were still thinking in terms of trench fighting and great continental wars of position, the Marines were applying themselves to the problems of assaulting fortified beaches. Between Gallipoli and Guadalcanal, the Marines developed the doctrine, organization, tactics and equipment necessary to wage this difficult and complex warfare because we knew it was the answer to the conditions future wars would create.

The doctrine also led to the reorganization of the Marine Corps and from this forward thinking emerged the Fleet Marine Force, a revolutionary offensive unit.

In the years before the war we made amphibious technique the keynote of all Marine training. In my opinion, this was the most significant development in the art of war ever conceived and all our maneuvers took the form of simulated landings on heavily defended beaches, attacking the impossible positions that the old school of military opinion, drawing on World War I and earlier conflicts for analogies, declared would not yield to assault.

We laid the foundation for our belief in maneuvers and

proved our doctrine sound in combat. Marines trained in this type of warfare could assault and capture positions which were deemed impregnable. It sounded startling but it was true. Given adequate naval and air support, they could go ashore on any beach and take any objective. I could have landed them in the mouth of hell if the Joint Chiefs of Staff had picked that target. (Iwo Jima was a fair substitute.) Success was a question of proper planning and co-ordination. The training and the spirit were there. Tested in actual combat on the tough road from Guadalcanal to Tokyo, the doctrine stood firm. True, we progressed by trial and error—many errors in some cases—but each error was converted into a lesson applied to the next operation. The Marines were committed to a novel principle of war, the principle of doing the impossible well. In fact the way they captured some of the most heavily fortified positions in the world made amphibious warfare appear easy.

Back home, when people picked up the paper to read of another Marine landing, they accepted victory as the natural corollary and paid no further attention beyond scanning developments. In the public mind, victory became merely a question of *when*, not *how*, and the public lost sight of the difficulties we had to overcome. The deceptive ease with which we gained our victories, due to a combination of training, morale and equipment all functioning like parts of a perfectly adjusted machine, even blurred the Navy perspective and made it increasingly difficult for us to obtain the amount of naval gunfire necessary to insure the success of our landings.

In this connection, the reader must realize how essential to a landing is the prior naval and air bombardment of enemy positions, which destroys defenses and softens up opposition before the assault waves hit the beach. The stronger the defenses the heavier, more prolonged and more effective should be the bombardment, over periods as short as three days and as long as ten days. During the war our old battleships, including some of the revitalized ghosts of Pearl Harbor, were invaluable in this work. They were able to stand close inshore and use their heavy armament with terrific effect.

The Navy reaction to our successful landings was to wonder if they were giving us too much gunfire and prejudicing their primary mission, which was to protect us against possible Japanese naval action. Perhaps, the Navy reasoned, the Marines could get along with less gunfire. As if a few rounds of ammunition mattered when it was a question of reducing casualties! The way I have always reckoned, shells are cheaper than lives. One of my biggest and most hopeless fights with Admiral Nimitz and with almost every other Admiral associated with me on an operation, was to get them to see my viewpoint on naval gunfire.

At Iwo Jima, I asked for ten days' bombardment and had to compromise on only three days' fire to prepare for the Marine landing on perhaps the strongest fortified island in the world, where every yard of volcanic terrain was covered by Japanese guns. The Navy idea of battle economy often reached unbelievable proportions.

The big colored map in Admiral Nimitz's planning room at Pearl Harbor showed our advance toward Japan but he could not have recorded that progress unless the Marines had taken those islands for him. The Marines made it possible and instead of enjoying easy victories, as they appeared to the superficial observer, the battles were bloody and hard fought.

I have been blamed for the relatively high casualties suffered by the Marines under my command in the Central Pacific. I have been called "butcher," "cold blooded murderer" and "indiscriminate waster of human life." One mother wrote Secretary of the Navy James Forrestal (now Defense Secretary) during the Iwo Jima operation as follows: "Please, for God's sake, stop sending our finest youth to be murdered on places like Iwo Jima. Why can't objectives be accomplished some other way?" To which the Secretary replied: "There is no short or easy way."

This is not an attempt to excuse the Marine casualties. To do so would insult the memory of the brave men who died so willingly for their country. The total U. S. Marine Corps casualties from December 7, 1941, to August 31, 1945, in all theaters, including the Central Pacific, were 89,585. Excluding wounded, these are the details:

Killed in action	15,130
Died of wounds received in action	3,392
Missing, presumed dead	901
Total	**19,423**

In addition, 106 officers and 1,841 enlisted men were taken prisoners of war. These included the 4th Marines in China and the Philippines; survivors of the Marine detachment aboard the USS Houston sunk off Java; personnel of the Marine barracks at Guam and the Marine detachment commanded by Colonel James Devereux, responsible for the heroic defense of Wake Island, nearly all captured in the early days of the war when the Japanese overran the Pacific.

Compared with Army casualties the Marine percentage was higher. However, statistical comparisons fail to give the complete picture. The proportionately higher Marine ratio is accounted for by these facts:

1. A larger percentage of Marines served overseas. (Marines 90 percent, Army 70 percent.)
2. The Marines were fighting a different type of war.
3. The Marines were assaulting more difficult objectives.

Former Secretary of War Henry L. Stimson recently stated: "Troop transport and assault landings are traditionally the most difficult and most dangerous of all military operations." Every time the Marines landed it was a Normandy on a smaller but more intense scale. In two wars I have fought Germans and Japanese. Throw a hand grenade into a German pillbox and they come out with hands reaching for the sky and shouting "Kamerad!" Throw a hand grenade into a Japanese pillbox and they throw it right back at you.

It has been said that the Army is long on strategy and short on tactics while in the Marine Corps we are short on strategy and long on tactics. Perhaps so; but one point must not be overlooked, particularly in any comparative assessment of the Pacific war. Our two converging drives on Tokyo had two distinctly different command set-ups. MacArthur was in supreme command in his own theater and could pick his own targets. He picked the easiest. Mine were picked for me by the Joint Chiefs of Staff in Washington, who indicated the objectives and left me the task of capturing them.

I have no desire to belittle the Army's contribution to our common victory but in defense of the Marines I must put on record the fact that when the Army had a difficult amphibious objective at Okinawa, the operation took three times as long as any Marine operation with the exception of Guadalcanal. When the First and Sixth Marine Divisions finally were thrown in, momentum was added. Total casualties were higher at Okinawa than in any Marine operation, although the Army enjoyed the initial advantage of landing unopposed. My Pacific experience was that the first half mile from the beach took the heaviest toll in lives.

Since I first joined the Marines, I have advocated aggressiveness in the field and constant offensive action. Hit quickly, hit hard and keep right on hitting. Give the enemy no rest, no opportunity to consolidate his forces and hit back at you. This is the shortest road to victory in the type of island war the Marines had to fight and is most economical of lives in the long run.

In the words of Frederick the Great, "By making your battle short, you will deprive it of time, so to speak, to rob you of men. The soldier who is led by you in this manner will gain confidence in you and expose himself gladly to all danger."

Marines were trained along these lines for their job in the Pacific and they responded to leadership of officers indoctrinated in the principle of short, lively, intense campaigns. We took the Pacific islands the only possible way. Any other method would have prolonged operations and cost more lives.

War is a costly undertaking and the Marines paid the bill. The Duke of Wellington once said, "Nothing except a battle lost can be so melancholy as a battle won." This is the summation I must make on the Pacific war: If the Marines had received better co-operation from the Navy our casualties would have been lower. More naval gunfire would have saved many lives. I had to beg for gunfire and I rarely received what the situation demanded. I had to fight not only for gunfire but for aviation, for the requisite number of staff officers to accompany me on operations and against Navy interference. The Navy transported us, landed us and protected us against Japanese naval and air attack. We could not have reached the islands without the Navy, but at that point their duties should have ended. Instead, they tried to continue running the show.

The Navy's mental arteriosclerosis made it hard for me in other ways. Procurement of equipment was a source of trouble. This difficulty dates back to long before the war but it was emphasized in operational planning. In 1939, when I was given command of the First Marine Brigade in the Caribbean, I concentrated on the amphibious aspect of training because it was obvious war was coming and therefore imperative that the Marines be ready. However, it was not simply a question of training men. Equally important were the development of equipment and weapons for use in amphibious warfare and the task of bludgeoning Washington into providing money and materiel.

It was a long and continuous fight to get what I wanted. I was constantly being slapped down by the Navy Department for what they dismissed as "grandiloquent representations." When I did convince the top Navy brass of the practical nature of my requirements, opposition took a different form. The new weapons I asked for suddenly presented insurmountable procurement or manufacturing difficulties. During this phase there was no immediate or overt opposition to my ideas. They were always well received but somewhere in the corporate mind of the naval oligarchy these ideas often vanished until I dragged them out again and got them on the planning table.

The ramp boat was typical. In China, the Japanese had been using ramp boats along the coast and up the shallow creeks for years. We did not possess a single boat of this type. Yet, without it, the Marines never could have landed on a Japanese island and the Army would have been crippled in Europe. To get the boat, we went straight to the builder, Andrew Higgins, discussed plans with him and he built the ramp boat while the Bureau of Ships was still dazed by the temerity of the suggestion.

With World War II in Europe spurring preparedness efforts, my private war for weapons and equipment began to bear fruit and in command of the First Brigade in the Caribbean I intensified Marine training for the amphibious task ahead since I was convinced the United States would join the battle against Fascism on two continents. If the Battle of Waterloo was won on the playing fields of Eton, the Japanese bases in the Pacific were captured on the beaches of the Caribbean, where the problems involved were worked out in Marine maneuvers.

Certain strategic Japanese islands were captured by plans drawn up as early as 1920—so sure were we of the course of history. On the beaches of Culebra, an island off the Puerto Rican coast which was the principal Marine training base, we superimposed maps of Japanese bases and made trial assaults which became reality a few years later. These dress rehearsals for the Pacific war were the most vivid I ever witnessed. I often remembered them against a background of smoking Japanese islands.

These Marine exercises were no secret from the Japanese. When we attacked Guam in 1944, I was convinced by the Japanese commander's disposition of his forces and the location of his defenses that the enemy had obtained a copy of our original plan for the recapture of Guam, rehearsed years before.

Unfortunately for the Japanese, the plan had been altered since it was first written. Originally we intended landing on the east coast of the island but this was changed to beaches on the west coast—north and south of Apra Harbor. Strong forces waited for us on the east coast, obviously misled by the discarded plan, and we went ashore on the west coast without too much opposition, although the main enemy strength was concentrated there. Typically, the Japanese military failed to take into consideration the possibility that our plan might have been altered in subsequent years.

A Japanese agent would have had no difficulty in obtaining the plan. Before the war we had a childish habit of broadcasting our military activities by publishing them in service journals available on the news stands, but we circumvented Japanese intelligence by neglecting to reveal that the original plan for Guam had been scrapped.

Marine operations in the Pacific underscored the nation's growing understanding of the functions of the Corps in relation to national defense. In prewar days, the Corps was popularly associated with the idea of an international police force. When missionaries were threatened in China or businessmen got into trouble in Central America, the cry went up, "Send for the Marines!" We were regarded as an international riot squad, instantly available to handle any disturbance involving Americans on the street corners of the world. In a larger sense, the dispatch of Marines to the Mediterranean, the new danger spot in the world picture, was another instance of this peacetime employment.

To be sure, this is a part of our duty and has taken us all over the globe, but it is a limitation of our basic program. The Marines always have been an integrated, well organized military unit, very advanced in tactical thought. Ten years before it started Marine Corps planners were forecasting the character of the Pacific campaign in World War II. That was a period when acceptance of the inevitability of World War II was just as unpopular as mention of World War III is today.

While we were envisaging World War II, we could not foresee the mental climate in which the war would be fought. World War II, although the most completely successful in our history, was also the most peculiar. Generals who lost battles and Captains who lost ships were promoted and decorated. A General took his wife and family to war with him. Generals competed with Admirals to acquire the largest number of stars. Generals, both Army and Marine, who were relieved from command for inefficiency, were continued on active duty in important commands. The correct disposition of top echelon insignia was as careful a staff study as the correct disposition of troops in our operations. Never in our history did gold braid sweep so high up naval sleeves nor so many stars adorn Army and Marine shoulders.

When I served in China I met a curious personage holding

the rank of Admiral-General. This Oriental package show, presented with suitable fanfare, shook me, but the height of our fantasy in high command was even more theatrical. We had Generals who were Admirals and Admirals who wanted to be Generals. Generals acting as Admirals are bad enough but it was the Admirals who wanted to be Generals who imperilled victory ✳ among the coral islands.

Coral was a great ally of the American forces in the Pacific. With coral we built airstrips, roads, piers and breakwaters and saved thousands of tons of shipping that would have been necessary to transport material from the United States if this natural product had not been abundantly and readily available. Coral is a living organism. After being blasted from the reefs that impeded our landing and utilized in military construction, it continued to work for us instead of against us. I would hesitate to place in the same useful category a lot of our brass in the Pacific.

CHAPTER II

~~~~~~

FORTY YEARS of military service climaxed by the greatest war the world has ever known covers a generous slice of history. Before I proceed to the events of that war as seen through the eyes of the Commanding General of the Fleet Marine Force, Pacific, I think I should tell something about myself, because those forty years were the crucial period of Marine Corps development.

How I got the name "Howlin' Mad" I don't know but it was pinned on me while I was stationed on Luzon, the main island in the Philippines. After being commissioned Second Lieutenant in 1906, I was assigned to Olongapo, our naval base on Subic Bay, which indents the northwestern extremity of Bataan Peninsula, later immortalized in American history. Olongapo wasn't much of a base at that time but it had a garrison, and here Marines were introduced to the Philippines.

For my first command I inherited "A" Company, 2nd Regiment, from Captain "Hiking Hiram" Bearss. This was a great honor for a young officer just out of training school. Command of a company usually was assigned to a Captain, not a Second Lieutenant and, besides, "A" Company and its commanding officer were famous in Marine circles. Hiking Hiram was one of the greatest travelers on foot in the Corps. He spent all his leisure time tramping and on his own two feet had been everywhere a man could go, except perhaps to the top of Mount Everest.

Samar, in the eastern Philippines, was his favorite proving ground and he had hiked all over the island, taking mountains, carabao trails and swamp paths in his stride. He always hiked with his shirt tail flapping outside his pants and the Samar natives must have derived their first amused impressions of the mad *Americano* as they watched him swinging along the trails.

Hiking Hiram infected his company with his own enthusiasm and it held the record for the toughest training march in the Philippines—Olongapo to Dinalupihan, 65 miles of the worst foot-blistering, back-breaking terrain to be found anywhere. Insect life and the damp heat of Northern Luzon helped take every ounce of stamina out of a man tramping under competitive conditions, which were heavy marching order, consisting of rifle, ammunition, five days' rations and extra clothing weighing forty-five pounds.

Naturally, "A" Company's performance was a challenging reputation to pass on to me straight from the States but I wasn't abashed. At school I was a sprinter and I knew what training meant. I started hiking and worked up an enthusiasm that soon led me on long treks all over the island. While my buddies spent their weekends absorbing night life in Manila, I was hiking along mountain trails and hacking through the jungles. When the right moment arrived, I paraded my company of 98 men and told them I was going to attack and beat Captain Bearss' record. Probably the men thought I was presumptuous but we started out. It was a day and a night trip, with a camp in the jungle, and I beat Hiram's record by three hours.

I suppose I did use tempestuous language to keep the men moving because I was determined to break the record. Somewhere along the line, or perhaps in the telling of the story afterwards, the name "Howlin' Mad" was coined. Despite the reputation it has given me, I protest that I am not given to sudden, uncontrollable outbursts of temper or to bawling out without cause. I would rather reason with a man than try to browbeat him. However, I do speak frankly, freely and emphatically when injustices occur, when official stupidity obstructs plans, or when the brass, big or small, tries to take liberties with my Marines. My vehemence has been magnified into habitual irreverence, which is incorrect.

"Howlin' Mad" stuck to me through my career but when I was born on April 20, 1882, at Hatchechubbee in Russell County, Alabama, a village twenty-seven miles from the Georgia border, I was named Holland McTyeire Smith after my great-uncle, Holland Nimmons McTyeire, who was a Bishop in the Methodist Episcopal Church, South. My great-uncle not only was a distinguished divine but a notable scholar and writer on religious subjects. Chinese Methodists in Shanghai named a girls' school after him, which Madame Sun Yat-sen and Madame Chiang Kai-shek attended. He was the first president of Vanderbilt University, which he helped to establish by talking Commodore Cornelius Vanderbilt into financing the project.

My father and mother hoped that by naming me after this ancestor I would follow in his footsteps. It was a great disappointment to them when their son showed no inclination to enter the Methodist ministry. Both my father, John Wesley Smith, Jr., and my mother, who was born Cornelia Caroline McTyeire, were very religious and my early years were strictly disciplined along Methodist lines, but my career must have been preordained by the character of other forebears.

My paternal grandfather, John Wesley Smith, was a Home Guard captain in the Confederacy. My grandmother on the paternal side was Martha Patrick, a direct descendant of Patrick Henry. My maternal grandfather, William C. McTyeire, was a sharpshooter in the Confederate Army. His proud possession was one of the new rifles obtained from England. This weapon was greatly superior to the old smooth bore gun, but as the Confederates had only a few, they were distributed only to the best shots and averaged about one rifle to a thousand men, which made my grandfather an outstanding soldier, indeed.

I don't know whether it was juvenile skepticism or just bloodthirsty curiosity that prompted me to ask him one day, "Grandpa, are you sure you ever killed a man in the war?"

He looked at me with an earnestness I had seldom seen in his face and said, "Holland, I'll tell you a story."

Settling back in his chair he began, "One evening in December we were in the Shenandoah Valley and from my position on the south bank of the river I heard a Yankee soldier call out, 'Johnny Reb! Got any tobacco?' "

"I yelled back, 'Yes! You got any coffee?' He called back to say he had.

"We both agreed to leave our weapons behind and come down to the stream to exchange tobacco for coffee and return to our posts without shooting at each other. We made the exchange all right but the Yankee got back to his post before I reached mine and whizz! a bullet almost clipped my ear. I ducked behind a rock and grabbed my new English rifle and shot the Yankee before he could take cover."

Then Grandfather added, "One of his comrades ran out to drag him in and I was so damn mad I shot him, too. Son, I've always been ashamed of that second shot."

My father was born in Harris County, Georgia. His family had been greatly influenced by the visit to the United States of John Wesley, the great English preacher, and the event was perpetuated by the family use of the two names, John Wesley. This custom caused some confusion in my father's life because my grandfather frequently received my father's letters. To avoid further blurring of his identity my father changed his name to John V. Smith.

The War of Secession impoverished the Smiths like many other Southern families. My father was able to attend the Alabama Polytechnic Institute at Auburn for only one year. His ambition was to become a lawyer. Diligence and perseverance overcame the handicaps the war created and in 1881 he was admitted to the Alabama Bar. In 1890 he was elected to the office of Court Solicitor for the State of Alabama and later was appointed President of the Railroad Commission, where he served four years. He practised law in Montgomery County and was a member of the State Legislature. My father died in 1913.

My mother was a remarkable woman. Alabama born, she died in Montgomery on August 7, 1946, at the age of 83. My father left her a meager estate but she possessed a keen business sense and by careful management developed the property to such proportions that her two children were comfortably off. My younger sister, Corrie Caroline, shortened by the family to Corrie C., married Robert Platt Boyd, an engineer employed by the State of Alabama, and died in Monroe, Louisiana, in 1920.

My mother took an active part in the Methodist Church. She was a woman of strong character. When I was three, the family moved from Hatchechubbee to Seale, in the same county. Seale is the Russell County seat, twenty miles from Columbus, Georgia, and therefore a place of considerable local importance.

The Central Georgia Railroad runs through Seale where the town marshal was notorious for his toughness in dealing with tramps who rode the freights. Generally, the tramps gave the town a wide berth, jumping off the trains outside the town and picking them up on the other side. During the interval they harassed the villagers with petty thefts.

One tramp tried to force his way into our house. My mother picked up the revolver that my father had taught her to use and fired at the tramp, who disappeared down the dusty road as fast as he could in his broken shoes. I don't think my mother hit him but the word got around and we had no more visits from unwelcome vagrants.

My childhood was brightened by a Negro servant who came into our life under unusual circumstances. One day when I was six an old Negro, driving a wagon pulled by a jack and a jenny, passed our house in Seale. The house was a square white building standing on a hill overlooking the town, surrounded by five acres of land on which was raised everything we ate. There was a parlor, living room, dining room, kitchen, four bedrooms and a large room with a tin bath.

The Negro's name was Uncle John Milby. He was a former slave and had been a jockey in his youth. As he drove his wagon down the road, my mother noticed blood streaming from a wound in his forehead. She hailed him and asked what had happened. Uncle John answered rather shamefacedly that his wife had hit him with a flat iron.

My mother invited him to the back door and, bringing a basin of warm water, in which she threw a handful of salt, she bathed the old man's wound and bandaged his head. While she was busy, Uncle John noticed the servant house in the back yard.

"Missey," he began shyly, "who lives in dat house?"

"Why, nobody now, John," my mother replied.

"Yes'm, they does," the old man said, "cos I'se movin' in."

Uncle John did move right in and he lived with us twelve years. He taught me how to ride, to hunt, to fish, to make bows and arrows, to set traps—and how to chew tobacco at the age of twelve. A little stream called Silver Run meandered near the house and here we caught catfish and perch. We shot quail and doves in the nearby woods.

My father always prided himself on possessing a fast horse and during Uncle John's stay with us he purchased a beautiful Hambletonian which, strange to say, was named Henry Ward Beecher. Uncle John, being a former jockey, made that horse the fastest in the county and together we travelled the roads, challenging any horse we met. Henry Ward Beecher invariably left every other animal far behind.

In all my life, I have never loved anyone more than I loved Uncle John. The formative years of my boyhood were in his capable, tireless and cheerful care and he taught me things about humanity that I never found in books. Our house was built in an "L" and my room was on the ground floor. On cold nights in winter—and it does get cold in Alabama—Uncle John used to climb through my bedroom window and curl up on the Brussels carpet in my room, which was much warmer than the servant house across the back yard. My mother and father never knew.

About the time Uncle John joined our household I started to school. Though Seale was the county seat, it boasted only one small school and one teacher, who taught all subjects to all ages from six to sixteen. He was expected to know Latin, geography, arithmetic, geometry, English literature, algebra—in fact, the complete curriculum of a well-staffed scholastic institution—and also to maintain discipline among unruly youngsters in a school averaging forty students.

The school, a dingy frame building the size of a good barn, was equipped with wooden benches and desks, with a few maps and pictures on the walls. The six-year-olds sat on the front benches and worked their way up, as I did, to the rear benches by the time they reached the age of sixteen. Ten years in that school left an indelible impression on the minds of the pupils. The room was heated by an old iron stove, wood-burning, which meant that the older you got the farther you moved from the stove and the more inured to cold you had to become to survive.

With such a pedagogic repertoire, it was only natural that in a small town like Seale, the teacher entrusted with the responsibility of moulding the lives of its youth was greatly respected. He was always addressed as Professor. I remember Professor Conyers, Professor Bass and Professor Dill. In my last years at Seale, from 1896 to 1898, the school board got expansive and added a lady teacher as assistant. Her name was Miss Annette Howard and she was an old maid, stern in expression but liked by all her pupils. She was free with the switch but she applied it with equal justice to all.

I was now sixteen and the old school at Seale had nothing more to offer, so in 1898 I entered Alabama Polytechnic Institute as a sophomore. The Institute is a military school at Auburn, in Lee County, next to Russell County, and that time the military commandant was Colonel B. S. Patrick. The rank was purely honorary but the school had a definite military flavor. We wore the Confederate gray uniform and followed a dull routine of parades, drills and rifle exercises which seemed puerile to me. I objected to every military detail. Everything military about the place offended me and the fact that I barely graduated is a pretty good indication of my interest in the preponderantly military side. But still I loved my Alma Mater.

However, two extra-curricular activities justified my three years at the Polytechnic. I became a good sprinter and a student of Napoleon.

It was purely by accident that I discovered I could sprint. As a military school, Alabama Polytechnic was ruled by the seniors, to whom was delegated considerable disciplinary authority. One night while on unauthorized liberty, I was detected by the seniors and I made a dash back to college to escape them.

One of the upperclassmen was the 100-yard champion and he chased me. I beat him back to the campus and when I told my upperclass fraternity brothers at the Alpha Tau Omega house about it, they ordered me to go out for track. Without any special training I did quite well and later at the University of Alabama I lost only one race in two years. At one meet I won the 100-, 220- and 440-yard dashes as well as the mile. Not a bad record for a single day.

While my grades were not very high at Auburn, I did well in history. Before I went to Auburn, I had fallen under the magic of Napoleon's genius and read everything about him I could get my hands on. In Seale, I had to buy books out of my allowance and consequently my reading was limited. Furthermore, my father strongly disapproved of this hero worship and promptly confiscated any book he found dealing with Napoleon. To counteract what I considered an unreasonable prejudice, I took to hiding my books under the house, which stood off the ground.

At Auburn things were different. The college had an excellent library and I read everything it offered on Napoleon, to the detriment of other studies. The Corsican's character fascinated me, his prowess awed me, and his rapid marches and countermarches across the map of Europe, defeating one adversary after another, implanted in my mind military principles that served me well later, although paradoxically the Auburn military atmosphere nauseated me.

The trait that counted most heavily in my youthful assessment of Napoleon was his offensive spirit. Inevitably, later in my life the halo I had visioned around his head began to tarnish when I appreciated the tyrant, the unscrupulous plotter, the enemy of freedom he became. It never occurred to me at that time that years later I would be wearing the Croix de Guerre awarded me by the French Government for fighting to save the land of Napoleon from her traditional enemy.

While I was at Auburn the most momentous decision of my life was made. Had the decision gone otherwise, this book never would have been written.

Shortly after I entered the Polytechnic I was offered a desig-

29

nation to take the examinations for entrance to the Naval Academy at Annapolis. Bored as I was by the pseudo-military air of Auburn, I still was an adventurous youngster, yearning to do and see things, and I was attraced by the Navy. Therefore, when Congressman Henry D. Clayton, representing our congressional district, offered me the designation I was delighted. Why it was offered I learned later. My father was a prominent man and there was some question of his entering the race for Congress against Clayton. The Congressman got wind of this and the designation to the Naval Academy, which he knew I wanted, was a discreet bribe to head off father's possible opposition.

I never accepted the designation or sat for examinations because my father and mother would not hear of it. They were both born during the Civil War period and they carried the mental scars of the conflict deep in their beings. They were still unreconstructed and would not permit me to accept an offer which, in their minds, would be a surrender to Yankee ideology.

Such an attitude would appear unreasonable today but when I was a boy in the South these ideas were live, glowing embers of a fire that had not been extinguished, remnants of a pride that could yield but not surrender. Unforgettable associations helped preserve this attitude. It was in Montgomery, where my parents spent many years of their lives, that the congress of delegates from the seceding States adopted the Confederate Constitution and inaugurated Jefferson Davis as President in 1861.

Destiny hangs by a slender thread. Instead of joining the Navy I became a Marine, following a brief and undistinguished flirtation with the law which convinced me I was not destined to become a John Marshall or an Oliver Wendell Holmes. In 1901, at my father's insistence, I entered the University of Alabama law school. My father had a comfortable practice and he figured his son would make a satisfactory partner but I never had the slightest interest in law.

Two years at the University, except for my sprinting which gained me campus popularity, were practically wasted and I barely graduated in 1903. After graduation I entered my father's office and the firm became Smith and Smith, with the junior member disliking his job more intensely every day. I suffered a further impediment to any chance of a successful career. Acquaintances always introduced me as John Smith's son and this made me realize that as long as I practised law I would be only John Smith's son. Like most young men, I had independent ambitions and they were far removed from the musty labyrinths of law.

My few appearances in court only emphasized my unfitness as a lawyer. The last time was in Montgomery, when I appeared as assistant to the County Solicitor in the prosecution of a Negro charged with attacking another Negro with a knife. I did what I considered a first class piece of work and made (I thought) a fine argument. The judge looked at me pityingly and the defense lawyer rested his case and sat down, almost unable to believe that anybody could present a case as badly as I did. The defendant was acquitted immediately and I walked out of the court room, vowing never to enter again.

That humiliating experience finally decided me: I would abandon law, which obviously was not my metier, and join the Army. This plan had been slowly forming in my restless mind ever since youthful aversion to uniformed drudgery at Auburn started to wear off. My inclinations were definitely toward a military career and I had already worked up to first sergeant in a cavalry troop of the Alabama National Guard.

I was now 21 and ready to make something out of life that the law couldn't offer. My father was reluctant to see me desert the family profession but he didn't stand in my way when I announced my plans. Instead, he gave me his paternal blessing and I went off to Washington to see our Congressman, Lieutenant Colonel Ariosto A. Wiley, who had served in the Army in Cuba during the Spanish-American War. Colonel Wiley heartily approved of my intentions but it was not easy to realize them. At the War Department he introduced me to Secretary Mills, who was cordial and sympathetic but wrecked my plans for an Army career by saying that no examinations for Second Lieutenants would be held until November, 1905. That was more than a year away and I couldn't wait.

As we were leaving the War Department Colonel Wiley, fully appreciating my disappointment, suddenly had an idea. "How would you like to join the Marines?" he asked. I know it sounds odd today but I answered, "What are the Marines?" Honestly, I didn't know. Nobody ever mentioned that branch of the service to me and even in my reading I never encountered the Corps. No attractive recruiting posters showing Marine life overseas plastered the country in the early years of this century.

Colonel Wiley explained to me the organization of the United States Marine Corps, its history and its functions. His little lecture on the street outside the War Department was the most convincing I have ever heard. I am sorry I can't recall it exactly because it could be usefully incorporated in Marine archives as a gem of extemporaneous lucidity and conviction. His talk immediately won me over and we went to see Secretary of the Navy William H. Moody. Mr. Moody told me he was looking for some boys from the South to complete the proper geographical distribution of commissions in the Marine Corps and said he would give me a chance. I was overwhelmed and thanked him profusely.

In Washington a school run by a Mr. Swaverly prepared candidates for Army, Navy and Marine examinations. I enrolled in a class of about forty young men studying for service careers. Looking back I remember among my classmates, who became lifelong friends, were Major General Ralph S. Keyser, Lieutenant Colonel Edward W. Sturdivant, Colonel Andrew B. Drum, Colonel Victor I. Morrison, Colonel David M. Randall, and Brigadier General M. E. Shearer, all stalwarts of the Marine Corps.

Examinations for entrance to the Corps were held in February, 1905, at the Marine Barracks in Washington and I passed successfully. It was the proudest day of my life, even prouder than the day when, with Secretary of the Navy Forrestal standing at my side, I watched my men raise the Stars and Stripes on Suribachi, the climax of my years in the service of my country. At last I was starting a career I felt would satisfy all my longings and ambitions.

I received a commission as Second Lieutenant and was assigned to the School of Application, known today as the Basic School, at the Marine Barracks, Annapolis, Maryland. Then came another proud day—the day I first wore my Marine uniform. At that time the Corps uniform consisted of a dark blue blouse with elaborate frogs across the chest and braid around the hem. The pants were sky blue, with a broad red stripe running down. A blue cap completed the outfit. Afterwards this uniform was discarded for one more practical but I was deeply thrilled when I first wore it. To me, it represented admission to an old, honored and distinguished company of men who had helped shape our country's history.

It was an intense, thrilling year at the School of Application. I began, as never before, to appreciate the qualities of my fellow men as we drilled on the parade ground, attended classes and studied or yarned far into the night.

In my class were fifty embryo Marine officers. The Commandant of the School was Colonel Lincoln Karmany, a magnificent man, the very embodiment of the ideal Marine officer. He had a long military record and was a strict disciplinarian but he was essentially kind and sympathetic. We all left school inspired to emulate him.

After graduation I had time only for a hasty leavetaking because I was assigned to my first station: the Philippines. Leaving Washington in April, 1906, with other officers of my class, I entrained for San Francisco where I boarded the USS *Sheridan,* an old transport employed to carry Marines to our most distant station. The *Sheridan* sailed on April 16, 1906, and as we passed through the Golden Gate and saw the buildings vanish in the fog around Telegraph Hill and the deep, blue Pacific heaving ahead I never dreamed what tragedy was in store for the unique California city I always loved.

Two days later an earthquake rocked San Francisco, followed by the terrible fire that killed so many people and nearly wiped out one of the most beautiful, glamorous cities in the world. We knew nothing about all this at sea. Radio telegraphy was in its infancy and few ships were equipped with this new system of communications. We heard nothing of the disaster until the ship was within visual signalling distance of Honolulu. Once ashore, we bought up all the newspapers and read the tragic news. Sitting at a table in a local hotel reading the papers, the fatalistic implications of the San Francisco disaster set me thinking. As I have said, destiny hangs by a slender thread. Had our ship been delayed a few days my life might have taken a totally different course—had I escaped death in the flames.

The *Sheridan* eventually docked in Manila and we trans-shipped to a small freighter that carried us out of Manila Bay and around Bataan Peninsula to the naval base at Olongapo in Subic Bay. Olongapo was only a small naval station on the east coast of the Bay and Olongapo itself a small native village of straw huts and wooden shacks. The base had repair facilities for small ships but later the drydock *Dewey* arrived and handled destroyers and light cruisers.

The Marine barracks was a group of old Spanish buildings of whitewashed brick and wood captured during the Spanish-American War. It had wide, airy rooms and accommodated about 1,100 men, who slept on cots and enjoyed a clean and sanitary existence. This is more than can be said of some of the officers, including myself. I shared a single room in the officers' mess, a separate building standing away from the barracks, and I've never been so pestered with bedbugs in my life. My iron cot was covered only with a light bamboo matting but despite this starvation diet the bedbugs thrived. Some of the other officers occupied mat sheds in the barracks area, no better than my quarters. Proper service buildings were not erected until later.

Living conditions didn't bother me too much. I was young, this was my first station and my new career was opening satisfactorily. Discipline was severe in those days of the Marine Corps. Senior Captains presided over the mess and a Captain in those days was only once removed from a king. In our mess were eleven Second Lieutenants and the only time we were allowed to open our mouths was to put food in. All our conversations were confined to whispered asides among ourselves. Direct communication with the mess president was unthinkable.

34

Still, looking back, I realize that such discipline was good for us. We were young and inexperienced and needed to be kept in line. I didn't object to the discipline though I am naturally gregarious and usually chafe under restrictions. Also, I was fortunate in my command. "A" Company, 2nd Regiment, that came to me from Captain Bearss, had an old time noncommissioned officer in First Sergeant Joseph J. Jackson, who was later commissioned and promoted to Captain in World War I. Jackson was a godsend to a shavetail. His advice saved me from lots of trouble.

Olongapo eventually became so crowded that with my company I was sent to the old barracks on the rifle range at Santa Rita, two and a half miles away. Here we had plenty of room and excellent training facilities. At Santa Rita I learned a lesson that stayed with me all my life. One night I met two Marines who were in the last stages of a drinking bout. They had been drinking *vino*, not just ordinary wine but a fearful native drink that robbed men of their senses. It was a white liquor distilled from rice and *nipa* leaves. I tried to take the bottle of *vino* away from the two men but they lunged at me. As they converged on me from two sides I stepped back, grabbed them by their collars and banged their heads together.

The concussion, plus the drink, knocked both men out and I had them thrown into the brig and put in double irons. *Vino* is violent stuff and in those days both wrist and leg irons were used on violent prisoners.

I jumped on my horse—all Marines had horses—and rode into Olongapo to report the incident to Lieutenant Colonel Eli K. Cole, Commanding Officer of the 2nd Regiment. I shall never forget that interview. What he said to me about an officer laying hands on a Marine burned in my memory and I left his presence a subdued and wiser young man.

Yet it was not a completely unpleasant incident. Later, while hiking along the trail with my company, we ran into a heavy rainstorm. I ordered camp made and rolled up on the ground in my poncho and single blanket. When I woke up in the morning I found myself snugly covered with two extra blankets.

They belonged to the men whose heads I banged together. The two were never punished after they sobered up and became the best couple in my company. However, I am not relating this aftermath in an attempt to disprove Colonel Cole's well-deserved lecture. It just happened that way.

A welcome break in my life at Olongapo came when I left for Cavite Naval Base, in Manila Bay, to manage the Marine baseball team playing in the Manila League. The team did fairly well but after the season I got into trouble with the Commanding Officer at the Marine Barracks. For the first and only time in my career I received an unfavorable fitness report and for my sins I was transferred to McManny Point, on the east coast of Subic Bay off Grande Island. The report was quite justified although something was to be said in extenuation. I had too many jobs. I commanded a special duty detachment and also served as Post Quartermaster, Post Exchange Officer, Post Mess Officer and manager of the baseball team. It was too much for a young officer of my brief experience.

At McManny Point I had my first experience of violent death in service. We were emplacing guns for the defense of Subic Bay against possible Japanese action. The Treaty of Portsmouth ending the Russo-Japanese War only two years earlier left the Japanese indignant against the Americans who, they claimed, had robbed them of the fruits of victory. They were cocky after defeating Russia and thought they could take on the United States, or anybody.

The guns were not large, 4.7 inches. They had been removed from the USS *Albany*, an old cruiser that had been decommissioned and broken up. Marine gun crews were assigned to test the armament but when we fired the first gun it exploded, killing one man and seriously wounding several others.

Even at that time, Japanese intelligence was following our defense program. On a weekend hike around McManny Point, I discovered a series of wooden pegs leading from Lingayen Gulf, on the northwest coast of Luzon, to our batteries at McManny Point. The pegs were definitely identified as Japanese markers but we took no notice of them.

36

However, it wasn't the Japanese threat that took me away from McManny Point. It was malaria carried by the clouds of mosquitoes over this marshy spot. With 85 percent of my command, I contracted the disease and was invalided home in September, 1908.

Shortly after my recovery I embarked upon another enterprise. I got married and, like the couple in the fairy tale, we have lived happily ever after. My wife tells the story somewhat differently but I stick to my version. After graduation from the School of Application, I was invited to a dinner party at the Annapolis home of Mrs. Karmany, wife of Colonel Karmany, and there met Miss Ada Wilkinson, of Phoenixville, Pennsylvania.

At a convenient opportunity, I seized her with both hands, backed her into a corner and said to her, "You've never seen me before in your life but you've met your future husband." This Marine approach was a new experience for this lovely Yankee girl and she was more or less impressed. I saw her three more times before I sailed for the Philippines and our relationship improved steadily.

On my return three years later, we were married at her home in Phoenixville on April 12, 1909. A man's first duty to the woman he marries is to provide a home for her. I started married life by ignoring this principle. Instead, the Yankee girl I married, who had never been away from her own hearth except to attend boarding school, started a nomadic life with me and did not have a real home until thirty-eight years later when I retired from the Marine Corps and we settled in La Jolla, California, in a house overlooking the sea.

In the first year of our marriage Ada moved fourteen times. At the dictates of duty and accompanying her husband around the world she has set up home with Japanese amahs, Chinese cooks, Filipino houseboys and Dominican and Haitian servants. I can assure those who think only the Marine's life is hard that actually it is the Marine wives who are the sturdy pioneers.

President Jose Santos Zelaya of Nicaragua opened the next chapter in my life. Two Americans were shot after being tortured by the so-called Liberal head of Nicaragua and in December, 1909, I left with the Marine expeditionary force ordered to Nicaragua and Panama. Zelaya was ousted by the Conservatives and Adolfo Diaz was elected president in 1910, a choice satisfactory to our State Department. Thereupon the Marines returned to the United States in April, 1910, without firing a shot.

This was my first experience with the Marines as an instrument of international order but the expanding functions of the Marine Corps, so far as I was concerned, left far less an impression on my mind than the revelation of the status of the Corps in the eyes of the other two branches of the armed service. The initial trip to Corinto, Nicaragua, and the way the Marines were treated on board ship aroused in me a deep resentment against the attitude of the Navy and sired a determination that above all else I would devote my energies to obtaining recognition for the Marines as an integral part of our armed forces. The impression I got of our status was something like Kipling's:

> While it's Tommy this an' Tommy that, an' "Tommy fall be'ind";
> But it's "Please to walk in front, sir," when there's trouble in the wind.

On the Nicaraguan expedition and, in fact, on all other trips made by Marines abroad, except to the Philippines, no regular transports were provided. Men piled on board any ship assigned to them and slept anywhere they could find a place to spread their blankets. I have often bedded down on deck. This is all part of a Marine's life. He is trained not to expect luxuries and he takes things as they come. A foxhole in the jungle is as good as a cot in the barracks.

What burned me up on this expedition, and on others later, was how unwelcome we were on board ship. Instead of being treated like comrades going abroad to protect our country's interests, we were regarded by the Navy as interlopers, unnecessary passengers who caused trouble, disrupted routine because we happened to be aboard, and debarked with the ship's personnel thanking God they had got rid of us at last.

Not that all Navy personnel was glad to see us go. Marines were always fair game for bluejackets. At that time the Marine had no access to ships' service stations or canteens. He had to buy his little extras through the bluejackets. On the Nicaragua trip bluejackets cornered the market in tobacco and candy. Bull Durham selling in the canteen at five cents a package was resold to the Marines at fifty cents and one dollar. Candy was sky high.

With my regiment, I was on board the USS *Buffalo* and this discrimination extended to the officers. The junior mess charged us $45 a month when the actual cost to Navy officers was less than $25. This profiteering so outraged me that I swore a solemn oath to my Maker that if I ever reached a position where I could do it I would fight to the bitter end this injustice against the Marines, officers and men.

In 1939, when I took the First Marine Brigade to Culebra, the opportunity occurred to make good on this oath. Similar attempts to squeeze Marines were made but at this time I was a Brigadier General and the scheme failed. I threatened to prefer charges against any naval officer, regardless of rank, who attempted to charge my officers more than the mess bill paid by naval officers, plus a ten percent charge for laundry and general wear and tear. The result was Marine officers were no longer imposed upon and the fight was taken to Washington, which conceded the justice of the issue.

This was a great victory for the prestige of the Marine Corps, the first of many. Thereafter my officers were placed in the same category as the Army and their mess bills were paid by the Government. A point like this might appear to be a minor one in the administration of a huge military organization but it helped make the Marine Corps an equal partner with the other two branches of the armed services.

After Nicaragua and Panama I was ordered to Puget Sound and was soon off with another expeditionary force—potential rather than active. A Marine detachment was dispatched to North Island, Coronado, California, where we were ready for the revolution against Porfirio Diaz, dictator-president of Mexico. Fighting involved Tia Juana, the Mexican city just over the

California border, but the Marines sat out the revolution at North Island, about fifteen miles away. Diaz abdicated and fled to France on May 4, 1911. Francisco Madero succeeded him as president and our job was ended before it started.

Back in Seattle, Washington, a happy event occurred in my family life. My son, John Victor Smith, was born and I had time to see him through the toddling age before I was assigned once again to the Philippines, and later to sea duty on the USS *Galveston* with the rank of First Lieutenant. In the fifteen months with this cruiser I visited China and trained with the Marines at Chefoo, the American summer station on the Shantung Peninsula.

While I was in China waters in 1914, World War I broke out in Europe and the Japanese attacked Kiaochow, the German base on the south coast of Shantung. The base had been constructed over many years as one of the Kaiser's pet projects and its powerful 10-inch guns, rising from almost impenetrable concrete walls, had given Kiaochow the reputation of impregnability. The Japanese landed a few miles away up the coast in September, 1914, and took the fortress by flank attack just as they captured the great Singapore base from the British early in 1942.

Upon returning to the United States in 1916, I found trouble brewing in the Caribbean. A revolution had broken out in Santo Domingo, where a procession of presidents had brought no peace and Desiderio Arias, War Minister, was the latest contender for power, revolting against President Jiminez.

In the expeditionary force ordered to Santo Domingo to "maintain order"—and that meant suppressing the revolution—I commanded the 8th Company, 5th Marines. A force of Marines had already landed at Monte Cristo, a small port on the north coast, and, in modern parlance, had secured a beachhead with some opposition. We came along later with orders to march—or fight our way—south to Santiago de los Caballeros, a town sixty miles inland.

This was my first amphibious landing. Sandy beaches, sheltered by thick woods, stretched along the coast but we never used them. Instead, we landed in ordinary ships' boats at a small jetty outside the town. Only a poor dirt road ran inland to Santiago, passing through heavily wooded country, and it took us several days to reach our destination.

The rebels had dug deep trenches in the road to impede our progress and when we passed these obstacles we had to remove trees cut down to block our march. The rebels kept up a sharp fire from the woods. At one point, fire was so heavy that I took a small party of Marines and headed for the source. What followed was the most dangerous incident in my life up to that moment, almost as dangerous as some experiences in the Pacific when the Japanese were throwing everything around. Our party was cut off and we found ourselves surrounded by about a hundred Dominicans, who outnumbered us at least ten to one. We had to fight our way out and only sound Marine training saved our lives.

Once we reached Santiago the revolution ended and Arias was defeated. American forces garrisoned the island and I was given command of the Marine garrison at Puerto Plata, in the southeastern corner of the island. Our action had assumed the status of formal intervention. Dr. Henriquez y Carvajal was elected president. Because he required American military strength to maintain him in position, the Military Government of the United States in Santo Domingo was established on November 26, 1916.

The next few months were spent in routine garrison duty but while I was at Puerto Plata the news came through that the United States had declared war on Germany. One day I received a code message I was unable to decipher. The message came from the USS *Charleston*, which was en route to Santo Domingo, and was relayed from the ship to me at Puerto Plata. My commanding officer also was unable to decode the message, so it was forwarded to the headquarters of General John H. Pendleton, commander of the Marine Expeditionary Force, at Santo Domingo, the capital city now known as Ciudad Trujillo.

Although I had no way of knowing it, I had a pretty good idea that the message ordered me and my company back to the United States. While headquarters were decoding I ordered my first sergeant to pack up 8th Company and be prepared to move at once. My guess was correct. It was war and we were ordered to get ready to go to France. Never in my career did things move so quickly as in the next twenty-four hours. My relief arrived from Santiago and when the *Charleston*, the ship that received and relayed the message, reached Puerto Plata, I was packed up and ready to move on board with my company.

The United States declared war on Germany on April 6, 1917. Two months later I was with the First Division en route to France, where we landed at St. Nazaire on June 26, 1917. My company was on board the *USS Henderson* on the transport's maiden voyage. As the *Henderson* sailed out of New York Harbor the ship bringing my wife home from Santo Domingo entered. She had been very ill when I left the island but I didn't know how desperate was her condition. She had been carried to the coast on a truck, strapped to a stretcher, then rowed out two miles to sea and slung aboard ship. Our baby was with her.

Not until the following August did I learn that she had undergone a serious operation and barely recovered. Throughout our married life, my wife has contrived to save me from the knowledge of possible disaster until afterwards. With her, the Marine Corps has come first, personal considerations second. My transport passed her ship in New York's lower bay as the largest convoy that had ever left an American port sailed for France.

CHAPTER III

THE ATLANTIC can be very pleasant in June, and it was on its best tourist behavior for the benefit of our convoy, which took fourteen days to reach St. Nazaire from New York, dodging German submarines we never sighted. The trip on board the *USS Henderson* gave me ample opportunity to review life as it had unfolded behind me and to take stock of the unforeseeable future.

I had been eleven years in the Marine Corps; eleven active, exciting years that had taken me from Russell County, Alabama, half way across the world to the Philippines and China and back again to the jungles of the Caribbean islands. Leaning on the rail of the transport watching the green Atlantic swell, surrounded by cruisers, destroyers and all the panoply of American might on its first armed venture into the European sphere in World War I, I began to realize that I was better fitted for service life than for any other career.

Eleven years in Marine uniform had given me confidence in my own judgment and in my ability to deal with men and to handle troops under fire. On the day we were trapped in the Dominican jungle and fought our way out against dangerous odds, I became a fatalist. I am not superstitious; the black magic of the Haitian hills never interested me; but I have complete faith in my own destiny. To me, France was just another tour of duty.

Returning from Santo Domingo, my company was designated the 8th Machine Gun Company, attached to the 3rd Battalion of the 5th Regiment. I had been promoted to Captain and my battalion commander was Lieutenant Colonel Charles

43

T. Westcott, Jr. Commanding the 5th Regiment was Colonel Charles A. Doyen who, with his staff, was on the *Henderson.* This regiment was the Marine contribution to the first American expeditionary force.

Off the coast of France, the American escort turned us over to French destroyers, which took us into St. Nazaire with an air cover of French planes. The entire coast was littered with wreckage as we steamed up the English Channel. Apparently, the European battlefield ended only at the water's edge.

"Vive l'Amerique!" roared the huge crowd waiting for us in the French port. We were the first American troops to land and the French went wild, as every man in the vanguard of the American Expeditionary Force will remember.

My regiment went into camp outside St. Nazaire and later moved up to a position in the French line. I got my first taste of French Army life when I was sent to train with the 70th Battalion of Chasseurs—French light infantry. The American *soldat-marin* evidently became popular. I was the first of our Marines the French troops had ever seen, and either my novelty or *camaraderie* impressed them, for they honored me by making me honorary private, first class, French Chasseurs, a rank I always have been proud to hold. Many years afterwards, when I was a Brigadier General in the Marines, I was promoted to honorary sergeant in the 30th Battalion.

My stay with the Chasseurs was brief. The American military effort was expanding daily and I was sent back with my company to St. Nazaire to help in the job of unloading transports which filled the harbor. When a regular port debarkation staff was organized, I was withdrawn from this duty, detached from the 3rd Battalion and ordered to the Army General Staff College, which had just been established at Langres. I was the only Marine officer to complete the first course and thenceforth my sphere of activity broadened.

The months that followed until the Armistice of November 11, 1918, were busy and significant. They were months of hard work when fresh American strength was turning the tide for the weary Allies, and American troops showed their caliber in some of the fiercest battles of the war. The Marines did their share and added luster to their reputation as fighting men.

By the addition of the 6th Regiment, the original Marine contingent was increased to a brigade and our official designation became the 4th Marine Brigade, Second Division. Colonel Doyen was promoted to Brigadier General and I was made Brigade Adjutant. The Allies were fighting for their lives in the Verdun sector and along the Aisne and the Marne against the massed attacks of the Kaiser's armies, which had been reinforced from the Eastern Front by the collapse of Russia.

Brigadier General Doyen was relieved and was succeeded by Brigadier General James G. Harbord. Major Harry T. Lay replaced me as Brigade Adjutant and I was retained on General Harbord's staff as administrative officer.

Harbord was one of America's great soldiers. A veteran cavalryman and a hard fighter who had risen from the rank of private, he had been selected by Pershing, another of the same soldierly breed, to come to France as first Chief of Staff of the AEF. Subsequently, Pershing gave him our Marine Brigade (then attached to the Army), a fine command, as the Commander-in-Chief explained, a reward for Harbord's good work on the staff. Harbord understood Marines and respected them. We reciprocated his feelings, with the result that the 2nd Division's Army-Marine team created by Harbord carried out some of the most distinguished combat operations of the first war. I always took Harbord as a model, and was proud to enjoy his good opinion.

After the battle of Belleau Wood, the Army claimed my services from the Marines. In June, 1918, I was transferred to the 1st Corps, First Army, and served as Assistant Operations Officer in charge of communications in the Aisne-Marne sector and the great Allied offensives of St. Mihiel, the Oise, the Meuse and the Argonne.

Then came the Armistice and the march to the Rhine. From the First Army I was transferred to the Third Army, also as Assistant Operations Officer, and three weeks later I was officially detailed to the Army General Staff, one of the few Marines ever admitted to the rolls of this vaunted group. My only notable accomplishment with the Army of Occupation was at Coblenz, where I graduated from the Army School of Equitation among cynical Army horsemen who thought that a Marine was a sailor and couldn't manage a horse.

"All Marines are good riders," I told them. "If you don't believe me, drop in at our equitation school at Quantico and we'll show you our trophies."

My rank was now Major and it was plain that a Marine's job on the Army staff was finished. I wanted desperately to go home, so I started the channels humming but there didn't seem much hope of success, at least for some months. Too many other men had the same idea.

My orders came through in March, 1919, and I went to Paris, where one day I had a stroke of luck. I met Captain James J. Raby, in command of a battleship, the USS *Georgia*, and I shared with him my nostalgic yearnings.

"Look here, Smith," he said, when I had finished sobbing my heart out, "I'm sailing for the States tomorrow from Brest. If you can make it by sailing time, I'll give you the Admiral's cabin."

Here was a chance I could not miss. The life of a lone Marine, swamped by Army echelons, was getting me down now that the fighting was over. Home never looked sweeter and this was a way to get there. I called on General Harbord, my former chief in the Fourth Brigade, now commanding the all-powerful "SOS" or Service of Supply, and he expedited my orders. The next day I was on board the *Georgia*. As I came up on deck with the battleship heading for Norfolk, I pulled off my spurs and heaved them over the side. I was back with my own people, going home.

I slipped into the United States as discreetly as possible because I needed a rest and wanted to see my family at Phoenixville. Time had passed so quickly in France that it hardly seemed possible nearly two years had elapsed since I had seen my wife and our boy Victor. That leave was a perfect domestic interlude between my tours of duty.

With World War I degenerating into a battle around the

peace table, my first assignment at home was to the Marine Barracks at the Norfolk Navy Yard, where later I took charge of the Officers' School for Service Afloat. Despite its name, this didn't mean going to sea. The school indoctrinated new Corps officers in sea duties and naval practice and administration so that they could march on board ship and feel as much at home as naval officers.

For some time, ideas had been slowly taking shape in my mind on the changing concept of modern warfare and the new role thus created for the Marines. My first big chance to develop this line of thought came in December, 1920, when I was ordered to the Naval War College at Newport, Rhode Island, with Major Lauren S. (Pop) Willis, now Lieutenant Colonel, Retired. Between fifty and sixty officers attended, ranging from Admirals downward. A number of Army officers also were taking the course, but Pop Willis and I were the only Marines. Naturally, the two of us saw eye to eye, particularly on matters relating to the Marine Corps.

The reputation of the College is very high: through its halls have passed our greatest naval leaders. Traditionally, it has molded American naval strategy and affected other spheres of our national defense policy. As a laboratory of germinating ideas, the College could be expected to exercise a profound influence upon the approach to our war problems, yet I found it bogged down in obsolescence. The lessons learned from World War I appeared to point backward instead of forward and the mass of pertinent, timely information furnished by the war just concluded had been ignored in favor of long established principles which a novice could see would never apply successfully to future problems. Despite the war that drew the European and Asiatic continents closer to the United States, the thinking at the War College was as static as that of the French when they built the Maginot Line.

President of the College was Rear Admiral William S. Sims, who was America's Special Representative and Naval Observer in Great Britain during the early years of World War I and commanded the U. S. Fleet in European waters upon our declaration of war on Germany. He had been promoted to Admiral, but after the war, in the middle of 1919, he was detached from his command and reverted to his former rank after appointment to head the War College. His Chief of Staff at the College was Rear Admiral C. P. Plunkett, who was in command of American railroad artillery in France when we mounted 14-inch ships' guns on specially constructed cars and added mobility and power to Allied artillery.

I have never met two men so utterly dissimilar in personality, ideas and perception. Admiral Sims was an old line sailor, well salted in tradition, hidebound and inelastic in his belief in naval sufficiency and superiority. In his own particular field he was a brilliant man. He had revolutionized naval gunnery and put our fleet on a higher level of efficiency than ever before in its history but his perspective was completely and narrowly naval.

On the other hand, Rear Admiral Plunkett, who had seen service ashore with land units, realized the limitations of naval power. He could appreciate situations where naval power would be important as it had been in the past but would not suffice. In other words, a new type of warfare, definitely planned and cutting through precedent by employing specialized troops working with the close support of the Navy but independent of the Navy.

The point at issue, which I introduced into all discussions, was the employment of Marines in an amphibious form of warfare. Sims and Plunkett were diametrically opposed in their ideas on the subject. The senior Admiral—like many Navy officers before and since—insisted this was a function of Army troops or bluejackets. The junior Admiral agreed with me that Marines were the logical choice.

At the War College we studied naval plans involving problems both in the Pacific and the Atlantic. We selected islands and continental bases and studied their assault operationally from a naval viewpoint but it was my constant endeavor to write into these operations a Marine plan of attack. This had never been done before and I believed that the time had come when the Navy should recognize this necessity.

Under the old Navy doctrine, a landing was a simple and

haphazard affair, involving no planning and very little preparation. Assault forces were stowed in boats 5,000 yards off the beach and given a pat on the back, with the hope that all would go well. Warships threw a few shells into the beach and that was all. Nobody took these landings seriously, because the mere appearance of a large naval force off shore was supposed to inactivate the enemy. Naturally, if an enemy fleet appeared, the Navy would engage it, but this contingency always could be calculated in advance and a safe superiority of strength provided.

Most naval minds refused to contemplate the endless new problems that must be solved to make a landing successful. It scarcely occurred to them that the enemy might resist and fire back, undaunted by the naval demonstration. Even the bitter lessons the British learned at Gallipoli had little effect on the War College.

Let us consider the primary conditions involved. No special troops existed which had been trained for this task. Not a single boat in the naval service was equipped for putting troops ashore and retracting under its own power. The practice was to use 50-foot motor sailers, cram them with Marines or bluejackets, and tow additional men in ordinary ships' boats. This method restricted the choice of landing beaches, because the boats could turn only in a wide circle and had difficulty getting back to their mother ships after landing the men.

Determination to put my ideas across resulted in a long and acrimonious struggle with the Navy. When I voiced objections to the accepted naval doctrine I was brushed off with the reminder that the Marines were only a secondary branch of the service anyway. The Marines, it was conceded, could be employed for landings chosen as the progress of operations dictated but only when commanded by a naval officer and reinforced with bluejackets.

To the men who captured the most heavily defended positions in the Pacific, this sounds fantastic, but it was the Sims doctrine at the War College when I was there. Had the controversy remained on a purely theoretical level, I would not have objected so strongly. But Sims had an unflattering opinion of the

49

Marine Corps and was not hesitant in expressing it. He considered the Marines the lowest form of naval life, much inferior to the lowest rating of bluejackets. He did not dismiss the Marines as useless. They could be employed on minor landings only in cooperation with bluejackets, for Sims considered his men capable of performing their duties as well ashore as they did afloat, disregarding the fact that they were not trained for shore duties.

The Marines came second in his thinking and he never overlooked an opportunity to say so. He coldly dismissed them as orderlies, messengers, drivers, naval guards on shore establishments and suitable for employment on minor expeditionary duties only. Borrowing his thinking from British Navy usage, where Marines are sometimes employed in this capacity, he also considered us a lot of flunkies.

The truth is—and I say this in all comradely respect for the Royal Marines—the British Marine represents every admiral's embodied ideal of the perfect Marine: heel-clicking, loyal, immaculately turned out, wise in his way like a graying family retainer—and, like a family retainer, carefully restricted in latitude of opinion and activity. How the Royal Marines reached their present status is another story, and properly one for their own chroniclers, but I must say that their present existence on sufferance and condition that they be limited to minor odd jobs, custodial duties and ceremonies, is a sad commentary on what unthinking admirals and scheming generals can do to stop a courageous corps from developing its own capabilities. It is only good luck and the grace of God which has so far saved the U. S. Marine Corps from a similar inter-service "bum's rush"—as a leading member of Congress put it during the recent merger debates.

Sims' viewpoint was a relic of the peculiar form of snobbery regarding the Marines common in the Navy at that period and occasionally surviving until the beginning of World War II. It was the same spirit I encountered on board ship en route to Nicaragua and it was dangerous because such a prejudice can sway a man's judgment. Sims could never see a fighting man in a Marine.

Naturally these slighting references annoyed Willis and me and finally aroused my resentment. They did not, however, deter me from my determination to push the Marine argument. I knew my ideas on planned and supported landings were sound, and an additional incentive to drive them home was the desire to obtain the recognition of the Marine Corps as brothers in arms with the other two branches of the fighting services.

Given the opportunity to plan and fight, the Marines were qualified by experience and training to undertake these special landing tasks, for which the Navy was unfitted. When the big opportunity did come in the Pacific the Marines demonstrably proved their fitness. Back in 1920 the struggle for the acceptance of these principles, for which I fought during the intervening years and even in the dark, early days of war with Japan, was only just beginning.

Even at that time Marine planners had a far more realistic view of amphibious probabilities than the Navy. Sims' insistence on the employment of bluejackets dates back to old Navy days when the men swarmed ashore with cutlasses and rifles and bayonets, and the enemy automatically surrendered. The new landing technique upon which we were working, and which was absolutely essential to reduce Japanese positions in the Pacific, emphasized the necessity for careful preparation, for communications, for logistics and close support from naval ships to cover the progress of the assault forces ashore.

I am no airman, but the widening scope and increasing effectiveness of air power made me realize the value of this weapon in the support of ground troops. I foresaw the day when the Marines would land according to a coordinated, carefully prepared plan of action, assisted by naval and air arms, and assault strongly fortified positions with no possibility of failure instead of going ashore in a haphazard, extemporaneous swarm, trusting to hit or miss methods.

Here I ran head on into what happily is today discarded naval doctrine. The use of warships in the way I advocated brought strong objections. All arguments produced the same answer: warships could not stand up to fire from heavier shore batteries and, simultaneously, engage in an effective bombardment of shore positions. The advantage always lay with the shore batteries.

In my efforts to write into these naval operation studies a Marine plan of attack, I stressed the need for heavy and concentrated support from naval gunfire, a subject I cannot refrain from mentioning time and time again because of its vital bearing on the success of amphibious warfare. The original Navy reaction was that such a proposal was impracticable. Warships would be required to carry two types of ammunition: high explosive for land bombardment and armor-piercing for action with an enemy fleet. Such a double load would tax magazine capacity.

This view had not been abandoned entirely twenty-three years later at Tarawa, when indecision between the job in hand and the anticipation of the Japanese Fleet resulted in ineffective naval support for the Marines.

I had to mass all the argument and illustration I could to overcome these technical objections but I disposed of them and then progressed to the real battle—the status of the Marines in amphibious operations.

"Holland, you're walking on eggs!" warned Pop Willis. "Don't ever forget that. We've gone a long way in getting the Navy to see things our way but don't push them too hard."

But I was a bad boy. I always have been a bad boy in inter-Service arguments and I often am amazed that I lasted so long in the Marine Corps. In this instance, I knew my arguments were sinking in and to have stopped fighting would have been like quitting the beach when you're dug in.

The Marine Corps at that time was so small that our troops were insufficient for a major landing, but at least the men we had were trained and disciplined. Now, I have great admiration for the American bluejacket. He is one of the finest sailors in the world, but you can't expect him to excel on board ship and then go ashore as an equally excellent infantryman. Most bluejackets are ill trained in small arms and can use neither rifles nor machine guns with efficiency. To throw them into a Marine force without adequate training is dangerous. This statement proved correct during the landing at Vera Cruz, Mexico, when wild fire from the bluejackets killed as many Marines as did the Mexicans.

In my defense of the Marines, I found an unexpectedly staunch ally in Rear Admiral Plunkett. Plunkett also was a veteran sailor but had profited by his experience in land operations in France with his railroad artillery. He was tough, too, like a Marine. Plunkett had seen Marines in action in France and knew what they could do.

One day during a discussion the dogmatic Sims remarked, "Marine officers are not qualified by precept and military education to command large forces in war. They are suitable for minor operations but they cannot be entrusted with major operations."

This smug dismissal made my blood boil, especially after being in action in France with the Marines, but Plunkett came to the rescue. "I'm afraid you're wrong there, sir," he said. "In France, Marine officers commanded divisions and brigades and unquestionably proved their ability as leaders. The Second Division was one of the best outfits we sent over and the 4th Brigade the equal of any brigade in the whole war."

Plunkett was referring to the Second Division commanded by Major General John A. Lejeune, subsequently Commandant of the Corps, and the 4th Brigade, commanded by Brigadier General Wendell C. Neville, also Commandant in later years. We both had seen these Marines in action against the Germans, who were acclaimed the world's best soldiers.

To any fair-minded person, the Marine record in France spoke for itself, but an Army representative at the College shared Sims' view. Strangely enough, although Marines are part of the Naval establishment and family, this similarity of viewpoint by Army and Navy brass is often found when Marines are involved, and persists to this day, even in the so-called amphibious sections of the Navy Department, where the smooth counsels of Army "experts" will often override the more blunt but down-to-earth views of Marine advisers.

I realized my proposal hit not only at established policy but at naval tradition. Never in the long history of the Marine Corps had a Marine commanded an operation. Command had always been given to a naval officer. My contention was that naval officers, while fully qualified to fight at sea, were not trained to command troops ashore, a task that required intimate knowledge of the intricacies of land warfare. Not only was I pressing for acceptance of new military principles but also for recognition of the ability of the Marines, as an independent and co-equal branch of the service, to command operations on the beach.

In spite of the Sims doctrine, I felt I had made a favorable impression on the War College. The principle of Marine participation on equal terms had never been recognized before. Most naval officers were incapable of envisioning a large Marine force operating without naval guidance, although the history of the Pacific campaign subsequently showed how shortsighted they were. I won my point. For the first time, within my knowledge, a complete plan for the employment of Marines ashore under their own command was written into a naval operation, and I am proud that I wrote it!

The plan itself was a departure from ordinary naval technique. On a higher plane was the satisfaction the Marines gained. From that day forward, the status of the Corps improved and we were no longer regarded as a "secondary force."

Perhaps it was the outspoken advocacy of Marine doctrines at the Naval War College that was responsible, after the completion of the course, for my transfer to the Washington Office of Naval Operations, War Plans Department, and my appointment to the Joint Army-Navy Planning Committee. This was in November, 1921, and for the next eighteen months I was the first and only Marine to serve on the Committee. It was a great honor. I was a Major and junior officer on the Committee but I considered the appointment a tribute to the Corps. At long last our ideas were penetrating the thick upper crust of what we in the Corps considered the obsolescent overlay of national defense policy.

The Committee was headed by the Army Chief of Staff and

the Chief of Naval Operations and members, drawn from their staffs, were: Army: Colonel Edgar T. Collins, Colonel John L. De Witt, Lieutenant Colonel John W. Gulick and Major John J. Kingman. Navy: Captain Luther M. Overstreet, Captain Sinclair Gannon, Commander Gilbert Rowcliffe, Commander Wilson Brown, Commander Russell Willson and myself. The Marines definitely had secured a beachhead in high defense councils.

In 1923, our insistence on intensive training of the Marines in their new role led us to look around for suitable training sites. Nothing on the coast of the United States offered the conditions we needed. The solution to our problem was found in the Carribean, where the terrain approximates that of Japanese islands beyond Hawaii.

I was assigned to find the necessary areas and I was happy to see our ideas begin to take on reality. Two areas were selected on the Puerto Rican islands of Vieques and Culebra. Vieques is nine miles off the east coast of Puerto Rico and has an area of fifty-seven square miles, largely lowland, with a small range of hills running down the center. Culebra, eight miles north of Vieques, has an area of eleven square miles—slightly larger than Iwo Jima. I rented the whole of Culebra and suitable beach territory on the arid, sandy eastern tip of Vieques. Owners were pleased to rent land to the U. S. Government, and I arranged yearly tenancies based on local conditions. Marines still go down to Culebra for training but the government pays only for the period we actually use the land. These areas fell into disuse during the war while we were using the beaches of Hawaii.

After selecting the areas and arranging the financial details I went to Panama and reported to Admiral Robert E. Coontz, Commander-in-Chief, U. S. Fleet, and returned with him on the USS Seattle to inspect the sites and get his approval. Thereafter, we had modified terrain needed for specialized amphibious training and for the development of new amphibious weapons.

The two islands are tropical and the beaches suitable for landing purposes. There is little coral but otherwise conditions are very similar to the Pacific. We didn't require any permanent installations beyond the airfield we built on Culebra. As training simulated actual combat, we put up tents instead of barracks. The men received useful embarkation and debarking practice, leaving their home bases in the United States in transports and unloading at Culebra and Vieques, under physical conditions not greatly different from the real thing. These two islands played a vital part in preparing the Marines for the Pacific.

About this time the Marine Corps was baffled by a mystery that was the rumble of a distant gun in my ears. One of our most brilliant strategists was Lieutenant Colonel Earl H. (Pete) Ellis, with whom I had served with the 4th Brigade in France. Like myself, Pete returned to the United States with forebodings and directed his analytical attention to the Pacific, where Japan was fortifying her mandated islands.

The product of his studies was one of the most prophetic war plans ever drafted, based on the anticipation of a Pacific conflict. It was Wellsian in its grasp of the shape of things to come and many of its salient points served as a blueprint for the actual campaign after Pearl Harbor.

As an example of his calculations, in 1923 Pete Ellis predicted that only one reinforced regiment would be needed to capture Eniwetok atoll in the Marshalls, now one of our atomic experimentation bases. Only one reinforced regiment—the 22nd Marines—was used when we took Eniwetok in 1944.

Pete Ellis' plan illustrated the close attention Marine planners were devoting to the Pacific. To test the soundness of his views, he obtained "leave" and roamed around the Pacific among the former German islands to which the Japanese denied access to other nationals. He succeeded in getting ashore at Palau, in the Carolines, but there he "disappeared." We never learned the manner of his death. The Japanese gave out the story that he drank himself to death and they probably were right: conceivably, he was poisoned because the Japanese knew his purpose.

The mystery of Ellis' death deepened when a young chief pharmacist's mate from the U. S. Naval Hospital in Yokohama volunteered to go to Palau and recover the body. He cremated the body but returned to Yokohama a mental case, unable to give a coherent story of his trip or any intelligent information about Ellis. His condition improved, and it seemed possible he would regain enough mental equilibrium to tell his story, but both he and his wife died in the ruins when the 1923 Japanese earthquake demolished the hospital.

One thing the Japanese could not kill was the spirit of inquiry that led Pete Ellis to sacrifice his life, although not all Marine thinking was as advanced as his. Assigned in 1926 to the field officers' course at the Marine Corps School, I was appalled to encounter there almost the same degree of outmoded military thought as I had found at the Naval War College.

The school was commanded by Colonel Robert H. Dunlap, with Major W. W. Buckley as Chief of Staff. Most of the officers on the staff had no battle experience. They were excellent theorists, could quote chapter and verse, but had never been in action and therefore could not handle situations which refused to square with theory. They were on the conservative side, no more capable of grasping reality than some of the officers at the Naval War College, and still floundered among the outdated doctrines of World War I.

From the first day of the course, I found myself deep in difficulties because I objected to the emphasis placed upon defensive tactics. The mission of the Marine Corps is primarily offensive. Any other role deprives us of our effectiveness. For a small, well trained force, capable of great mobility, the best employment is offensive, not defensive. This is a sound military principle.

At the Marine School in Quantico, as well as at the Army School in Leavenworth, the classroom strategists preached that the principles of attack were confined to a superiority of numbers, which is contrary to the opinion of the world's greatest soldiers. Mobile, well trained troops, imbued with *esprit de corps,* should not be confined to a defensive position if there is the possibility of a successful offensive.

Napoleon proved this a century ago. He fought most of his battles with numerically inferior forces but he moved them so rapidly and used them so boldly that he compensated for this initial handicap. One of his greatest maxims was, "The art of war (with inferior forces) consists in having larger forces than the enemy at the point of attack or defense." Stonewall Jackson could not have succeeded had he fought his battles on the theory that he must have numerical superiority before he attacked.

I completed the course, but so wide was the divergence between workable theory and fact that I almost flunked communications. In France I wrote every plan of communications for the First Army Corps and my plans worked successfully in the uncertainties and changing conditions of battle. For this service I received the Meritorious Service Citation from General Pershing. At school I had trouble in obtaining a satisfactory mark in communications. The staff was dealing in textbooks and my experience had been in the practical problems of maintaining communications under fire. Textbooks proved far more formidable than combat obstacles.

I had two reasons for spending the next four years as Post Quartermaster at the Marine Barracks in the Philadelphia Navy Yard. First, I wanted to send my son to the Penn Charter School in the Quaker City, which enjoyed a high reputation both for scholarship and character building. Secondly, I was eager to learn something about logistics—the military science of transport and supply—to round out my background for the war I knew was coming.

A Quartermaster's job isn't very exciting but these four years proved invaluable to me. They gave me an insight into the great problems of equipping an army, problems that magnified in scope when we had to assault islands thousands of miles from our bases. At Philadelphia I learned, as I never learned before, the complicated system of planned supplies, food, clothing, ammunition, equipment—from gas masks to shovels—all wrapped up in that comprehensive word logistics. This experience helped strengthen my insistence on planning as the basis of amphibious warfare.

We still lacked equipment. I got a pretty good illustration of our deficiencies in 1932 when I went to sea again as Battle Force Marine Officer. I was transferred to the USS *California* as FMO on the staff of the Commander Battle Force, U. S. Fleet. Our home station was Long Beach, California. Incidentally, in two years I had the unique experience of serving under four four-star Admirals. They were Admirals Frank H. Schofield, Richard H. Leigh, Luke McNamee and William H. Standley.

That year we held combined exercises off the coast of Oahu, the main Hawaiian island on which Honolulu stands. Joint Army and Navy exercises on a smaller scale had been held off Hawaii before and the 1925 operations actually were based upon Gallipoli and its related problems, but in 1932 we were engaged in the first large scale operation held so close to Japanese bases. It was a test of our strength and of our knowledge of amphibious warfare, with Japan actually in mind. A lot of big brass came along to watch the show.

Supported by the Fleet, the Marines went ashore, waded through the surf, secured a beachhead and carried out all the details of the plan. But what a dismal exhibition! I realized that we had a great deal to learn before we approached anything like efficiency in amphibious warfare.

The Marines landed in standard ships' boats, which were unsuitable for crossing reefs and riding the surf. It was obvious that our elementary need was more efficient landing craft, a retractable type that could get in and out of the surf. Moreover, we didn't have sufficient boats to get enough men ashore at one time to constitute an effective assault force. So small was the number of men we were able to land that the suppositional enemy would have wiped us out in a few minutes.

The Oahu operation revealed our total lack of equipment for such an undertaking, our inadequate training, and the lack of coordination between the assault forces and the simulated naval gunfire and air protection.

"If the Japs had been holding that island, we couldn't have captured it," I told myself. "In fact, we couldn't have landed at all." I realized how badly prepared we were and how urgent was our need for further study and improvement of our methods. The doctrine of amphibious warfare was still in the theoretical stage.

Major General John H. Russell, Commandant of the Marine Corps at that time, was keenly alive to the realities of the situation. In the autumn of 1933, he produced a solution to our organizational problem by fathering the idea, which the Chief of Naval Operations approved, of the Fleet Marine Force. The creation of the FMF was the most important advance in the history of the Corps, for it firmly established the Marine Corps as a part of the regular organization of the U. S. Fleet, available for operations with the Fleet ashore or afloat.

I shall deal later with the history of the FMF, Pacific, which I commanded during World War II, but at the present stage the FMF can be best described by quoting Navy Department Order 245, dated November 27, 1946, which states:

A fleet marine force is defined as a balanced force of land, air and service elements of the U. S. Marine Corps which is integral with the U. S. Pacific and/or Atlantic Fleet. It has the status of a full type command and is organized, trained and equipped for the seizure or defense of advance naval bases and for the conduct of limited amphibious or land operations essential to the prosecution of a naval campaign.

In a nutshell, everything we had striven for was realized in its creation—recognition, independent command ashore, specialized duties. For the first time, a permanent organization for the study and practice of amphibious warfare was brought into existence. The force comprised only 3,000 officers and men in the beginning, with the major elements stationed at Quantico. When I commanded the FMF, Pacific, it was 264,565 strong and its creation paid off during the war.

A year after the birth of the FMF its code for living was written. On General Russell's direction, the new doctrine of landing operations—the Marine Corps School "Tentative Landing Operations Manual"—was formulated, and it has governed the conduct of every amphibious exercise and campaign since 1935, including the war from North Africa to Okinawa. The Navy manual in use up to that date had been a dead letter for thirty years and bore no relation to modern conditions.

Completed in 1934, after years of intense study by Marine

officers, "Tentative Landing Operations Manual" broke ground for a new science in the realm of warfare, a means for carrying an assault from the sea directly into the teeth of the most strongly defended shore. By 1938, after the Fleet Marine Force had thoroughly tested these doctrines, the Navy adopted the entire "Tentative" manual, put a new cover on it, and re-issued it to the Service under title of "FTP–167, Landing Operations Doctrine, U. S. Navy." Three years later still, in 1941, when the Army suddenly realized that the forthcoming war must of necessity be amphibious, General Marshall in turn adopted the "Navy" text of FTP–167, put it between Army covers as "Field Manual 31–5," and promulgated it to the Army as their own doctrine on landing operations. The foreword to FM 31–5, however, does state that it was taken *en bloc* from FTP–167—which is perhaps as good a way as any for the Army to admit that, seven years after Marine Corps Schools had definitively covered a subject, the War Department General Staff was now forced to copy verbatim what Marines had long ago originated.

An interesting footnote to the Marine Corps School's manual is that it was based almost entirely on failures. The entire previous record of amphibious warfare had been spotted with fiasco and disaster, culminating in Gallipoli, during World War I, which convinced most professional heavy thinkers that assault of a defended beach was another of the "impossibilities." In spite of all this, however, our officers went to work on what they could find, dissecting every failure and locating the weak spots and failure-factors. After almost fifteen years of trouble-shooting and experimentation, in 1934 they could write the "Tentative Landing Operations Manual" with confidence. It demonstrates the caliber of their work that those 1934 doctrines not only carried us through Tarawa, Normandy and Iwo Jima, but still stand, to this very day, as the basic amphibious methods of the United States.

Passage of a badly needed Selection Bill also helped streamline the Corps. This too was inspired by General Russell and, in my mind, did more for the Marines than any other legislative act. The Corps was overloaded with officers who had been promoted by seniority. Many were too old for their grades and others were non-progressive and out of line with the new trend of Marine thought. The Selection Bill made possible a clean sweep of the higher ranks and prepared the way for a healthy list of promotions in which merit was recognized.

During this period I could not keep my eyes off Japan. The ominous portents became clearer when I served as Chief of Staff to the Department of the Pacific in 1935. Japan had invaded the Asiatic mainland and overrun Manchuria into North China. From my post in San Francisco, I observed the huge cargoes of scrap iron and oil going from West Coast ports to Japan. The war in China did not require such preparations. The stockpile was being built for war against the United States.

I wrote to General Russell insisting that every effort should be made to intensify our training program in amphibious warfare and to modernize our equipment. The Japanese, I pointed out, had attained a high degree of efficiency in this particular type of warfare along the coasts and rivers of China.

During World War II at Saipan, I read a monitored broadcast in which Tojo and Company complained bitterly that we had copied the technique of amphibious warfare from Japan, even to landing boats and equipment.

My letters to the Commandant served their purpose and accorded with the widening conviction in Marine Corps councils of the nearness of war and the necessity for accelerating our program. The strength of the Corps at this period was 1,224 officers and 16,014 men, limited by Congressional action to twenty percent of the strength of the Navy.

Out of a blue sky in March, 1937, came orders transferring me to Marine Headquarters in Washington and later to the post of assistant to the new Commandant, Major General Thomas Holcomb. I was now a Colonel but I had never served with General Holcomb before, except in the same brigade in France, where he was battalion commander and afterwards regimental commander.

My first post in Washington was Director of Operations and Training. I now was in a position to supervise the building of a modern amphibious force along the lines we had developed for years and to obtain the necessary equipment to insure its success. The amphibious force was the Marine answer to the new concept of war being accepted by the world and the Marines were in training on both the Atlantic and the Pacific coasts to emphasize that answer.

We didn't have long to wait. The Nazis marched into Poland. On September 3, 1939, Great Britain and France declared war on Germany. The United States had been in World War I and it was my honest belief that we could not stay out of World War II.

CHAPTER IV

~~~~~~

THE OUTBREAK of war in Europe caused little surprise in Washington military and naval circles. For months the signs had been plain to read. The only question in my mind was: How long will it be before the United States gets into the war? We were drawn into World War I, and it seemed inevitable that we would be involved in World War II, first in Europe and ultimately in the Pacific, if and when Japan joined the Axis and started casting covetous eyes across the Pacific after she was firmly established on the Asiatic mainland. The stockpiles I had observed being accumulated on the West Coast for shipment to Japan could have only one purpose.

Nobody could honestly say that in Washington we did not appreciate the danger of the situation. The prospect of this country's being involved in the European war was readily admitted but, ironically, there was little realization of the necessity for full preparations for that war. It was another case of everybody knowing what was going to happen but nobody doing much about it.

Frankly, we were not prepared for war—not by a long shot. The armed services had long been starved for funds and the country's defenses were operating on a shoestring because the Army, Navy and Marine Corps were hogtied and hobbled by the insane refusal of the American people even to consider the possibility of having to fight another war. We, as a grateful people, build magnificent memorials to our war dead but we begrudge spending a nickel for defenses strong enough to insure that we shall have no more dead heroes.

Proof of the common attitude toward our defense needs

64

came in 1938 when Rear Admiral Arthur J. Hepburn was appointed by Congress to head a board to study and recommend additional naval bases in the Atlantic and the Pacific. Congress then proceeded to wreck the report by rejecting, among other things, a plan for fortifying Guam, the Mid-Pacific island that was to cost us 7,902 casualties, dead and wounded, to recapture.

Rear Admiral Joseph K. Taussig appeared before a Congressional committee and predicted a war with Japan as the basis for the Navy's needs for additional facilities. So horrified was official and public reaction to his frank speaking that, as a reward for his patriotic services, Taussig was threatened with a court martial and transfer to inactive duty. Such was the American ostrich that required a Pearl Harbor to blast its head out of the sand. Unfortunately, the explosion came too late to save the Pacific Fleet.

In addition to public inertia, the Marine Corps had its own troubles, not stemming from lack of foresight or inability to assess military necessities. Despite ample warning, it was not until the fall of 1942, three years after the Nazis marched into Poland and nine months after the Japanese attacked Pearl Harbor, that we were able to place a fully trained but only partially equipped Marine division in the field although we had two divisions organized.

The Marine Corps has always suffered from the difficulties inherent in a younger brother relationship; a small unit attached to a large force like the Navy which, crippled by its own meager appropriations, tossed us the crumbs. This scant ration was not always doled out intelligently or sympathetically.

Let me explain to the reader our relationship with the Navy. Although Marines primarily are land troops and perform most duties ashore, we are part of the naval establishment. We have our own Commandant but operationally we are commanded by the Commander-in-Chief of the U. S. Fleet in the particular theater where we are serving. We derive our being from the Navy. All Marine procurements come through the Navy. A Navy Budget Officer scrutinizes and passes or rejects all recommendations. This officer is generally a senior captain, frequently a competent sailor familiar with his duties on board ship but certainly not qualified to pass on equipment and supplies needed for an amphibious force like the Marines.

I have objected to this Navy Budget Officer system for years. Surely a self-contained force like the Marine Corps, which can be trusted to conduct a war ashore, also can be trusted to budget for its own needs. We could do it more efficiently than the Navy because we know what we want. The Navy has its own particular supply problems to handle. However, this is the system and it survives to this very day. The Marines cannot obtain the most insignificant item without naval approval. Every pair of socks, every pair of shoes, every undershirt, every round of ammunition, every gun, every tank must be passed on by the Budget Officer, whose mind is thousands of miles away with a broad deck under his feet, the rolling ocean around him, and an efficient executive officer to run his ship.

As Director of Operations and Training in Washington, I included in one of our appropriations schedules an item for half a dozen artillery trucks to haul ammunition. The Budget Officer at that time was a captain who later achieved dubious renown at Pearl Harbor. When his eye encountered this item he paused and asked, "Why don't you do like the Army and use mules and wagons to haul ammunition?"

I choked back the obvious riposte, "There are enough jackasses in the Navy to do the pulling but where would we get the wagons?"

On the credit side of our budgetary methods—and whether it stems from the Navy or Marine Corps, I don't know—it is a matter of record that, dollar for dollar, the taxpayer derives more return from his Marine Corps than from any other armed service. In 1940, for example, we had the world's premier Marine Corps, which cost the country approximately $1,800.00 per individual Marine, whereas we then had the world's eighteenth army, at a cost of almost twice as much per soldier. In all fairness, it must be added that an army is bound to be somewhat more expensive, because as you get increased size, you lose efficiency and accumulate overhead. If in no other sense, though, the Marine Corps will continue to be a national asset simply as a yardstick to enable the public to assess the efficiency (both professional and budgetary) of the Army.

On my way down to Culebra in the spring of 1940, mulling over the responsibilities of new duties assigned me in the West Indies, I often thought of that horse-and-wagon budgeteer. His remark was a cross section of official thought and typical of the obstacles which Marines constantly met in Washington. Such an attitude was incredible, but there it was in the full flower of obtuseness.

At that time I was in command of the 1st Marine Brigade, Fleet Marine Force, with headquarters at Quantico, Virginia. Before leaving the West Coast for Marine Headquarters in Washington, Major General Holcomb, our Commandant, promised me that I would be with him only two years. I was not, and never have been, attracted to an office job. Active field duty is my meat and drink. As it happened, however, instead of two years I actually served thirty months in Washington before I was given brigade command.

The 1st Marine Brigade, with the 1st Marine Air Group attached, was the landing force in Fleet Landing Exercises No. 6, or Flex–6 as it was officially truncated—the sixth of a series of maneuvers held annually in the Caribbean or on the West Coast to test the progress of amphibious training.

For six years we had been putting into practice the new Marine doctrine but still lacked adequate equipment. Starved for funds, the Marine Equipment Board had done its best with the means available, and at Culebra we had made a number of practice landings in boats provided by our antiquated Bureau of Ships, which could do no better than furnish us with outmoded tank lighters, non-propelled artillery lighters and useless personnel landing craft. We did not possess a single ramp boat, although the Japanese had been using ramp boats in China for years. Lack of proper transports, shortage of personnel and a limited production schedule for new weapons also hampered us while the ships needed by the Atlantic Fleet for the 1940 neutrality patrols reduced the strength of the naval units participating in the landings.

Nevertheless, the 1940 exercise was the most advanced and realistic attempted to date. The outbreak of war in Europe had quickened the tempo of training and as I regarded Japan as our official enemy, Flex 6 assumed for me a new significance. I had to fight official apathy and lack of imagination in Washington to put my ideas across. Few of the top brass could visualize the coral islands leading to Japan and the form of warfare the Marines would have to fight to capture them.

Rear Admiral Hayne Ellis, Commander, Atlantic Fleet, commanded the "Farragut Attack Force"—so called—which included Battleship Division Five, comprising the old BBs *Texas*, *Arkansas* and *Wyoming*; Cruiser Division Seven less one ship; Destroyer Squadron Ten; Submarine Division Eleven and a "transport" group. I quote transport because, in reality, we had no transports. This group comprised the old battleship *Wyoming*, the supply ship *Capella* and one "APD," a World War I four-stack destroyer converted into a troop transport.

We embarked at Quantico and Norfolk aboard any ship available, taking with us 1,000 tons of supplies distributed throughout the fleet. The total Marine landing force was approximately 3,000 men, considerably less than a full brigade although we called ourselves a brigade. I had two battalions of infantry, a small battalion of artillery, a small engineer company, a small signal company, a small supply company and five light tanks whose armor was so thin that one clout from a claw hammer would dent it.

These five-ton tanks had been built experimentally with the claim that they particularly fitted Marine requirements. This claim was highly exaggerated. The tanks were fast, but after each operation the temperamental vehicles had to go back to the shop for repairs. The only way we could express our appreciation was to name them after the man who authorized them—Admiral Harold R. (Betty) Stark, Chief of Naval Operations at the time. Our Bettys were mechanical misfits, but they were better than nothing.

During the three landing operations comprising Flex 6, we held training and field exercises ashore on Culebra, the island I had last seen when I rented it for Marine training in 1923. On the south coast of Culebra is the little village of Dewey, named after the Spanish-American War hero, but the island is sparsely populated. It is hilly, with deep valleys and plenty of scrubby trees and tall grass for cattle fodder. Culebra has no fresh water. Rain water was collected in great concrete catchment basins and when this natural supply failed we brought fresh water in barges over from Puerto Rico, a few miles across the straits.

We landed our heavy supplies at Dewey's small pier while the men ran their boats up on the beach and got their first taste of island landing. It was a deceptively mild prelude to the assaults made in war. We made camp in tents and I established my headquarters in a small frame building near the airfield in the center of the island, where the 1st Marine Air Group was stationed.

On my staff at this time were men who subsequently linked their fortunes with mine in the Pacific and served with distinction throughout the war. My chief of staff was Colonel Julian C. Smith, later Commanding General of the Second Division at Tarawa. My G-1 was Lieutenant Colonel John T. Selden; G-2, Lieutenant Colonel A. D. Challacombe; G-3, Lieutenant Colonel David R. Nimmer, later Commanding General, III Amphibious Corps Artillery, and G-4, Lieutenant Colonel George R. Rowan. The Brigade Surgeon was Commander Warwick T. Brown, USN.

We were fortunate in having a man like Rear Admiral Ellis in command. He had considerable experience in training Marines for landing operations and enjoyed the respect and admiration of officers and men. He rendered us every possible assistance, was sympathetic to our shortcomings and placed at our disposal every facility his limited force could supply. Moreover, he lacked that bombastic pomposity too often found in certain naval officers who attempt to assume responsibility over matters with which they are not familiar.

Contrasting unpleasantly with Hayne Ellis' forebearance and understanding of Marine problems was an experience I had with the chief of staff of another admiral during maneuvers. I was testing radio telephone communications between ship and shore and sent a trick message designed phonetically for audibility and clarity, accepted as perfectly sensible by communications men although it sounds childish to the uninitiated.

This was the message: "I now can see twenty-nine men under a tree." The test was routine, everything checked and I forgot about it until I was back on ship that night. There I was promptly taken to task by the chief of staff for sending what he called "a silly, unmilitary message" and wasting the time of his communications officer.

Three landings in Flex 6 were held between February 15 and March 8 on Culebra and the neighboring island of Vieques. Included was a night landing from rubber boats. Introducing reality, we used submarines for reconnaissance missions and for landing scouts, and we constructed underwater defenses to obstruct access to the beaches. Naval gunfire covered shore operations and the training emphasized control of fire and the capabilities of different types of ammunition on targets to be expected in war.

Before passing to an analysis of Flex 6, which was the turning point in our amphibious outlook, let me give the reader a tabloid of an amphibious landing from ship to shore. From transports at a point off the enemy coast, men and equipment are loaded into boats, organized into waves and sent to the beach at intervals to capture the objective, which in war already has been subjected to intense preliminary naval bombardment and air attack in order to neutralize or reduce opposition to the assault forces. This sounds simple enough but the loading of the boats, the formation of the assault waves, the timing of the waves, the overhead protection by airplanes and the supporting fire from warships must be co-ordinated to the nth degree.

All possible information regarding the beach and the area beyond the beach must be obtained. This is done by study of maps, charts and air photographs, reconnaissance of scouts landed at night, and even by survey of the coral floor by underwater demolition teams of expert swimmers. Until the assault forces hit the beach, command is in the hands of the Navy. Once ashore, command passes to the Army or Marine shore commander.

Obviously, plans must be elastic in the event they are disarranged by the unexpected strength of enemy resistance, gunfire and mines, boats breaking down, adverse tides, high surf, bad weather and other unpredictable contingencies. In principle, however, an amphibious operation is the same for a company of a hundred men as it is for a corps of thousands. The Marines followed this pattern from Guadalcanal to Iwo Jima.

After the basic exercise at Culebra, we returned to Quantico with a far clearer picture of our needs. Despite deficiencies in matériel, I felt that Flex 6 showed we had made tremendous progress and that both Navy and Marines were indoctrinated in the principles involved in the new science of warfare.

The chief deficiencies were technical and quantitative. We still did not have enough landing boats of the right kind. We needed more boats capable of retracting after debarking their passengers. During Flex 6, we tested twenty-five special landing craft of three different types, as well as new tank and artillery lighters, with varying results.

In general, operations were confined to the use of ordinary ship's motor boats totally unsuited for work in the surf, which runs as high as six and eight feet at Culebra. The only way these boats could be handled was to head them for the beach until they almost touched bottom and then drop a stern anchor until the men could pile overboard. This way the troops got soaked to the armpits. Not particularly objectionable in warm weather, this saturation is very uncomfortable in cold weather. It also wets all equipment, fills the men's shoes with sand and makes marching difficult ashore. At Culebra, landing waves were disorganized when anchors were fouled and boats swamped in the surf.

For years the Marine Corps had been trying to secure proper boats but we got neither adequate appropriations to build them ourselves nor enthusiastic support from the outmoded Bureau of Ships, whose job it should have been to provide us with the craft. For Flex 6 the Bureau provided a dozen boats copied from the type used by Cape Cod fishermen, with modifications. These quaint models might stock the New England fish markets but they were unsuitable for assault landing purposes. Eight landing skiffs from the Bureau were no better. Two Navy tank lighters proved mechanical handicaps, almost denying us the use of our precious five tanks. They would have got us nowhere in combat, except killed, since they habitually functioned on only one of two engines.

So much for the debit side of the boat account. On the credit side was the first appearance of the prototype of the Higgins boat—the craft that, in my opinion, did more to help win the war in the Pacific than any other single piece of equipment. In the pages of this book I shall have a great deal more to say about the Higgins boat because without it our landings on Japanese-held beaches in large numbers would have been unthinkable.

Basically, the original Higgins boat used at Culebra, which was called the Eureka, resembled the modified model used successfully in the Pacific, North Africa, Sicily, Italy, Normandy and every other theater; mother and father of the LCVP (Landing Craft Vehicle Personnel) the standard landing craft, and a big and diversified family of LC's. Andrew Higgins told me he developed the boat in 1926 for use in the shallow waters of the Mississippi River and along the Gulf Coast, where it could run its bow up on river and bayou banks and back off easily. We did not get it until fourteen years later, but it was the same shallow-draft type with a tunnel stern that could nose up on the beach and retract. It suffered one defect, which wasn't remedied until later. The boat had no ramp that could be lowered, permitting the men to debark directly on the beach instead of jumping over the side.

The Marine Equipment Board had obtained five Eurekas, which proved their superiority on the Culebra beaches that spring. Not only did these boats mark a definite advance in landing facilities but I could see in their improvement and modification an answer to the Marine prayer—a retractable, shallow draft ramp boat, superior to the Japanese wooden type, that would carry us over the reefs to our island objectives.

72

Between the spring of 1940 and the spring of 1941, when we held Fleet Landing Exercise 7, we made great strides, under the urgency of the European war, in equipping amphibious troops. Back in Quantico, I was informed that the Navy had embarked on a ship purchase program to provide us with transports and was buying up all sorts of passenger liners that could be converted to our special assault needs. We already had one transport, the USS *Henderson*, but she was used solely for carrying Marine replacements to overseas stations and could not be employed as an assault transport, a term and a ship function that our amphibious needs had developed.

The first two vessels for transports, renamed the *McCawley* and the *Barnett* after Marine Corps Commandants, were purchased in New York, and I delegated a number of Marine officers to examine the ships and advise the Navy on the changes we desired. Washington obviously realized the gravity of the international situation, and our big brass was making up for lost time. The old battleships were no longer suitable for carrying amphibious troops. We needed a special type of ship, carrying men and cargo, and equipped to launch landing boats rapidly and easily. Once put to the task and backed by an awakening public apprehension of danger, the Navy did its job ably.

Even with the acquisition of these new transports it became evident that great improvements would have to be made before we could employ them to maximum advantage. The davits were ponderous and slow, necessitating development of new davit and deck machinery. The water supply was inadequate for the number of troops the ships would carry, and there were other drawbacks. But it was a start, before the Navy began building special assault personnel and cargo transports, and we were encouraged.

When I commanded the landing forces in Fleet Landing Exercise No. 7, we employed assault transports for the first time. This exercise lasted from February 4 to February 16, 1941, and was a joint Army-Marine operation. Since the previous exercise, important developments had occurred. Our experience in Culebra demonstrated that it was possible to expand the 1st Marine

Brigade into a division with little effort. My staff officers were competent and well trained, functioned in a superior manner and showed themselves fully qualified to serve as divisional officers. Before embarking on Flex 7, the Brigade completed several months' intensive training at Guantanamo, Cuba, an alternative training area, and while in the Caribbean was redesignated, on February 1, 1941, the First Marine Division.

Flex 7 was historic as the final prewar exercise in the Caribbean. It was a joint exercise involving elements of the First U. S. Army Infantry Division (then under overall Marine command for amphibious training) and the First Marine Division. My Marine division was below divisional strength and its three infantry battalions, plus two Army battalions, placed the exercise once again on a brigade, not a divisional, basis.

Naval forces included Battleship Division Five with our three old friends, the *Texas, Arkansas* and *Wyoming*; Cruiser Division Seven comprising four ships; Destroyer Squadron Two (less a division) and an aircraft group including two aircraft carriers and the 1st Marine Air Group. After the previous exercise we had recommended the use of carriers and this was adopted. Instead of a makeshift transport group we actually had three transport divisions: our own three ships, the *McCawley, Wharton* and *Harry Lee*; two Army Transports and three APDS (destroyer transports). Unified command of all participating forces was under Rear Admiral Ernest J. King, who had succeeded Hayne Ellis as Commander, Atlantic Fleet.

During the Culebra exercise I had occasion again to assert my authority in behalf of my Marines. I have already described the incident of the mess bills on board Navy ships but the impositions went much farther. The Marine was always the whipping boy. On board ship there was an acute shortage of fresh water and the Captain of the *McCawley* accused his Marine passengers of stealing it, despite strict orders to conserve. For a period of 24 hours, he shut off all fresh water outlets, except those required for cooking, but afterwards 10,000 gallons were still missing. I sent Captain Victor H. Krulak, a member of my staff, to investigate and he found that the Marines were not to blame. The ship's petty officers were diverting fresh water from the tanks to flush their toilets.

Overcrowding was another irritation. On one transport, where conditions appeared unreasonably congested, I discovered the Captain had set aside much needed space on the top deck as a promenade for his dog. That officer was detached from his command shortly afterwards.

The purpose of Flex 7 was threefold: to train Army and Marine divisional units in landing operations; to test the efficacy of existing doctrine governing these operations; and to train commanders in joint command and staff procedure. Rear Admiral King was not an easy man to get along with; he was far different from his predecessor, who had such an enlightened grasp of amphibious problems and appreciated the shore commander's viewpoint.

King was a brilliant man, as he proved later throughout the war as COMINCH (Commander-in-Chief, U. S. Fleet) and Chief of Naval Operations. He was dynamic, energetic, severe and quickly impatient with men who couldn't think as fast as he did. On the debit side, he was a domineering man, a frosty product of naval tradition, and he sometimes interpreted the term "command" too literally for harmonious conduct of a complex undertaking like an amphibious landing. With all these defects—which were in reality the defects of his virtues, as the French say—King's diamond-like hardness and perfectionism were destined to stand the United States in good stead.

The Caribbean exercise was probably the first occasion in King's career when he was connected with an enterprise in which he knew less about training the forces involved than the officer primarily responsible for the training, who was his junior. But he never admitted this fact.

The Marine never tries to tell the sailor how to run his ship. He recognizes that the ability and experience of the sailor fit him to operate his vessel without outside interference. Conversely, the Marine does not expect the sailor to tell him how to conduct landing operations, for which the Marine's ability and training equally fit him.

On board Admiral King's flagship, the USS *Texas*, we bitterly disputed the selection of landing beaches. I had my own ideas, based upon long experience, of what we needed to permit full exploitation of the training program. King would have no part of it. He insisted on making his own selection and chose a beach on the nearby island of St. John, which, in war, would have been plain suicide for an assault force. His beach was shallow, blocked by impassable mountains and was totally unsuitable for the landing of troops, artillery, tanks and supplies.

I pointed out to him that landing on his beach would be useless unless we had a beachhead. Now *beachhead* is a term developed in the progress of amphibious warfare to describe a topographical and tactical element. It is synonymous with *bridgehead*, the term used by the Army to describe a suitable point on the enemy side of a river which can be fortified to protect a crossing. In amphibious warfare, beachhead means an area beyond the actual beach which can be held to protect the landing of supplies on the beach and used as a base to continue the assault.

"Beachhead!" King was caustic. "I'm getting sick and tired of hearing the word 'beachhead.' It's beach, I tell you, not beachhead. Why don't you Marines get it straight?"

"Admiral, we do get it straight," I replied. "A beach is one thing, but a beachhead is another. A beachhead is a place where you can get your men, tanks and supplies on, and also get them off if you want to move inland."

Beachhead and *operation* were the two most common military terms to emerge from World War II as additions to the English language, but it was useless to argue with a man like King.

So with the remark on *beaches* his directive stood, and I was handicapped from the very beginning. He ordered me to make the landing with nothing to go on but the general information contained in the sailing directions compiled for mariners. These were all very well for coastwise traders, but useless to a Commanding General preparing to put a large force ashore on unreconnoitered, "hostile" territory. King had airplane photographs of this particular beach which he could have given me, thus providing the accurate detailed information we badly needed. Instead, he kept the photographs to himself. I never was able to figure out why he kept them. After all, the Navy and the Marines were "fighting" on the same side. Or so I thought.

It was obvious that if the exercise was to serve any profitable purpose we could not—and should not—use King's beach. It would wreck all our plans. I told the Admiral that landing at that point would be of no value whatsoever and, furthermore, if we went ahead, the choice of such a landing beach would cause a good deal of criticism among the younger officers. It was opposed to all they had learned in training, since it was a narrow beach with no egress to the rear. His decision, if he insisted upon it, would seriously reflect on the judgment of the higher command in the minds of the men who knew such a choice was wrong in amphibious warfare. My argument won the day and grudgingly —for he had built a career on being right—he cancelled his directive.

This was one of many controversies showing basic differences which sometimes existed between Navy and Marine thinking. King had another idea for a landing, this time on the southern coast of Puerto Rico itself. In this case the beach had an impassable canal behind it and to approach the canal would have necessitated a ninety degree turn through a narrow channel parallel to the beach. Enfilading fire from the "enemy" across the canal would have wiped us out.

Before accepting this beach I asked permission to fly over it. King, now more reasonable, lent me his plane. From aerial inspection, it was obvious the beach was wholly unsuited for landing. The area in the rear was marshy, and a letter from my medical officer, Commander Brown, reinforced my objections by pointing out the district was infested with flukes and also had the highest incidence of malaria in the Caribbean.

Another fact I rammed home before we abandoned the project was that no effort had been made to obtain trespass rights for that particular area. It was Puerto Rican private property and we would have been snowed under with claims once we set foot ashore there without permission. Conditions were different at

Culebra and Vieques. There we rented the beaches and could do as we liked. But not on Puerto Rico.

By this time Admiral King was convinced that I knew my business. He agreed to my plans and supported me fully. Army and Marine forces held alternate landing exercises, valuable for future joint operations. These landing exercises also were useful in training personnel of the new transports in debarkation duties, so we could compile data regarding the transfer of men from ship to landing craft, essential in planning a ship-to-shore schedule. Equipment and boats were still short despite our efforts since the previous exercise to make up the deficit.

Ideas were flowing around the design for an amphibious tank and we nearly produced one involuntarily during the exercise. A tank was travelling ashore on a lighter under tow when the lighter careened and the tank slid into the sea. We would have lost the vehicle entirely had not the tank settled in an upright position and although it became completely amphibious we managed to salvage it.

I established headquarters ashore on Culebra but even there it was difficult to escape the influence of the high naval command, reluctant to relinquish the slightest degree of control. A Navy staff fashion at this period was white blouses and black trousers. Arrayed like this King and his staff came ashore to inspect my positions. They looked like Soviet Commissars at a midsummer festival in Red Square.

In so far as these visits showed interest in operations ashore, I welcomed them but I felt the military experience of King and his staff did not qualify them to judge my positions and formations. King told me confidently during discussions on the beach that he had some military experience. I asked where he got it. He said he commanded a regiment of midshipmen at the Naval Academy in 1902. I let the matter drop.

Another visitor to the maneuvers was Secretary of the Navy Frank Knox, who joined the jeering section. The Marine utility uniform, which Knox had never seen, impressed him more than any other phase of the operation. He was accustomed to seeing the Marines on parade in dress blues or pressed forestry greens, so he was shocked when he saw their bedraggled battle uniforms, saturated with dust and splotched with brown earth.

I explained that the men were living under battle conditions and were working and sleeping in foxholes, for which this particular outfit had been designed. The Secretary appeared to accept the explanation but when he returned to Washington he reported to our Commandant that his Marines looked like "a lot of bums." Knox had forgotten—or perhaps never known—that the appellation "bums" was first used in English to describe one of the most successful armies of modern times, Sherman's. In any case, however, the Secretary's reference was not intended as a compliment.

Although Flex 7 suffered from lack of equipment, the results were by no means negligible. Satisfactory boat training and practice of supply functions in landing were carried out. All participating units finished training with a better appreciation of the intricate problems involved in a joint undertaking, even on the small scale of this particular exercise.

However, my naval troubles were not at an end. I still had to deal with the admiralty temperament. One night at dinner King mentioned a communication which I denied receiving. This denial so angered him that he jumped up from his place at the table, walked over to his desk at the side of his cabin, dashed off a message and then resumed his seat.

Later during the dinner, this message, demanding acknowledgment, was handed to me across the table by King's chief of staff. This excessive formality was humiliating, especially in the presence of other officers seated around the Admiral's table. It was also amusing. In the correct manner of acknowledging official dispatches I looked King gravely in the eye and intoned, "Your so and so received . . .," following the acknowledgment formula. He said nothing, and the meal proceeded to after-dinner coffee, which was bitter in my mouth.

After Culebra, I left the USS *Texas* with the feeling that by insisting on carrying out my own theories I had incurred King's disapproval and that, in all probability, I would be relieved of command. This conviction was strengthened by the absence of an official farewell. The Admiral failed to see me over the side, according to naval custom, and I went on board the transport *Harry Lee* certain that my services would soon be terminated. This feeling persisted despite the fact that, during Flex 7, President Roosevelt authorized me to assume the rank of Major General ("without pay and allowances") although I did not "make my number" until the following October. King was promoted to Vice Admiral at the same time.

I knew, nevertheless, that I had done my job, and this feeling of pride and satisfaction helped bolster my morale. Next day a letter arrived by special boat from the flagship. I looked at the envelope and felt that this was the end. I took the letter into the privacy of my cabin, because it would have been impossible to conceal the blow from the others if I read it on deck. Here was what King, the caustic, had written:

> At the close of the recent intensive landing force exercises, I wish to express to you and to the troops under your command in this area my feeling of satisfaction that such well-trained troops, so well commanded, are an integral part of the Atlantic Fleet, and my confidence in their capacity to do their full part and to do us all credit in whatever active operations may come our way. Well done!
>
> E. J. KING

It was, in many ways, the finest commendation I have ever received, and it taught me that, unlike many another in high places, Ernie King would say his worst to your face, would never go behind your back, and would reward performance with a generosity as unexpected as it was King-ly.

After Culebra a need developed for facilities at home to free us from dependence upon the Caribbean Islands, which at some future date might be denied us. An intensive search of the Atlantic Coast from Maine to Florida was made and the investigating Board of Officers hit upon New River, North Carolina, where broad beaches and ample rear areas provided the necessary conditions of terrain. Through the influence and assistance of the Hon. Clifton A. Woodrum, Congressman from Roanoke, Va., appropriations were obtained for the purchase of this area in the winter of 1940. This gave us training grounds for land operations as well as a landing beach for boats.

New River became the largest Marine training base in the United States and its size, 110,000 acres, enabled us to give substance to what were only dreams in the restricted area of Culebra and Vieques. By the following August, our exercise was almost as large as some of the island operations in the Pacific.

For the force landing exercise starting August 4, 1941, the largest of its type held in the United States, 1,500 yard beaches were laid out and designated by letters for each assault division. Across them we put ashore 16,500 officers and men of the First Army Division and the First Marine Division, 300 vehicles and 2,200 tons of supplies. Forty-two naval vessels and four aircraft carriers participated. Vice Admiral King, Commander, Atlantic Fleet, was again in overall command but was not present.

Such a high degree of realism was attained that following the seizure of a beachhead, an advance of nine miles inland was made before withdrawal was ordered, a necessary ingredient of a well-balanced training plan. Marine parachute troops were employed for the first time and 266 landing craft of different types were used.

Analyzing the results, the maneuver was again hampered by lack of equipment and personnel, especially in the field of communications. Initial phases of the landing suffered from shortage of tank lighters and of motor transport ashore. There were other deficiencies which an enterprising "enemy" could have exploited, but in my mind the debut of the Higgins boat, complete with ramp, more than compensated for these deficiencies.

The Bureau of Ships, true to its stolid habits, supplied a diversity of craft but our five 26-foot Higgins ramp boats set a new mark for performance and reliability. At last we had the boat we wanted. Of the several types used, our five Higgins ramp boats and sixteen Higgins tank lighters "proved the most satisfactory," my official report reads. Actually, this was sheer understatement. They proved to be some of our most potent war weapons.

Now that we had the New River training base and Washington began to loosen up with appropriations, there was no limit to what we could do. Mass production training was one of the innovations. We built the first mockup: a platform resembling the side of a ship over which men learned to debark using cargo nets hanging over the side. It looked like a huge movie set strayed from Hollywood but was far more substantial. Over its side graduated thousands of men who carried the lessons they learned in North Carolina to surf-swept atolls of the Pacific. The mockup cost $175,000 and to wring the money out of Washington, our resourceful Quartermaster, Brigadier General Seth Williams, performed a miracle.

The New River installation enabled us to embark upon the first large scale amphibious training program, which made the big August maneuver possible. In June, 1941, I was given command of the First Joint Training Force, a provisional corps organization consisting of the First Army Division commanded by Major General D. C. Cubbison, the First Marine Division commanded by Brigadier General Philip Torrey and other troops.

The primary mission of this corps was to prepare a two-division expeditionary force for employment under the Commander, Atlantic Fleet, in amphibious operations in the Atlantic. War was threatening the United States. This largely underscored all planning and primary emphasis was placed on combat readiness. However, the group originally envisioned as an expeditionary force increasingly became a training staff.

The reason for this transition is understandable if we recall what now seems so unbelievable, that in 1941 the United States had not a single amphibiously trained unit—even in the most elementary principle—except the minuscule Fleet Marine Force. In Army field service regulations of the day (and even much later) landing operations occupied tail-end spot in a list of so-called "special" operations of the remote-contingency type, being spotted just behind "Partisan Warfare." A few Army observers had looked over our peacetime Fleet Landing Exercises, and, in the San Clemente maneuvers of 1937, a small provisional force of West Coast soldiers had received elementary indoctrination, but, at the end of the war-games, this had been disbanded.

The subject of amphibious warfare was a dead letter in all of our service schools (except those operated by the Marine Corps at Quantico)—largely because few people believed either that major landing operations would ever be needed, or that, in any event, they could succeed. I often look through back files of Army professional journals of the period, but I have yet to find a single article dealing with the problem of amphibious assault, unless a stray Marine officer managed to find his way into print. Nowadays, this is all changed: the public can readily be excused for believing that the amphibious miracle of ten years ago was nothing sensational; and now that the technique has been proven to be successful and essential, it has found a horde of self-appointed sponsors, each of whom competes to claim credit for its evolution.

As a result of this lack of any amphibious know-how (let alone trained units), it became the obvious duty of the Fleet Marine Force to convert itself into a training-command, and this was what we became.

During June, July and August of 1941 we trained intensively at New River but results pointed up the necessity for radical change. At Fort Story, Va., I acted as umpire in a landing by the First Army Division. The weather was bad and interfered with plans but the operation was so inefficiently conducted that I wrote to Admiral Stark, Chief of Naval Operations, recommending the creation of a special organization devoted exclusively to amphibious training. After completing training at New River in August, the First Joint Training Force was redesignated the Amphibious Force, Atlantic Fleet, with headquarters at the Norfolk Naval Base. The force comprised Army and Marine units under my command. Army, Navy and Marine personnel were selected for the training staff with Rear Admiral Henry K. Hewitt eventually in overall command.

After the departure of Admiral King from the amphibious command we had a number of admirals in charge but no sooner were they indoctrinated in amphibious principles than they were transferred. One of them refused to be indoctrinated and his stay was brief. Duties of an amphibious admiral include a certain amount of flying but this particular officer said his wife would not let him fly. He moved on after a few weeks.

Rear Admiral Hewitt was outstanding as directing head of the new enterprise. While he came to us with little background in amphibious training, he applied himself earnestly to our particular problems and made rapid progress. He was intelligent, sympathetic and willing to accept recommendations. Our relationship was pleasant and "all hands" were happy.

On the West Coast, a similar organization known as the Second Joint Training Force was created under command of Major General C. B. Vogel, USMC, and later became known as Amphibious Corps, Pacific Fleet. The Corps comprised the Second Marine Division, the Third Army Division and other forces. When Vogel left for the Pacific a year later I succeeded him.

This was the nucleus of the command which prepared all six Marine divisions for war in the Pacific, and, what was fully as important, imparted all the U. S. Army ever learned in basic amphibious knowledge. I have heard it remarked, with some superiority, I must say, that our Army had 28 amphibiously trained divisions by the end of World War II, whereas the Marines never had more than six. What this glib observation omits, intentionally or not, is the fact that the first three U. S. Infantry divisions ever to become amphibious units, the 1st, 3rd and 9th, were trained by the Marine Corps; these were likewise the total of assault infantry divisions which executed our North African landings. Furthermore, in addition to these crucial three divisions, Marines trained the 7th, 77th, 81st, and 96th Infantry Divisions. That means, in recapitulation, that we gave the Army seven of those vaunted 28 amphibious divisions (including the first three) With seven Marine-trained divisions, even the Army, I should think, would find relatively little difficulty in carrying on with training the rest.

The Fleet Marine Force doctrine spread through all services in all theaters of operation. Admiral Hewitt and Vice Admiral Alan G. Kirk, key members of whose staffs had trained with me applied the doctrine to landing operations in North Africa

Sicily, Italy and Southern France. Vice Admiral Daniel E. Barbey, who had been chief of staff to the Commander of Training in the Atlantic Fleet, carried the doctrine to the Southwest Pacific. The First Marine Amphibious Corps took it to the South Pacific and the Fifth Amphibious Corps continued to practice and refine its basic tactics in the Central Pacific.

Our doctrine had begun a revolution in warfare.

CHAPTER V

O N SUNDAY, December 7, Ada and I were invited to lunch at the Army and Navy Country Club in Arlington, overlooking the beautiful Potomac. Our hosts were Brigadier General Robert L. Denig, USMC, and Mrs. Denig, and even for a service party it proved a disjointed affair for every one of the fifty-seven guests. Contrary to precedent, the last to arrive was the General's Aide, who mumbled flustered excuses about being detained at the office.

During each course several officers were called to the telephone. They returned looking dazed, made their excuses to their hostess and departed "on business" until our ranks slowly thinned to a nervous shadow of the original party. Finally General Denig excused himself with the promise to find out exactly what was taking his guests away so abruptly.

He returned, looking very grave, and called the few of us left to the radio outside the dining room. H. V. Kaltenborn was speaking: his low, authoritative voice unusually stirring. "The Japanese are attacking Pearl Harbor," Kaltenborn announced and went on to give the meager details available of the attack on the Pacific Fleet. Everybody was shocked into momentary silence. Then the storm broke.

One Navy officer vowed the message was a fake, probably remembering the Orson Welles Men from Mars broadcast that had terrified the nation. Others pooh-poohed the idea of such an attack on our great mid-Pacific naval base. What's more, they argued wildly, the Japs wouldn't dare! By this time most of the guests had gone, including Colonel Graves B. Erskine, my Chief of Staff, who returned to Quantico. Still refusing to accept the fact of the attack, two die-hards lingered behind, anchored to the radio.

My reaction was the direct opposite. War had come and from the direction the Marines had predicted, although we had expected to be involved in the European conflict first. Yes, it was war, and the country was not prepared.

I am not a man given to panic, so Ada and I proceeded with our plans for that Sunday afternoon, which included a concert at Constitution Hall. As we drove past the Army and Navy Building, where the services lived in harmony before they dispersed to separate wartime quarters, we saw armed sentries with steel helmets and live ammunition in their cartridge belts. There they were to stand—until peace came.

For me the concert was a respite, an interval during which I was able to accustom myself to the idea of my country once more at war. There was nothing for me to do at Quantico that Sunday; emergency measures must wait until the next day. I don't recall what the orchestra played that afternoon and I only remember the audience coming to its feet with the first stirring note of "The Star-Spangled Banner."

Back at the Marine base, I made preparations for a partial blackout and ordered dispersal of the few planes on the aviation field. As my command was training, not combat, I commenced to survey the wartime task of the Marine Corps from the viewpoint of both intensive and extensive training. I knew that the Corps would develop during the war out of all proportion to its peacetime strength. I knew that we would fight an amphibious war in the Pacific. There was no need to outline our needs. The Navy had only to dust off the files in Washington to find all our plans and requisitions, which had been waiting there for years.

By Act of Congress, the strength of the Marine Corps was still restricted to twenty percent of the Navy. However, the Selective Service Act of the previous year had increased the Navy's intake of men and we were free to increase our enlistments proportionately. At the time of Pearl Harbor the Corps' strength was 66,319, all volunteers, and after December 7 recruits poured in faster than we could handle them. Since all Marines are volunteers, we always have been able to maintain our high physical standards and during the war they were not lowered to any great extent.

While we trained recruits we had to keep in mind the priority claims of the First Division, which would be the first sent overseas. At the outbreak of war the First was in fairly good shape, though below strength. In order to build up our training staff, we were compelled to drain the First of both officers and non-commissioned officers. And, in addition to training troops for land duty, we were called upon to furnish Marines for the increasing number of naval ships requiring Marine detachments. It long had been a Corps custom to assign only the best trained officers and men to sea duty. We built up the First with new recruits and when the division sailed for New Zealand in the spring of 1942 it was a well-trained outfit.

We had shortages of everything but men. Training was ahead of production and we ran our equipment red hot. Our greatest shortage was ammunition for rifle and artillery practice. The country had allowed its reserve to sink so low that if the Japanese had continued from Pearl Harbor with an amphibious force and landed on the West Coast they would have found that we did not have enough ammunition to fight a day's battle. This is how close the country was to disaster in 1941.

We needed anti-aircraft guns, anti-tank guns, 50-caliber machine guns, 37-m.m. guns, more 75-mm.'s, 105 and 155-mm.'s, heavier tanks, bazookas, flame throwers, planes, all of which existed in design and required only to be manufactured. We had no special assault personnel ships or assault cargo ships to transport us or our equipment.

Amphibious wars are not fought with ships and guns alone. We needed better marching shoes for the jungles and hard coral rocks. Our garrison shoes were too light. We needed utility uniforms and camouflage suits. The First Division was issued white mosquito nets because they were the only nets available. We had to dye them green to make them less conspicuous jungle targets before the First left for the South Pacific. We needed medical equipment, tents, cots, blankets, mess gear, cooking equipment, belts, belt buckles, sight covers for rifles and hundreds of other items ranging from buttons to trucks of all tonnages, bulldozers and tractors.

One bright spot in the supply picture was the landing boat. We had got rid of the crazy, unseaworthy boats the Bureau of Ships had tried for years to foist on us and had concentrated on the Higgins ramp boat, which we were receiving in increasingly satisfactory numbers.

The Marine boat fight with the Navy had been long and frustrating. On the one hand, we encountered the antiquated ideas and obstinacy of the Bureau of Ships. On the other, we suffered frustration through lack of funds. Pearl Harbor did not end the struggle. Except for availability of funds, it grew more intense in 1942 and showed how difficult it is to loosen well-anchored tradition and how dangerous to national defense such tradition can be.

For twenty years the Marines had experimented with all types of landing craft until our needs crystallized in the Higgins boat and we maneuvered, bullied and coerced the Navy Department into adopting it. We tested shallow draft boats, skiffs, Coast Guard boats, Cape Cod fishing boats and many other types. One day a number of boats seized from rum runners operating off the Florida Coast were turned over to us. They may have been good liquor carriers but they were useless for assault troops. Both the Navy and the Marines had established development boards working on plans for a practical assault boat.

We knew what we wanted. The basic boat we envisioned, which became the standard landing craft in all theaters and was used by all the Allies, had the following characteristics: length, 30 to 36 feet; draft, two feet; speed, 10 knots with a 120-mile fuel endurance; capacity, 18 to 38 men.

Certain other conditions were essential: seaworthiness and stability in the open sea; ability to land through the surf and retract; armor for the coxswain, the engineer and the gunner; lightness, so that the boat could be hoisted by ships' booms and davits.

The appearance of the Higgins Eureka boat at the 1940 Caribbean exercises was the first approach to these specifications. As I said before, the Eureka was designed in 1926 for the shallow waters of the Mississippi. It had an unusual type of bow and its builder called it a spoonbill. Andrew Higgins developed two models with a tunnel stern; one where the propeller was completely within the tunnel and the other with a half or semi-tunnel stern. His modification of his Mississippi boat performed well in its first military test.

Higgins, who offered the Eureka to the Navy in 1927, renewed his offer year after year but it received little consideration in Washington. The Marines, however, were greatly interested. Higgins visited Quantico in 1934 and discussed his boat with us. The Corps had no funds at its disposal to undertake the construction of such a boat but we did not lose interest, which Higgins appreciated. In 1937 he went to the Navy again and furnished them with drawings and complete specifications regarding the boat. After a long delay, he was informed that the Navy had only $5,200 available for an experimental boat and he agreed to build one for that sum. He also accepted the Navy stipulation that the boat should not exceed 30 feet in length.

Higgins built his boat, the first Eureka type for landing purposes. He told me it cost him $12,500 but he considered it money well spent. The Marine Equipment Board was impressed by the potentialities of the new boat. Only the length was against it; the Marines preferred a landing boat nearer 40 than 30 feet long but the Navy was adamant on this point.

Andrew Higgins, a fighting Irishman, won the opening phase of the boat battle single-handed, with loud Marine applause. The Navy placed several experimental orders with him for the 30-foot boat, which he filled more or less under protest. As he told me, he was in bad odor because he kept insisting that the boats should be longer.

During a memorable conference at the Navy Department he again brought up the question of length, which was running the Bureau of Ships ragged, and urged that the boats be built 39 or even 40 feet long. Why should the Navy stick to a 30-foot boat? he demanded. The explanation given him, with chill naval logic, was this: boat davits already placed on a number of ships had been standardized to handle 30-foot boats.

"To hell with designing a boat to fit the davits!" Higgins roared. "Why don't you design davits to fit a proper sized boat?"

He was so exasperated that he returned to New Orleans and, at his own expense and without orders from the Navy, built a 36-foot boat and shipped it to the Norfolk Navy Yard with the demand that it be tested. When the Marines heard about this, they whooped. After passing Naval tests, the boat was sent to us at Quantico and we put it to further tests.

Through the unfathomable processes whereby the official mind finally emerges from darkness into light, the Navy eventually decided to standardize on the 36-foot Higgins boat. Higgins has always said that without Marine championship of his boat over the years, it never would have been tested.

The New Orleans scourge of the Washington bureaucrats displayed much the same scorn as I did for obstructive brass. When I was in command at New River in 1941 and 1942, during our critical equipment period, I was in constant touch by telephone with Higgins in New Orleans. He also visited me, bringing members of his staff to help us in our boat training. Higgins was never too busy to answer a phone call and give advice on a problem. If the matter was too involved to settle over the telephone he sent a representative to work it out with us at New River. Major Victor H. Krulak, who was my boat officer, acted as liaison officer with Andrew Higgins and he was a very busy man.

The Eureka had all the qualifications we demanded except one. Once on the beach, it had no way of discharging men or cargo except over the side. The answer to this problem was the ramp gate. Brigadier General Emile P. Moses, who headed the Marine Equipment Board, worked out the idea with Higgins in New Orleans. From these conferences emerged the famous boat that—in my opinion—contributed more to our common victory than any other single piece of equipment used in the war.

91

I wrote to Andrew Higgins on February 5, 1942, after we had tested his boats:

We believe that your new ramp type boat comes very close to perfection. We look upon your equipment as a part of our Force: quite as essential as tanks and guns and ammunition. I want to say that I never lose an opportunity to tell people in high latitudes that we have the best damn boats in the world, but only half enough.

Andrew Higgins also came to the aid of the Marines in the battle of the tank lighter, where we had another ally in the War Investigating Committee established by Congress on March 1, 1941, and headed by Senator Harry S. Truman. The Higgins ramp boat, officially designated the LCVP (R) (Landing Craft, Vehicle, Personnel, Ramp) was suitable for carrying small numbers of men or light vehicles. We needed craft to carry our tanks ashore and since technical developments were producing larger tanks these craft must be substantial vessels.

In the 1941 Caribbean exercises, the Bureau of Ships supplied us with three 45-foot tank lighters of its own design, capable of carrying one 16-ton tank or two 6-ton tanks. After the exercises I reported: "The Bureau type lighters are heavy, slow, difficult to control, difficult to retract from the beach and equipped with an unpredictable power plant." This was a mild stricture. They were unmanageable and unseaworthy in heavy surf. One capsized.

Notwithstanding criticism from the Marines and from the Navy afloat, the Bureau proceeded to award contracts for the construction of 96 lighters of this condemned design. By the end of the spring of 1941, clamor against the Bureau type of lighter was so loud that Admiral Stark approved our suggestion that Higgins be given a contract to design an experimental 45-foot tank lighter, with authorization to build more if the pilot model proved successful. We urgently needed lighters to keep pace with our training plans. Higgins had suited our book before and we believed he would again.

The Bureau of Ships put the job in Higgins' hands on May

27, 1941. He set to work with characteristic energy and had the lighter in the water in 61 hours. Produced in this incredibly short time, it was accepted as the stock model of all the tank lighters we used in the war, although there were subsequent refinements. The lighter was practically dedicated to the Marine Corps, since Higgins declined to take any action except through Marine channels.

He told me the full story of this wonderful job that set the Navy on its ear. The Bureau of Ships called him by telephone and asked him to design, develop and build a steel boat to carry combat tanks. Higgins promised to do the job if it were urgent but made one stipulation. He would deal only with the Marine Corps, not with the Navy. Brigadier General Moses and Lieutenant Colonel Ernest Linsert, Secretary of the Marine Equipment Board, flew to New Orleans to discuss Marine needs with the forthright boatbuilder.

At that time Higgins had on hand a partly completed shallow draft, twin screw, steel boat designed for use on the Amazon. The pilot house was finished and the Diesel engines ready to install. Overnight the hull was cut up and the Amazon river boat was converted into a vessel capable of carrying a heavy tank. It was fitted with a ramp gate. Though the new boat was improvised in haste, it was a great success in tests. The Truman Committee said that this boat, built in 61 hours, was superior to the Bureau of Ships lighter, which represented four years of design and development.

The Navy designated Higgins' newest boat LCM (3) (Landing Craft, Medium) and gave him an order for 49 more, ten to be delivered at Norfolk within fourteen days. Nine were in Norfolk in twelve days after Higgins received the verbal green light. I am sure everyone who knows anything about boat building will agree that this was a magnificent feat, showing a combination of imagination, resourcefulness and skill. In my opinion, these three terms sum up Andrew Higgins.

In the Navy, tradition never dies while there is a shot left in the locker. Although the Bureau type of lighter was damned by everybody from the Chief of Naval Operations downwards, the atrophied occupants of the Bureau advertised for bids on a batch of boats of its own type, which was still in the design stage.

Higgins protested and got the order reduced to ten boats. This accomplished, he neatly outmaneuvered the Bureau die-hards by building only the first of the lighters according to the Navy design and testing it before Navy observers, who saw the Bureau's pet craft was unsatisfactory even in calm water and probably would capsize in a rough sea. There was nothing new in this discovery. I had reported the suicidal character of this type of lighter months before but the Higgins demonstration put the defects on visual record. The Navy observers couldn't deny their own eyes. The upshot was the Higgins design won and he completed the order for nine 50-foot boats capable of carrying 30-ton tanks, necessary now that the powerful Shermans were coming into production.

These direct action methods of Higgins had a favorable effect on our equipment program. They were as much our battles as his and they provided us with the craft we wanted and knew was the most practical. Higgins went even farther with his demonstrations on our behalf. President Roosevelt held a conference at the White House on April 4, 1942, and called for 600 tank lighters as the basis of the new supply program. The Bureau quickly grasped the opportunity to push forward its own unsuccessful design and, despite the wide and emphatic condemnation that design had received, proceeded to order 1,100 lighters to be built along these lines.

Higgins was not a man to accept defeat easily. He arranged a sort of Monitor and Merrimac competition at the Norfolk Navy Yard between one of his own 50-footers and one of the Bureau type. The Higgins entry proved vastly superior, as everybody who knew the two boats predicted. The order was changed to the Higgins type and thereafter a good many yards started building us boats to the Higgins design.

My criticism of the Bureau lighters brought me a visit from one of the attorneys to the Truman Committee, who asked for copies of my correspondence, which Secretary of the Navy Knox authorized me to furnish. After reading some of my memoranda, the attorney told me I would be called before the Committee to testify. Much as I would have enjoyed the opportunity to place my views personally before the Committee, I had little to add to the criticisms which, over my signature, reposed in the Office of the Chief of Naval Operations.

Furthermore, I knew something about the inner workings of the official mind held up to censure. If I stood before the Committee in Washington and publicly stated my critical viewpoint I would never get out to the Pacific, which was my devouring ambition.

I explained this to my visitor and asked him to convey the facts to Senator Truman who, as a politician long versed in Washington's ways, would understand my reluctance. He obviously did understand because I was not called and the Committee drew on my memoranda in compiling its report, which strongly criticized the Navy, especially in regard to the lighters.

One observation the Committee made was: "It is clear that the Bureau of Ships, for reasons known only to itself, stubbornly persisted for over five years in clinging to an unseaworthy tank lighter design of its own" and, the Report added, "the Bureau's action has caused not only a waste of time but has caused the needless expenditure of over $7,000,000 for a total of 225 Bureau lighters which do not meet the needs of the Armed Forces."

I mention these facts because the Marines were the principal sufferers from the Bureau's crass obstinacy and were rescued chiefly by Andrew Higgins. I regard Higgins as a great patriot and his contributions to our common victory were extremely high. He was absolutely fearless in his dealings with government officials, from the President downwards, and his great sense of patriotism would send him charging into the White House, or into any department of the government where he could obtain results. He had a real affection for the Marine Corps.

Andrew Higgins was willing to go to bat with anybody and when we got lost in the morass of crippling detail and Washington procrastination, he came to our assistance. His heart and soul were pledged to building the vessels we so desperately

95

needed for amphibious warfare and it was coincidental—but extremely prophetic—that I found myself writing to him on December 6, 1941, "Often I propound this question: Where the hell would the Amphibious Force be without your boats?" History has answered that question.

Although I maintained close contact with Higgins by long distance telephone, straightening out our technical difficulties as they arose, and helping him with his troubles with the Navy Department, I was able to induce him to visit New River to solve one particular problem. Higgins had established his own school for Navy coxswains, where he trained them to handle his boats at his own expense. We were having trouble with our own coxswains, who seemed unable to get the best out of our landing boats.

So Higgins, with his staff, came to New River to demonstrate the correct handling of his boats in the surf and on the beach. Within a few days of his arrival, our boat handling greatly improved and our amphibious training gained new momentum, a reflection of the spirit of the man from New Orleans. I had quarters in one of the summer houses on the beach and here I established Higgins and his staff. I found him a delightful guest; witty, an excellent raconteur and a good judge of whiskey.

He was anxious that his boats should meet all our requirements and listened appreciatively to suggested changes. I remember that one suggestion was in connection with armor plating. We felt that the coxswain was too exposed. Higgins went to work and devised a shield that proved very effective. Other suggestions were incorporated without hesitation if they proved practical. Such was the Marine relationship with Andrew Higgins, first at New River and later in the Pacific.

He wrote me later:

. . . my contact with the Marine Corps is the bright spot in my recollections of those intense and hectic days, and out of this haze stands the bright memory of the time I spent with you and your staff at New River. I believe that the things we foresaw and did there had a profound effect on the winning of the war.

Our amphibian tractor program was encouraging. As far back as 1924, we had experimented with an amphibious tank called the Christie but had lost faith in it. In trials held that year the Christie was put over the side of a ship and it worked fairly well in the water. Unfortunately, the captain of the ship lost his nerve at the sight of this strange monster wallowing in the waves and put out a boom and slung it back on the deck. After that abortive experiment interest dwindled, though we never lost hope of one day having a waterborne tank as a troop transport and combat vehicle.

Substance was given to this hope in 1938, when the attention of the Marine Corps Commandant was drawn to a magazine picture of an amphibian tractor designed by Donald Roebling, Jr. Like our landing boat, his tractor was a product of the shallow waters and creeks of the South. Roebling, an engineer who had retired to Florida for his health, had built his tractor for rescue work in the Everglades. He called it the Alligator and his model, which he manufactured that year, included all the essential features of the military vehicle widely used since.

We did not get our Alligator immediately. Members of the Marine Corps Equipment Board were ordered to Florida and reported favorably on the invention but the Chief of Naval Operations declined to allot funds, already earmarked for critically needed landing craft and tank lighters, for the purchase of the tractor.

It was the old, old story of delay but we persevered in our recommendations and finally, in April, 1940, we received authorization for three trial Alligators. The vehicles were constructed of aluminum and proved their usefulness in tests and during Marine maneuvers. Seven months later—on November 5, 1940—the Navy ordered 200 steel tractors for the Marine Corps and the first model, officially designated LVT (1) (Landing Vehicle, Tracked) came off the production line in August, 1941. This was the open-deck type, first used at Guadalcanal and later, in November, 1942, in North Africa.

A second model, LVT (2), incorporated changes in design and came off the production line in 1943. This model was used at Bougainville, in the South Pacific, at Tarawa and the Marshalls. Armored and turreted models followed, and further changes based on combat experience resulted in additional versions, including two turreted models and a whole family of tanks—personnel and equipment-carrying, engineering, rocket-launching and field artillery.

When the war started we had a number of tractors for training purposes and others were assured as fast as the manufacturers completed the Navy order for 200. With these vehicles we were able to create an amphibian tractor battalion and when the First Division left for the South Pacific it was the first in history so equipped.

The top priority given this division for combat purposes compelled us to concentrate on its training, in addition to handling the large numbers of new recruits entering the Corps. The prime urgency was to put the First Division in the field as soon as possible. The Japanese were spreading all over the Pacific and they enjoyed the advantage of at least five years' amphibious combat experience, gained since their major strike in China in 1937. The New River installation proved a godsend in meeting this training challenge. With other training centers in that part of the country, its facilities were adequate to handle our intake in the East. Unfortunately, the West Coast was not so well equipped. We had a recruit depot in San Diego, California, and to this we added Camp Elliott, a large area nearby, and Camp Pendleton, an old Spanish hacienda with extensive grounds running along the coast near Oceanside, 40 miles north of San Diego.

Inevitably, New River's facilities were restricted by wartime limitations. We were denied the use of our beaches and could use only the shore areas. Almost as soon as war was declared Nazi submarines began to operate off the Atlantic Coast and constituted a grave menace to our amphibious training ships off the open beaches. I wrote to Rear Admiral Ferdinand L. Reichmuth, Commander, Amphibious Force, recommending that we secure an area in Chesapeake Bay for training. New River was an open roadstead and there was nothing to prevent enemy submarines coming in and sinking our training ships. Submarines could not enter sheltered Chesapeake Bay. Admiral Richmuth agreed with me and we obtained training grounds on Solomon Island and a naval gunfire bombardment range on Bloodsworth Island. Troops embarked from Norfolk in transports for this new area and, by an ironic geographic coincidence, the Marines trained on Solomon Island, in Chesapeake Bay, for their first assault in World War II, on the Solomon Islands in the South Pacific.

Deep in training for the Pacific war, we could not escape the impact of international events. After the 50 over-age destroyers were exchanged for the use of British bases in September, 1940, we manned strategic points in the Caribbean and in June, 1941, sent an expeditionary force to Iceland. The Iceland force was drawn from the Second Marine Division, which was officially activated on the West Coast at the same time as the First. It consisted of a strongly reinforced regiment (the 6th) and passed through the Panama Canal to my area before going north.

The force reported to me for transportation and embarkation, and went north as part of my command until it reached Iceland, where it came under command of the Army. Due to this curious command setup, the Commandant of the Marine Corps, whose troops were being employed by the Army, reported to the Secretary of War. This is the first and only incident I can recall in World War II when the Marine Commandant had two bosses; he reported to the Secretary of the Navy on all other matters, but to the Secretary of War on Iceland.

This attachment of Marines to the Army differed from the ordinary type, which we describe as an operational attachment. Under a seldom-used provision of law, the President may declare portions of the Marine Corps to be part of the Army, under Army regulations and under the Secretary of War.

At the urging of General George C. Marshall and the Secretary of War, this was done in the case of the Iceland force of Marines, which was then the only body of U. S. troops in readiness for instant overseas expeditionary duty. The provisional Marine brigade selected for this mission was fully organized and underway for Iceland within a week of receipt of orders. Although this type of attachment of Marines to the Army begat an infinity of extra paper work, plus separation of our men from their normal Naval source of supply (a most important consideration on an island supported and maintained by and for the Atlantic Fleet), Marshall insisted that we be placed under Army command. This was another example of the Army's insistence that Marines be kept away from independent responsibility and, although General Holcomb, our Commandant, protested the decision with great vigor, both on the grounds of principle and of horse sense, he was overruled by Army influences in the high counsels.

Training duties also went hand in hand with the primary mission of the First Joint Training Force, which was to prepare an expeditionary force for amphibious operations in the Atlantic, if circumstances warranted. After the outbreak of war we made an intensive study of the Azores, a group of Portuguese islands 1,000 miles off the coast of Portugal; and the Cape Verde Islands, another Portuguese group 500 miles from the western tip of Africa.

In the hands of the Germans, these islands, standing well out in the Atlantic, would have made ideal submarine bases for attacks on Allied shipping, as well as possible air bases for raids on the United States by long distance bombers. The Azores are 2,400 miles from the Statue of Liberty.

We knew that the Nazis were considering seizing these islands and we were prepared to prevent such action. Plans, based upon the use of a Marine assault force, were drawn up and proved that it would be a simple operation. However, the Germans failed to act and the troops intended for that operation were sent to the South Pacific.

At this time I was pressing the big brass in Washington to give me a combat command. Under Major General Archer Vandegrift, Marines had already come to grips with the Japanese at Guadacanal, and I was eager to get to the Pacific to be with my men. Then an inexplicable incident occurred. I was 60 in

1942, and an order came out that all officers of 60 or over must take a new physical examination. I did so, as a matter of routine. Afterwards a member of the Medical Examining Board, convening at the Navy Hospital in Washington, told me confidentially that the Board had found I was suffering from a severe case of diabetes.

Flabbergasted, I rushed from Quantico to Washington to see what all this monkey business was about. As I was walking along a corridor in the Navy Department I met Secretary Knox, who gave me an unusually warm handshake and invited me to lunch.

He confirmed the report I had heard but added that a group including Admiral King, COMINCH, Admiral Randall Jacobs, Rear Admiral Ross R. McIntire, the President's medical adviser and Surgeon General of the U. S. Navy, and himself had recommended that I should not be retired from the Marine Corps because he had seen me during training exercises in the Caribbean and I had seemed very fit.

To say I was astounded is to put it mildly. I never have had the slightest symptom of diabetes. After lunch I hurried to Admiral McIntire's office and told him—with considerable heat—exactly what I thought of the medical examination. On my insistence, he promised to give me another physical. I fear I left my temper inside the office, for I slammed the door when I left, even though he had promised me another examination.

Subsequently, I took three or four blood-sugar tests in Quantico. Certainly my blood pressure should have been high after my stormy experience in Washington but all the reports came back negative and normal. That made me even more certain that somewhere along the line somebody was trying to "get me." The only explanation—and a very feeble one, too—I could wring out of the Board was that the laboratory technician had made a mistake in the analysis.

Andrew Higgins, who had been my tutelary deity in many crises, filled in the gap later. He wrote me:

> I well recall the incident and after you walked out I heard you had been sent back to Quantico. I got pretty much riled about it.

As you know, fools jump in where angels fear to tread, so I went to see President Roosevelt about something, or it may have been on a pretext. I cannot recall which but I asked him point blank what was happening to General Howlin' Mad Smith.

He started to get huffish with me and, though he was the President, I talked to him pretty bluntly as to what I thought about some four-flushy Admirals and Generals I had met, and what I thought about the Marines by comparison. Before I left him, he had thawed out. I don't know whether it had any effect and it may have antagonized him, but I have often wondered what peculiar conspiracies were going on at that time.

After that incident, I was not troubled with physical examinations until I reached the Pacific Coast, where I underwent another routine checkup, with similar negative and normal results. But that Board report set me wondering, too, about a conspiracy that could deprive a man of an opportunity to fight for his country by killing him with a medical certificate.

In September, 1942, my opposite number on the West Coast, Major General Vogel, commander of the Second Joint Training Force, was sent to the South Pacific as Commanding General of the First Amphibious Corps, which comprised at that time only the First Marine Division and a few attached units. I left Quantico to succeed him. Although I was still assigned to training, this was one step nearer the Pacific theater of operations.

With headquarters at Camp Elliott, my training force consisted of troops at Elliott, Pendleton, and an artillery unit at Niland, a town on the edge of the desert near El Centro. Manpower in this area came from the East Coast and from the recruit depot at the Marine Base in San Diego. We organized the men into divisions as they arrived.

Working to fit these Marine divisions for combat duty, I also was entrusted with another training job. The Joint Chiefs of Staff had decided upon the Aleutians campaign and Lieutenant General John L. De Witt, of the Western Defense Command, turned over the Seventh Army Division to me for amphibious training. It was commanded by Major General Albert E. Brown. Our objective was Attu, which the Japanese had occupied at the same time they took Kiska and Agattu. The Commander of the Amphibious Force, Pacific, was Rear Admiral Francis W. Rockwell, who had been in command of the U. S. Naval District at Cavite when the Japanese struck in the Philippines and was evacuated to Australia with General Mac-Arthur.

It was fine working with a Navy officer like Rockwell. He understood amphibious operations and therefore appreciated the problems of both the naval commander and the shore commander. There was nothing Jovian in his attitude towards the Marines and it was easy to make recommendations to him for the most efficient training of the Seventh Division. In accordance with the authorization given by General De Witt, the division was streamlined for its amphibious mission.

I have always considered the landing of the Seventh in the dense fog of Attu, on May 11, 1943, an amphibious landing without parallel in our military history. Transport was not available to carry the entire equipment of a full division and even if it had been it was useless on the terrain of this bleak Aleutian island, where the sponge-like *tundra* bogged down all heavy equipment.

After the Seventh Division left Southern California, I followed them to Cold Harbor, Alaska, aboard the *USS Pennsylvania*. From Cold Harbor I flew to Amchitka with Colonel W. O. "Bill" Aereckson, USA, and then ploughed through the fog shrouding Attu, trying to catch a glimpse of the fighting. This was my first experience in battle with any troops I had trained and I was keen to see how they made out. But in spite of Bill's low flying, I saw very little through the cold, gray blanket. Attu was secured by May 31, after the Japanese made a *banzai* attack, cutting through our lines and penetrating to some hospital tents, where the crazed men murdered many of our patients before they could be wiped out.

If my Aleutians trip had produced nothing but the memory of that *banzai* attack, it was worth while. That mad charge through the fog made a profound impression and alerted me to the ever present danger of just such a final desperate attack during my operations in the Central Pacific. Before I left the Aleutians, I decided to amplify our training to include countermeasures against such an eventuality.

The only other result of the trip, painful to me, was that I developed pneumonia in the cold fog of the Aleutians and entered hospital in Adak. Fortunately, it was a mild case and I soon recovered and returned to Camp Elliott, in Southern California's more equable climate.

The month after I got back I was invited by Admiral Nimitz to visit Pearl Harbor and make a tour of the South Pacific with him. Nimitz was in San Diego at the time. I needled him into the trip because I wanted to visit the Pacific battlefront and see how my Marines were doing. We flew from San Francisco to Honolulu in his private Coronado and from there down to Suva, Fiji; Noumea, French New Caledonia, where the assault on New Georgia in the Solomons was being planned; Espiritu Santo, in the New Hebrides; and Guadalcanal.

Here I visited the first Marine battlefield in the Pacific war. Guadalcanal had special significance for me. The Marines who fought and died there were my Marines, the men of the First Division I had trained in the Caribbean and in the United States. It was a stirring experience because here, on remote Guadalcanal, our Marine amphibious doctrine was proven sound. Major General Vandegrift had achieved the impossible with a magnificent body of men, inadequately equipped but filled with the willingness to fight and to die fighting. Fate had robbed me of the opportunity to command my old division in its first battle in World War II but I was proud to have commanded the men in training.

On the flight back to Pearl Harbor I became increasingly depressed because I was not on active field duty. I should have been fighting with my men in the South Pacific instead of going back to training camp. I had understood in Noumea that Admiral Nimitz and Admiral William F. Halsey, Commander, South Pacific, intended making a change in the Marine command in that theater as our offensive operations expanded. I had hoped that, if such a change were made, this command would come to me. But it did not and I wondered sadly if I ever would get to the active theater of operations.

Seated by the window in the Coronado, watching the immensely thick and fantastically molded banks of clouds that form the perpetual Pacific ceiling, I was lost in this depressing speculation when Nimitz called me to the other end of the cabin, where he had been reading a magazine.

"Holland," he said gravely, "I am going to bring you out to the Pacific this fall. You will command all Marines in the Central Pacific area. I think that you will find your new job very interesting."

This was all the information that the Admiral gave me at the time but it was enough. It was the turning point for me: my road would lead out across the Pacific.

I threw myself heartily into the new training job that awaited me at Camp Elliott. After Attu was secured, the Joint Chiefs decided upon the capture of Kiska, and Amphibious Training Force 9, under Major General Charles H. "Pete" Corlett, was set up for the operation. The command was stationed at Fort Ord, California, and the Army troops were turned over to me for amphibious training.

After preliminary work in California, the Ninth was ordered to the Aleutians, with headquarters at Adak. Here it was joined by a Canadian brigade. I went to Adak with part of my staff to direct the training of both the Canadian and American troops under Arctic conditions. They were uniformed and equipped for the cold and a powerful naval force was assembled to support them against the anticipated strong resistance of the Japanese.

Commander of the operation was Vice Admiral Thomas Kinkaid and Army commander was Lieutenant General Simon Bolivar Buckner, who was killed nearly two years later at Okinawa. Pete Corlett had command of the combat troops and Rear Admiral Rockwell of the naval forces. I went along as an observer, since I had directed training.

The landing was made in full force on August 15, with barren results. The Japanese had evacuated Kiska, a fact I long had suspected. Air photographs taken on the rare clear days when photography was possible had convinced me of their withdrawal. I made arrangements with an Army flyer to remove the radio from his P-38 so that I could fly piggy-back with him from Amchitka to Kiska, where I could make low reconnaissance of the island and ascertain the situation for myself. He removed his radio all right but wrecked my plans by backing out at the last minute. It's damn hard to thumb a ride if you're a General.

I then tried to make a reconnaissance through official channels but the high command ruled this out on the ground that if a member of the reconnaissance party was captured the enemy would torture him into giving full information of the impending attack.

On board the *Pennsylvania* and at GHQ at Adak I was the object of ridicule because of my persistent belief that the Japanese had left Kiska. In my opinion, the key to the situation was the mysterious disappearance of 65 low wooden buildings, apparently used by the Japanese as barracks. Early air photographs showed them standing, in later pictures they had disappeared. Obviously the enemy had torn down the buildings and used the wood to build boats and rafts to take them out to waiting transports. This explanation caused the loudest laughter of all among the skeptical strategists of the mess.

American troops landed at Kiska after heavy naval and air preparation. They were on the island 24 hours and made no contact with the enemy. Then the Canadians landed and moved rapidly across the island, confirming that the Japanese had vanished. This was apparent when the first boat ran up the beach and not a shot was fired in opposition.

The Japanese probably had been gone three weeks and it was a crushing anti-climax to our massively mounted operation to discover we had been outwitted by a wily enemy exploiting the fog and our failure to make a proper reconnaissance. In the Aleutians we had all the means at our disposal to determine definitely whether the Japanese had evacuated Kiska but we failed to use them. This negligence on the part of the high command was inexcusable.

I went ashore with General De Witt, who was there also

in the role of observer, since all American troops involved were drawn from his Western Defense Command, and on the beach we found two roughly built boats and a pile of loose planks stripped from a building. The planks in the two boats had warped, making the craft unseaworthy. I had assigned members of my staff to the Army and the Canadians and they confirmed the thoroughness of the evacuation. The Japanese left nothing salvagable behind except some blankets and winter uniforms. A number of one-man submarines had been wrecked beyond repair.

There was only one incident at Kiska. Two Army battalions collided in the fog and opened fire. A number of men were killed and wounded before identification was established. Each group mistook the other for Japanese.

From the Aleutians, where the *williwaws* howl across the *tundra* and our men wore Arctic boots and parkas as protection against the bitter weather, my return to sunny Southern California was a pleasant transition, heightened by the knowledge that soon I would be heading for the Pacific to assume my new command.

Orders arrived shortly and after two years of waiting I was bound for the fighting war. I assembled my staff, which comprised Colonel Erskine, Chief of Staff; Major C. W. Shisler, G-1; Lieutenant Colonel St. Julian R. Marshall, G-2; Lieutenant Colonel Robert E. Hogaboom, G-3; Colonel Raymond E. Knapp, G-4; Colonel A. E. Creasey, Quartermaster; Captain J. B. O'Neill, USN, Corps Surgeon; Colonel J. H. N. Hudnall, Communications Officer; Lieutenant Colonel Peter P. Schreider, Air Officer; Lieutenant Colonel A. V. Wilson, USA, Corps of Engineers; Lieutenant Colonel Thomas R. Yancey, AUS; Major Charles S. Tracey, Transport Quartermaster; Major C. A. Woodrum, Jr., USMCR, my aide; Major J. L. Stewart, Assistant G-3; Major W. R. Lytz, USMCR, Assistant Engineer; Captain H. H. Steiner, USMCR, Assistant G-2; First Lieutenant L. S. Dyer, Assistant Communications Officer; First Lieutenant G. L. Rea, Assistant Quartermaster; Second Lieutenant R. A. Hamlin, USMCR, secretary to the Chief of Staff; and my faithful and irreplaceable orderly, Platoon Sergeant William L. Bradley.

Captain Mac Asbill, Jr., my aide, followed me later to Pearl Harbor.

For the second time in our 34 years of married life, I said goodbye to my wife and left to fight in a world war. When I sailed for France in 1917, our son Victor was a baby. When I left for the Pacific he was a Lieutenant in the United States Navy and I was twice a grandfather. Ada and I were extremely proud of Marion and Holland McTreire Smith II.

CHAPTER VI

IF THE UNITED STATES were the Arsenal of Democracy, the Hawaiian Islands were the Pacific locker when I arrived in Honolulu by Clipper from San Francisco on September 5, 1943, to assume the post of Commanding General of the Marines in the Central Pacific.

Huge camps spotted these beautiful semi-tropical islands. Towering stockpiles of equipment and mountains of supplies covered mile after mile of storage bases. Pearl Harbor, once the grave of the Fleet, was busier than any navy yard I had ever seen. Ships jostled one another for room in the blue water. Airfields were packed with planes and it scarcely seemed possible that less than two years before the Japanese had caught us sound asleep. We were a people girded for revenge.

Rear Admiral Richmond Kelly Turner met me at the airport. Kelly Turner and I were to be team mates in all my operations. He commanded the Fifth Amphibious Force while I commanded the expeditionary troops that went along with the Navy and our partnership, though stormy, spelled hell in big red letters to the Japanese.

I had met Kelly Turner in Washington when he headed the Operations Section (War Plans) at the Navy Department. He had commanded the amphibious operations in the Solomon Islands and brought to the Central Pacific considerable battle experience. On first meeting, he suggests the exacting schoolmaster, almost courtly in courtesy. He is precise, affable in an academic manner and you are tempted, in the first five minutes of acquaintance, to make the snap judgment that he is a quiet, softly philosophic man. Nothing could be farther from the truth.

Kelly Turner is aggressive, a mass of energy and a relentless task master. The punctilious exterior hides a terrific determination. He can be plain ornery. He wasn't called "Terrible Turner" without reason.

The broad lines of the Central Pacific offensive were drawn at the Quebec Conference in August, 1943, when President Roosevelt and Prime Minister Churchill discussed with the Joint Chiefs of Staff the grand strategy of the Pacific war.

In the South Pacific, the enemy movement toward Australia had been checked and Allied action in that theater, originally defensive, had swung over to the offensive. A large part of the Solomons was ours and General MacArthur had turned the tide in New Guinea. Japanese offensive action had ceased; ours was accelerating. The time was now ripe for a boldly planned drive across the Central Pacific from the east to coincide with our advance from the south.

In the global strategy to which the United States was committed, the war in Europe absorbed the bulk of our military effort and, until the defeat of Nazi Germany released from that theater troops for employment in the Pacific, we did not have strength for a frontal attack on Japan. However, we did possess sufficient naval and air superiority to start a war of attrition, capture bases in Japan's mandated islands in order to increase pressure on the enemy homeland, and whittle down her strength until we were able to launch the final assault.

A month before, Admiral Nimitz had been alerted by the Joint Chiefs to prepare for the offensive. This was approved by the Quebec Conference. The Gilbert Islands, strung across the Equator 2,000 miles southwest of Hawaii, were designated as the jumping-off point in the Central Pacific campaign. Here the Japanese had seized and fortified a number of low-lying coral islands in the main atolls.

In his official report, Admiral King explained:

Their location [the Gilberts] is of great strategic significance because they are north and west of other islands in our possession and immediately south and east of important bases in the Carolines and Marshalls. The capture of the Gilberts was, therefore, a necessary part of any serious thrust at the Japanese Empire.

Tarawa, the atoll in the center of the group, was selected as one target and originally Nauru, the phosphate island to the west, was suggested as the other. For reasons I will explain later, Makin, at the northern end of the group, was substituted for Nauru in the final plans.

We captured Makin and Tarawa. The people of America were shocked by the slaughter on the beaches and stirred by the heroism of the Marines. Makin was an easy job, with few casualties. Tarawa was a terrible baptism of blood for the new offensive. The Marines lost relatively more men in a few hours than they had ever lost before. Tarawa cost us 990 dead and 2,311 wounded. Twice the issue of battle was in doubt. We could have been driven back into the lagoon, defeated, but we were saved by the bravery and tenacity of individual Marines and were able to chalk up a final victory.

The question is inevitable: Was Tarawa worth it? My answer is unqualified: No. From the very beginning the decision of the Joint Chiefs to seize Tarawa was a mistake and from their initial mistake grew the terrible drama of errors, errors of omission rather than commission, resulting in these needless casualties.

The operation plan issued by Admiral Nimitz directed the capture of Makin, Tarawa and the nearby Apamama atolls as a prelude to gaining control of the Marshalls. I am convinced that we should have hit the Marshalls first, capturing Kwajalein, which we did two months later. Kwajalein Atoll, in the heart of the Marshalls, was the logical initial objective.

Tarawa had no particular strategic importance: as a base it had little value. The Japanese had concentrated their strength on Betio Island, the southwestern tip of Tarawa Atoll, which is only about the size of Central Park in New York City. Tarawa constituted no threat to our communications with the South Pacific or to our offensive in the Central Pacific. The Japanese had built an airfield on Betio as a refuelling base for planes on sorties from the Marshalls and the Carolines but little traffic was observed on the field and prior to our D-Day strike there were only two planes there. There were no dock or naval facilities for the Japanese fleet and only a shallow lagoon.

Roi-Namur (part of Kwajalein Atoll), the biggest base in the Marshalls whence air support could be drawn, was 600 miles to the northwest; Nauru was 500 miles to the west; and Truk, the great Japanese naval and air base guarding the Central Pacific approach, lay 1,500 miles to the northwest.

Tarawa should have been by-passed. Its capture—a mission executed by Marines under direct orders from the high command—was a terrible waste of life and effort. Rabaul, in the South Pacific, and Truk, in the Central Pacific, both far stronger and more vital bases, were by-passed without danger to our rear. They both had airfields, naval and military installations, submarine, dock and storage facilities.

To have ignored Tarawa's 4,000-man garrison would not have endangered our position. In the New Britain-New Ireland area 50,000 Japanese troops were pinched off and left to starve when Rabaul was by-passed. Acquisition of air bases on neighboring islands enabled us to bomb and harry the Japanese at will, secure in our knowledge that they could not escape and equally certain that to assault these bases would have cost us an incalculable number of men.

Rear Admiral Forrest P. Sherman, war plans officer to Admiral Nimitz, put his finger on the solution when we struck directly at the center of the Marshalls and captured Kwajalein, completely ignoring other Japanese occupied islands. He said, "We shall let them wither on the vine." To borrow his words, we should have let Tarawa "wither on the vine." We could have kept it neutralized from our bases on Baker Island, to the east, and the Ellice and Phoenix Islands, a short distance to the southeast. Or, as we did later in the case of Rota, with a garrison of 4,000 a few miles off the coast of Guam, used Tarawa as a convenient bombing and "gun unloading" target.

The futile sacrifice of Marines on that strategically useless coral strand makes me as sad today as it did then. Why did we attack Tarawa? The war was young in those days and perhaps the powers that be felt the need of a victory in the Central Pacific as a demonstration upon which to base future operations. My Marines provided the necessary victory but it was a fearful initiation, out of all proportion to the results, although it taught us lessons that were not forgotten in subsequent operations. But even the knowledge we gained did not justify Tarawa.

The Gilberts attack, known as Operation GALVANIC, was the largest we had undertaken at that stage. Shortly after my arrival at Pearl Harbor an impressive chain of command was established for all amphibious operations in the forthcoming offensive. At the top, in command of all Army, Navy and Marine forces, was Admiral Nimitz, Commander-in-Chief, Pacific Fleet, whose function was the planning, overall supervision of operations, logistic support and co-ordination between the three services.

Under him was Vice Admiral Raymond A. Spruance, Deputy Commander-in-Chief and Chief of Staff to Nimitz, who was detached to command the Central Pacific Force, consisting of the powerful Fifth Fleet of fast battleships, cruisers and aircraft carriers, the striking forces that kept the enemy at sea and protected us ashore.

Next was Rear Admiral Turner, commanding the Fifth Amphibious Force, comprising old battleships, cruisers, destroyers, supply ships, transports, minesweepers, a veritable armada of vessels for transporting, supplying and supporting the troops.

I commanded the V Amphibious Corps, the expeditionary troops, which were under Kelly Turner's command for the purpose of operational control but were administratively independent. As soon as the assault waves hit the beach the status of my command was parallel, not inferior, to Kelly Turner's. For the two phases of the Gilberts operation, there was further subdivision: Kelly Turner commanded the Northern Attack Force for the assault on Makin and Rear Admiral Harry S. Hill commanded the Southern Attack Force at Tarawa. These organizational details are necessary to explain the command relationships.

Headquarters of the V Amphibious Corps was in the Marine Barracks area in the Navy Yard at Pearl Harbor. Troops assigned here were quartered on Oahu at Camp Catlin, named after Brigdier General Albertus W. Catlin, hero of World War I. We had three Marine divisions in the Pacific and a fourth in combat training on the West Coast. The Second Division, under Major General Julian C. Smith, assigned to the assault on Tarawa, was training in New Zealand.

For the Makin phase, the Twenty-seventh Army Division (New York National Guard) under Major General Ralph Smith, was assigned to the V Amphibious Corps for operational control, a term which is frequently misunderstood and must be clearly defined here in order to explain difficulties arising later. The term means that I had no administrative control over the Army division. The Twenty-seventh was turned over to me for employment in a specified operation, in this case the capture of Makin, and when the operation concluded the division reverted to the Army. However, only one regiment was actually employed at Makin.

Crippled as I was by shortages of staff for the task of planning and training for the Gilberts at short notice, I set to work with all the data available. In my estimate of the situation regarding the original objectives, I decided that the capture of Nauru would require more troops than we could spare and that the cost in men, time and equipment of a landing on poor beaches against strong Japanese defenses did not justify the attack. I suggested the substitution of Makin for Nauru and after much argument with Spruance and Turner I won my point, which Nimitz approved. This was the first important decision I was able to push through.

Major General Julian Smith, Colonel Merritt A. Edson, his Chief of Staff, and other members of his staff, flew from Wellington, New Zealand, to Pearl Harbor, where plans for Tarawa were drawn up at my headquarters and approved at a joint conference with Kelly Turner, Julian Smith, and our staffs.

The Makin plans were drawn up by Major General Ralph Smith and his staff and were similarly approved after modifications.

Commanding Army troops in the Central Pacific at this time was Lieutenant General Robert C. Richardson, Jr., who was also Military Governor of the Hawaiian Islands. His nickname was "Nellie." Richardson caused more than a lifting of the eyebrows when he decorated members of his staff with the Legion of Merit for what he termed the "massive planning" of the Makin operation. All the approved plans for Makin came out of my office.

His penchant for such decorations was not limited to awarding them, as became evident later in the war when he accepted an Air Medal from the local air commander, in recognition of his long overwater sightseeing trips in a command airplane, to and from islands which had been rendered safe by Marines.

I made an official call on Lieutenant General Richardson soon after I arrived. He was amiable and welcomed me to Hawaii but it was evident that my appointment to command the V Amphibious Corps and lead the Central Pacific offensive was a great disappointment to him.

Richardson's resentment was not based upon personal objections. Of this I am sure. The reason was much deeper rooted. Although he commanded the Army troops in the Central Pacific, his paperwork headquarters being non-tactical and responsible only for the administration and logistic support of the troops, he was directly under Nimitz in the chain of command. But he had hoped that he, and not a Marine, would be given command of amphibious operations. This ambition to make the Pacific offensive an Army show amounted to an obsession with Richardson and other Army men. They ruled out the possibility of Marines playing anything but a secondary part.

The decision to give command to a Marine was made by Nimitz in his capacity as Commander-in-Chief. Most of the troops to be employed in the offensive would be Marines, so a Marine commander was the logical choice. Moreover, this highly technical mode of warfare, in which Marines had trained for years, demanded specialized leadership and my experience in training amphibious troops in the Atlantic, the Aleutians and on the West Coast must have influenced Nimitz in his decision. Richardson, on the other hand, had no amphibious background. He was a diehard horse cavalry enthusiast, who had been ordered to Hawaii from a swivel chair in the Army's high-powered Bureau of Public Relations in Washington.

The long standing General Staff thesis, that no Marine should ever be allowed to exercise high command, dominated Richardson's thinking and eventually expanded into an inter-Service controversy—largely of his own making—between the Army and my Corps, in which he intervened against me with Nimitz and with Washington. After Tarawa, for example, he reported in a secret "eyes-only" memo to Nimitz, that Marines were not competent to command amphibious operations and that my veteran V Amphibious Corps headquarters should be replaced by an Army Corps command over all the Central Pacific. Nimitz kept me in ignorance of this, but my old team-mate, Admiral King (ably seconded by Vandegrift), made short work of the suggestion when it reached Washington.

Hostility to my initial endeavors from high Army sources was never demonstrated openly. Subtle influences were set in motion and permitted to flow unchecked through receptive channels. In combat it was disquieting to feel that my actions were being observed, not with the idea of constructive analysis but with the sole purpose of finding fault. Richardson seemed waiting for me to make a mistake that could be magnified to promote the grand plan of an Army-controlled offensive, well supplied with Marine troops to do the fighting.

Had the Marines failed at Tarawa, no Marine would have commanded another major operation. Command in the Central Pacific would have passed to the Army. Since at this period there was not a single Army general with amphibious experience, it would have taken time to qualify commanders and, consequently, would have added months to the Pacific war.

The glittering prize of amphibious warfare, spectacular victory over Japan, dazzled not only Army eyes. The prospect pleased the Navy, who from the start made a determined effort to cut me down to size and show the fountainhead of authority.

In a memorandum to Spruance on September 12, 1943, Kelly Turner indicated his intention of taking over the training of the landing forces. This was an attempt to usurp my functions and was probably initiated under the mistaken impression that I was a newcomer to command and could be molded to naval subservience. It was an effort to undermine everything we had accomplished for the Marine Corps. As Commanding General of the V Amphibious Corps, I was in Hawaii to supervise the training of troops, their embarkation and everything else pertaining to them. I wrote Spruance four days later, strongly protesting, and pointed out that Turner, as Commander of the Fifth Amphibious Force, "would be granted operational control during the amphibious phase but that command of the landing force is a function of the Corps Commander. . . . The amphibious training of the units assigned to the landing force must be under his command."

That point was conceded but, with troops assigned, transports loaded and the expedition ready to sail from Pearl Harbor for the Gilberts, I was amazed to discover that in the general directive from Nimitz, my name had been removed from command. Apparently, the Navy intended to employ the V Amphibious Corps and leave me, the Corps Commander, twiddling my thumbs at Pearl Harbor. Incredible as it may seem, there it was— or wasn't. Nimitz had appointed me, ordered me and my staff to Pearl Harbor to take the job, entrusted me with the training of the troops and handed over all planning material and when matters had reached the final stage I was to be left behind.

The last minute change of orders sent me charging over to Spruance, who was as dumfounded as I was that his top amphibious officer wasn't going along. Admiral Spruance insisted that I go along. I had no knowledge of the person or reason behind that extraordinary maneuver until the day Vice Admiral Charles H. McMorris, who succeeded Spruance as Chief of Staff to Nimitz, admitted that he was responsible. He had the Navy idea that naval officers could do the job without Marine assistance, other than divisional command.

117

Looking back on this period from the vantage of years and distance, I sometimes wonder if we didn't have two enemies: the Japanese and certain brass hats in the Army and Navy. But at that time I was too keen to get into combat to allow intrigues to upset me disastrously.

For the two-phase Gilbert operation I considered the allocation of troops and targets as satisfactory as possible. Tarawa would be a hard nut to crack. Information on Betio wasn't too good. The island had been seized by the Japanese from the British early in 1942 and was strongly fortified. Our charts were old. Air reconnaissance photographs failed to reveal all details of the enemy's cunningly hidden defenses constructed during a year and a half of occupation. The Second Division was a good outfit, already battle tested, and Julian Smith had drawn up a fine plan for wresting the island from its garrison of 4,000 men, approximately two-thirds of whom belonged to the Special Naval Landing Force, the elite of Japan's marine troops.

Makin was different. The main island of Butaritari was lightly held. The garrison was only 290 combat personnel, plus 271 laborers, and therefore I considered Makin a minor operation, which a single regimental combat team from the Twenty-seventh Army Division could handle easily. Admittedly, I was a little uneasy about the Army troops because Ralph Smith had told me the Army Inspector General had given an adverse report on the division. In Hawaii, I had to high-pressure the Twenty-seventh to get the division into a dress rehearsal for the Makin operation. One of Ralph Smith's objections was that his equipment might be damaged.

I took the 165th Regiment (Reinforced) for employment at Makin. It was the best in the division but prior to departure it was reported that MP's had been mauled in an incipient riot over at the Twenty-seventh Division's camp. The trouble was reported to have started over the question of return to the mainland after more than a year's service in the islands. This discontent, plus the fact that the Army troops were not so well trained as the Marines in amphibious warfare, did not make

118

the Twenty-seventh an ideal division but, since Makin was only feebly defended, a reinforced regiment should take it easily.

The Second Division embarked for Tarawa from New Zealand. The Makin forces sailed from Pearl Harbor. I travelled with Kelly Turner on his flagship, the USS *Pennsylvania*. This was my first combat command and my sense of expectancy just about balanced the mental third degree I gave myself, turning over all the cognate problems in my mind. Makin presented no obvious difficulty. I was not so sure about Tarawa. One uncertain factor was the Japanese defenses. Another was the long, fringing reef stretching the length of the lagoon and curving shallowly along the north shore of Betio Island, where we were to land. The tricky question of tide could not be overlooked. The system of underwater demolition teams, which contributed so much to the success of later landings, had not been organized and we had no accurate information on actual beach conditions since the Japanese emplaced underwater obstacles.

Our landing plans were on a radically new basis. We had Higgins boats, both LCVPS (Landing Craft, Vehicle, Personnel) and LCMS (Landing Craft, Medium). In New Zealand, the Second Division had conducted special tests in shallow water simulating conditions anticipated at Tarawa.

However, we were too cautious to place our entire confidence in these craft. The Second Division also had a battalion of amphibian tractors, officially known as LVT's (Landing Vehicle, Tracked), the latest addition to our mechanized equipment and forerunner of other amphibious vehicles, including armored tanks. A few tractors, abbreviated to "amtracks," were used to haul supplies at Guadalcanal, but for the deceptive reef at Tarawa we planned to send the first three waves of Marines ashore in amtracks, using Higgins boats to complete the landing of supporting waves and supplies.

What a fight I had to get an adequate number of amtracks into the operation. And what a lucky day it was for the Marines when, after virtually a stand-and-deliver ultimatum, the Navy yielded on this supply request. It galls me to remember this instance of Navy stubbornness.

Officially, the Second Division had 75 amtracks but not all were operable. To insure success, more were needed. We used 125 all told, barely sufficient to carry in the first three waves, and during the battle the 125 dwindled to a mere handful due to reef hazards, enemy fire and mechanical defects.

During planning at Pearl Harbor, I was appalled to find Kelly Turner shortsightedly opposing the use of amtracks. He saw no need for them and said flatly he would not carry the vehicles on his ships. Our equipment, he stated, was adequate without these tractors.

I pointed out that it was essential we should have amtracks, as many as we could get, for carrying men and supplies across the reef, which landing boats might not be able to pass, and also for destroying underwater obstructions. On Oahu, I obtained irrefutable proof of the amtrack's efficiency in clearing a way through protected beaches. The amtracks walked clean through seven lines of barbed wire in tests. We knew that a double-apron barbed wire fence practically encircled Betio and a series of concrete tetrahedrons had been nearly completed. If the reef proved impassable for boats—and it did—the only way to get the men ashore was in amtracks.

When our disagreement reached an impasse I said bluntly, "Kelly, it's like this. I've got to have those amtracks. We'll take a helluva licking without them." And I added with finality, "No amtracks: no operation." The Marines took along their amtracks plus reinforcements, which they obtained this way: A shipment had arrived in San Diego too late to transport to New Zealand before the Second Division sailed. This shipment was rushed to American Samoa, where the Second Division picked up an additional fifty en route to Tarawa and we landed with the amtracks despite the reef.

Admiral Nimitz stressed the value of these amphibious vehicles in his report on the operation. He wrote:

The ideal defensive barrier has always been one that could not be demolished, which held up assaulting forces under the unobstructed fire of the defenders and past which it was impossible to run, crawl, dig, climb or sail. The barrier reefs fulfil these conditions to the letter, except when sufficient amphibious tanks and similar vehicles are available to the attackers.

D-Day for one of the saddest and most glorious battles in American history was set for November 20, 1943. I am not going to describe the fight for Tarawa. The story, brilliantly told by war correspondents and Marines, has been written into the annals of our country. Besides, I was not there. I was 450 miles away, on board the *Pennsylvania,* chafing under the inexcusable delay caused by the fumbling Makin operation. Makin should have been cleaned up in one day but fighting dragged out three days and chained me to this insignificant skirmish.

My only direct contact with Tarawa was through laconic messages from Major General Julian Smith reporting the shifting phases of the attack. Three days of pre-landing air and naval bombardment failed to knock out the defenses. So strong was Betio that our naval gunfire did not materially reduce resistance. Two thousand tons of naval shells and 400 tons of bombs had little effect. The Japanese were ready for us. Hardly had the transport fleet hove into sight, hardly had the assault force started embarking in amtracks and boats for the organization of waves when the shore batteries opened fire and our first casualties were caused by near misses.

What happened was that three of the four 8-inch Vickers guns, brought to Tarawa by the Japanese after the British surrendered Singapore Base, were still in action. Only one was knocked out by the initial bombardment. Our transports anchored far south of their proper stations and came within the range of enemy guns. H-hour (landing hour) was postponed twice while the transports shifted position to escape shore fire and were followed by the already loaded craft. Precious time was wasted in organizing assault waves because in the confusion boats were separated from their mother ships. Meanwhile, naval units moved in and silenced the big shore guns but for half an hour the Japanese gunners ashore had the transports at their mercy. Providentially for us, the Japanese seemed inept despite our feeble initial bombardment. Perhaps the bombardment did stun them and disrupt their communications. Otherwise, they might have sunk some of our transports and wrecked our plans. As it was, the damage they inflicted was minor.

After two postponements, H-hour was fixed for 0900. One Marine party already had reached the pier jutting out 500 yards from the north shore of Betio, where we had chosen our three landing beaches. Three waves of amtracks headed for shore, followed by landing boats. The reef was our undoing. It cost us many casualties on the first and second days of the battle. An attempt to lay down a smoke screen failed because the wind shifted. Also, an unaccountably low tide—which lasted for two days—lowered the water on the reef so that only amtracks were able to get ashore. The Higgins boats stranded on the reef, half a mile from the beach. Marvelous as they were, the Higgins boats couldn't run over dry coral.

At this point the failure of the bombardment to come up to the Navy's expectations became tragically apparent. Though the big guns had been taken out, there were dozens of smaller guns, from five-inchers down to vicious 37-millimeter anti-boat guns and machine guns in concrete emplacements and pillboxes. They were still operating, raining murderous fire on that half mile from reef to shore, where the men of the later waves jumped out of their boats and waded through the blood-stained surf into the swirling red hell that was Tarawa.

These details, of necessity, I learned later. On board the *Pennsylvania*, pacing near the communications shack and watching the dilatory Makin operation, I was unable to realize the gravity of the situation at Tarawa. The first message from Julian Smith read:

Successful landings on Beaches Red 2 and 3. Toe hold on Red 1. Am committing one LT (Landing Team) from division reserve. Still encountering strong resistance.

This message was timed an hour and a half after the landing and since his reference to committing another landing team from division reserve was not a cause for great alarm, in view of the resistance, it was not until that afternoon that I got a true picture of Tarawa.

A message from Julian Smith reported that heavy casualties had been suffered during the morning and added, "The situation is in doubt." I was holding the Sixth Regiment, Second Division, as Corps reserve. Julian Smith asked that this reserve be turned over to him. Without it he was uncertain of the final outcome. He was sending in his own reserve and this left him with a few artillerymen, engineers, mechanics, military police and headquarters technicians.

Kelly Turner was in his cabin resting after long hours on the bridge. I took the message directly to him. After a discussion we decided to release the Corps reserve for employment by Julian Smith in compliance with his request. No conditions were imposed on its release, though I was seriously disturbed by such an early request. The battle was only a few hours old. I had full confidence in the commander of the Second Division and in his ability to use the reserve advantageously. I have always believed in decentralization and when a man is given a job to do he should be supported fully. The Second Division was one of the best in the Marine Corps; it was well trained and well led and, though the picture looked black, I was sure Julian Smith would not fail. Having landed, the Marines would hold on. My faith in the Corps reassured me.

But, knowing the strength of Betio, I was extremely apprehensive. Julian Smith would not have asked me to commit our last reserve unless conditions demanded this desperate action.

No news is good news in the ordinary pursuits of life but in war no news is bad news. I had had no sleep the night before and after committing our last reserve to the battle of Tarawa, sleep again was out of question. No matter what happened to my Marines at Tarawa I could not be with them because Turner insisted that I remain at Makin. He promised to send me south as soon as the situation was well in hand. Makin, an operation the Marines could have completed in a few hours, came first and he was in overall command. I stayed aboard the flagship, waiting.

That night, alone in my cabin with my fears, I turned to a

source of solace that has never failed me. I opened my Bible and read about Joshua and the Children of Israel and their troubles and triumphs. During the war, I always read the Bible each night before I went to sleep. It was a great spiritual relaxation: an answer to the day's problems. My Bible was given to me by my mother when I joined the Marine Corps and she admonished me, "Holland, always read your Bible. Never be ashamed of being esteemed religious."

Two other books also gave me consolation. One was the Catholic Prayer Book and the other a collection arranged by Father Joseph F. Stedman, bearing the title *My Daily Readings from the New Testament and the Daily Mass Book*, distributed by the Chaplain's Aid Association. Coming from a Methodist family, I follow the faith of my fathers, but in the Pacific I was never without these two books and read a prayer from them each night. I have always felt a special sympathy with the doctrines of the Catholic Church because of the spiritual discipline the Church imposes.

Next morning I was buoyed by new hope, although the news on the second day was little better than on the first. Again the treacherous reef, the best ally the Japanese had, combined with enemy fire to hold up our landing. We still had only a precarious hold ashore but one factor was in our favor as we struggled to consolidate our position.

The Japanese were unable to counterattack. Had they counterattacked that first night they might have driven us back into the lagoon but the bombardment had achieved one positive result. Enemy communications, which were above ground, had been disrupted by naval gunfire and the Japanese were no longer a cohesive force but a series of scattered units. They had no system of runners for carrying messages and could not organize a counterattack.

The situation on the reef continued to worry me. Our supply of amtracks was limited and could not last indefinitely under operational strain. The dismal picture of my men trying to wade ashore against Japanese fire was before my eyes all day. I could do nothing to help them except pray for an early conclusion of the Makin phase so that I could take the first plane to Tarawa.

However, reasoning dispassionately, I was able to discover reason for hope. In spite of terrific obstacles we had succeeded in getting a few tanks ashore, as I learned later, and this cheered the men tremendously. On the evening of D-day, Lieutenant Colonel Presley M. Rixey had started landing the 1st Battalion, 10th Marines (Artillery), a 75-millimeter pack howitzer unit.

Except for some destroyer fire on the eastern end of the island, Navy guns were helpless because of the uncertain situation ashore: the chances of killing Marines were too great in continued close fire support. By the morning of the second day, Rixey had five sections in action, bearing on Japanese strong points at close range.

The second day of the battle for Tarawa was one of climax and anti-climax. The bottleneck of the reef looked very serious when I studied Julian Smith's earlier messages but 30 hours after the Marines went ashore came a message which relayed the news from Colonel David M. Shoup, shore commander, reporting:

Casualties many; percentage of dead not known; combat efficiency: We are winning.

With this message in my hand I knew that the darkest hour at Tarawa had passed. Throwing in the Corps reserve had swayed the balance. Not only had Marine combat training triumphed; so had our morale. I looked forward more eagerly than ever to standing beside my men at Tarawa.

At Makin, however, the Army troops were infuriatingly slow. Butaritari, the objective island, should have been secured by dusk on D-day. Any Marine regiment would have done it in that time. At Eniwetok, the 22nd Marine Regiment, under Colonel John T. Walker, captured Engebi, a far stronger island than Makin, in seven hours, but on the morning of the second day the end of the Makin operation was not even in sight. Army superiority in numbers alone should have overwhelmed the Japanese. The 165th Infantry (Reinforced) totalled 6,500 men against an enemy garrison of 290 armed with nothing larger than light artillery and machine guns.

I was very dissatisfied with the regiment's lack of offensive spirit; it was preposterous that such a small Japanese force could delay the capture of Makin three days. It probably was not the fault of the men. The 165th was not too well officered. When I returned to Pearl Harbor, I reported to Admiral Nimitz that had Ralph Smith been a Marine I would have relieved him of his command on the spot. His conduct of the operation did not measure up to my expectations at all.

Speaking as a Marine, faithful to service tradition, I was greatly disturbed by a certain incident at Makin. On D-day, Colonel Gardiner Conroy, commanding officer of the 165th Regiment, exposed himself while making a reconnaissance and was killed by a Japanese sniper. With him at the time was Lieutenant Colonel James Roosevelt, son of the President, who was a Marine observer attached to the Army. Two days later, I was shocked to find the gallant Colonel's body still lying where it had fallen. No attempt had been made by either his officers or his men to recover the body and give it a Christian burial.

The body lay a few yards from the main road traversed by troops, jeeps and trucks, in full sight of hundreds of men and only a short distance from the beach. It was inconceivable to me that soldiers of a regiment, whose loyalty is centered on the man directly in command, their Colonel, could permit his body to lie unrecovered for two days. There was no danger involved in recovering it and even if there had been, such negligence was inexcusable. To me this callous disregard of a soldier's common duty to his commanding officer was an ominous commentary on the morale of the regiment. I ordered Ralph Smith to recover the body immediately and bury it. In that order I used emphatic language.

Poor Conroy's death had an ironic aftermath. Back in Honolulu, Richardson, without any reference to me, let alone the Marine Corps, decorated young Roosevelt with the Silver Star for his part in the Makin operation, which consisted of being present. Had the matter been referred to me, a courtesy which should have been extended to the Commanding General, I would have strongly disapproved the recommendation. Jimmy Roosevelt proved himself a competent and courageous Marine on many occasions, but I always wondered how he felt about that decoration.

Another incident at Makin, well publicized at the time, involved a young Army lieutenant who was doing some wild firing. "Son, if you can't do better than that I'll have to take your gun away from you," I was quoted as saying. That admonition cast me in a paternalistic role which tells only half the story. The complete version is a sorry reflection on the undisciplined, trigger-happy Army troops on the island.

This is what happened: Accompanied by my aides, Major Woodrum and Captain Asbill, I was driving along the beach where hundreds of troops were unloading supplies. A company came through, firing indiscriminately right and left and forcing the unloading party to take cover in the belief it was enemy fire. Jumping from my jeep, I located the lieutenant in command and asked what he was firing at.

"I'm trying to clean out snipers in this area," he replied.

"Can't you see there aren't any Japs around here?" I shouted. "Our men are working all over the area and you come shooting at tree tops when any damn fool can see there aren't any Japs up there. Why, the enemy is thousands of yards up front."

"I was given orders to clean out this area," the lieutenant persisted. "And I think there still may be Japs around here. I'm shooting at everything so we won't be taking any chances."

This did make me howling mad. "If I hear one more shot from your men in this area I'll take your damn weapons and all your ammunition away from you," I said, revealing my identity. I was wearing my utility suit, without insignia. The shooting stopped and unloading was resumed.

One of the worst nights I ever spent in the Pacific was at the Command Post ashore on Makin when I slept under a mosquito net, on a cot set outside the tent. This was the first time the

165th Regiment had been in action and I hoped the presence of Ralph Smith, their Commanding General, and myself would be a good influence on the sentries posted around camp. I was mistaken. Shots whizzed over my head from a 25-yard range, drilled holes in the command post tent and clipped coconuts off the trees. I crawled out from under my net and implored the sentries to stop shooting at shadows. There wasn't a Japanese within a mile of the Command Post. My two orderlies, Sergeant Bradley and Sergeant Daniels, were less sanguine about their Army buddies. They spent an unmolested night in foxholes.

Only a brief examination of the situation ashore sufficed to show there was little opposition. I stressed to Ralph Smith the importance of cleaning up the island as soon as possible, and early on the morning of the third day I called for a report. I received one saying there was still heavy fighting at the northern end of the island, which delayed final capture. This seemed highly improbable, so I took a jeep and drove to the scene of the reported action. There was no firing of any sort. Two Army officers, Colonel Aereckson, Headquarters Support Aircraft officer, and Colonel C. B. Tenney, afterward Island Commander at Makin, joined me and we advanced to the front line of the battalion occupying that zone. It was as quiet as Wall Street on Sunday.

"Sometimes a General has to go up to the front and let the troops see him," I remarked. "That's the only way he can make them realize there's nothing ahead of them."

I was furious with Ralph Smith. I was anxious to go to Tarawa and here he was fiddling around with an operation that should have been ended long before in my opinion. His communications with his regiment were extremely poor and he showed little enterprise in improving them. He didn't know where his battalions were, and insisted on sitting by the phone, where he couldn't get any information because the phone didn't work.

Back at the Command Post I advised him to go and have a look for himself at what his staff called heavy fighting. There were very few Japanese alive on Makin and it was all over as far as I was concerned. I collected my staff and returned to the *Pennsylvania*, where I reported to Kelly Turner there was no further need for my presence at Makin. That afternoon, a short time after I left the island, came Ralph Smith's message: "Makin taken."

Later the same afternoon the best news I ever received came from Julian Smith. Organized resistance had ceased on Tarawa. Saipan and Iwo Jima caused me many anxious hours but the relief when they were "secured," the official end of operations, was nothing to the overflowing happiness I felt at that message from Tarawa.

Officially, Tarawa was secured at 1300, seventy-six hours after the Marines landed. Secured does not mean that fighting has ended. There is always the job of mopping up and cleaning out isolated pockets of resistance, but to all practical purposes fighting is over. The message meant Tarawa was ours; Makin was ours; and when Brigadier General Leo D. Hermle seized Apamama Atoll two days later, after Marine reconnaissance troops had landed, the Gilbert Islands were ours. For the first time in a week I slept soundly, free from the endless apprehensions that had tortured me, and I woke up refreshed, ready to board the seaplane to Tarawa.

No words of mine can reproduce the picture I saw when the plane landed after circling that wracked and battered island. The sight of our dead floating in the waters of the lagoon and lying along the blood-soaked beaches is one I will never forget. Over the pitted, blasted island hung a miasma of coral dust and death, nauseating and horrifying. Chaplains, corpsmen and troops were carrying away wounded and burying the dead. We had about a thousand killed and, added to this nightmare of mangled bodies, were the four to five thousand Japanese. The Marines took 146 prisoners but only 17 were Japanese. The others were Korean laborers.

As I stepped ashore from the barge to the jetty inside the lagoon on my way to Julian Smith's Command Post, I passed boys who had lived yesterday a thousand times and looked older than their fathers. Dirty, unshaven, with gaunt, almost sightless eyes, they had survived the ordeal but it had chilled their souls. They found it hard to believe they were actually alive. There were no smiles on these ancient, youthful faces; only passive relief among the dead.

I haven't the slightest recollection of what I said to Julian Smith when I met him in the battered Japanese shack he called his headquarters, although I remember vividly the faces of the boys on the beach. I do remember clasping his hand warmly and I must have congratulated him on his fine conduct of the campaign. He was elated over victory but, like myself, distressed by the casualties. We both knew the Marines would be criticized by the people back home, to whom the high price paid for Tarawa must come as a shock. I do remember that later I extended congratulations to members of his staff and to officers of the Second Division—that is, those who survived. Among 3,301 casualties at Tarawa, were 57 officers killed and 111 wounded. The ratio of dead to wounded—about one to two—was probably the highest in any battle of World War II.

With Julian Smith I made a tour of the western and central portions of the island, where the enemy had built his strongest pillboxes and blockhouses. My pride in the invincible spirit of the Marines was never greater. Only men with the highest morale and willingness to die rather than be defeated could have captured this well-nigh impregnable chain of fortifications. Japanese prisoners told me their officers boasted Betio defenses were so strong that a million men could not take the island.

Turning to Major Woodrum, I said, "I don't see how they ever took Tarawa. It's the most completely defended island I have ever seen."

That inspection trip left other impressions on my mind— impressions of our own inadequacies. Before the Marines landed and the Navy laid down the final bombardment, one of the Admirals messaged the Southern Attack Force:

It is not our intention to wreck the island. We do not intend to destroy it. Gentlemen, we will obliterate it.

Obliterate it? I entered every pillbox and blockhouse on the western end of the island and found only one had even been hit by naval gunfire. Not one had been destroyed. All of them had to be destroyed by the Marines with explosive charges and hand grenades. Dead Japanese lay everywhere but they were killed by Marines, not by Naval gunfire.

Instead of three days' preliminary bombardment, Betio needed at least ten. After that amount of fire, the Marines would not have faced guns that should have been knocked out before they landed. They would not have had to capture, almost bare-handed, positions the Japanese had fortified for 15 months. The strength of the blockhouses was tremendous. Concrete was five feet thick and superimposed were 8-inch coconut palm logs, reinforced with angle iron and railroad spikes. The Japanese then piled ten feet of coral or soil on this structure. Nothing but a direct hit with a 16-inch shell, or a 2,000-pound bomb could cave them in.

The Second Division had initiated a request to Major General Willis A. Hale, commanding the Army's Seventh Air Force, that 2,000-pound bombs be dropped on Betio. For some unexplained reason, this request was ignored so there was nothing left for the Marines to do but take the blockhouses by frontal attack.

The Japanese Command Post was a case in point. On the low-lying coral island it reared against the skyline like a two-story house, a massive building of reinforced concrete, coconut logs and sandbags. A Kingfisher reconnaissance plane from the USS *Maryland*, Hill's flagship, spotted it intact long after it was supposed to have been knocked out. He radioed his discovery to the task force and his message was acknowledged. But it was not knocked out.

Once more, the Marines took the blockhouse their own way. Bulldozers were moved up, the drivers sheltering behind the blades, and buried the entrance in coral and dirt. As the height of the rubble increased, gunports and other apertures were closed, immobilizing all Japanese resistance and completing the process of entombment. Marines then climbed on top of the blockhouses and poured gasoline down the air vents. A few hand grenades, and incineration followed. Rear Admiral Keijai Shibashi, the island commander, was the principal victim of this holocaust. The Marines took out 300 bodies. It was a grim procedure but the only course left to the Marines if they wanted to survive.

If Tarawa had to be fought, its only justification was the information we gained that saved lives and increased the efficiency of our landing technique in subsequent operations. We were entering a new, uncharted land, a field of military enterprises in which we were guided only by theory and peacetime maneuvers. At best, simulated attacks are poor substitutes for combat experience. This was our first frontal attack on a fortified enemy atoll and we were ignorant both of its capacity for resistance and of our own offensive limitations. The Marine doctrine of amphibious assault stood the test.

Timing of the operation and the selection of beaches were good. The three beaches on the north coast of Betio, inside the lagoon, were the only feasible landing beaches. Had we delayed our attack a few weeks, the Japanese would have completed their ring of underwater obstacles and made our landing even more difficult. Lieutenant Colonel (afterwards Brigadier General) Evans F. Carlson's raid on Makin in August, 1942, was a spectacular performance by his 2nd Marine Raider Battalion but it was also a piece of folly. The raid had no useful military purpose and served only to alert the Japanese to our intentions in the Gilberts. The intensive fortification of Tarawa dates from that raid.

Tarawa taught us the necessity for more naval gunfire and more air bombing before we undertook a landing. What was considered by the Navy a paralyzing amount of fire was directed at Betio, in our first wedding of naval guns and airplane bombs in the reduction of a fortified atoll, but until after Tarawa we could not calculate accurately the result of this type of attack on concentrated fortifications such as the Japanese had constructed. Moreover, the Navy was inclined to exaggerate the destructive effect of gunfire and this failing really amounted to a job imperfectly done. The Marines discovered this fact only when they tried to land. Air assistance was no better gauged than naval support and the strikes were poorly co-ordinated. The planes were not there when needed. The secret of amphibious warfare is concentration of your forces and meticulous co-ordination of all elements, plus as much naval gunfire and air bombardment as you can pour into enemy positions.

An island as small as Betio made it impossible to establish a beachhead as we understand the term in amphibious parlance. There was no depth beyond the beaches for landing supplies and organizing attacks. With every yard accurately and carefully covered by enemy fire, we had first to get a toehold and proceed to take the island all in one piece. This was the first time we had made an assault across a fringing reef covered by an uncertain depth of water and our calculations on water depth were badly in error. The Japanese were fully aware of the defensive possibilities of that reef from the vantage of their pre-sited guns, and they were helped by the inexplicably low tide which held for two days.

Another lesson the Navy should have learned was the need for better co-operation between all units. An Admiral should confine himself to the job of carrying the troops safely to the objective and then helping to protect them. He should leave details of landing and assault to the troop commander.

The reef at Tarawa emphasized the value of amphibian vehicles. The operation was as much a test of our technical equipment as it was of our landing technique. We should have had more amtracks for employment in the initial landing, with adequate reserves for vehicles knocked out by enemy guns or incapacitated by mechanical difficulties. The two or three types used stood up well. The average mechanical life of an amtrack is 200 hours; some of those used at Tarawa had already run 400 hours.

After Tarawa I made up my mind that all future landings would be spearheaded by amphibious vehicles, either the opendecked amtrack, of which a new improved model was already being made available, or amphibian tanks, carrying heavier guns, which were in production. This decision did not mean discarding Higgins boats. These craft could be used on unobstructed beaches, or through reef channels—as the work horse of amphibious landings—but for impassable reefs the solution was the amphibious vehicle.

Tarawa taught other lessons. It stimulated our desire to learn. It taught us more about the character of the enemy than all the textbooks and intelligence reports at staff disposal. In the strategical scheme for the Central Pacific offensive, it taught me that the instrument of high policy known as the Joint Chiefs of Staff was not infallible.

Tarawa was a mistake.

CHAPTER VII

BETWEEN OPERATIONS and planning for operations in the Pacific, life with the top echelons at Pearl Harbor could be very pleasant once you penetrated the inner defenses. The brass lived at Makalapa, a settlement spick-and-span as a ship's deck, on the hill behind CINCPAC, Admiral Nimitz's headquarters twelve miles outside Honolulu. Makalapa, the name of a crater, means "Flashing Eyes" in Hawaiian.

Makalapa residents had the choice of two fine views. Looking out to sea lay West Loch, a sheltered arm of Pearl Harbor, and Battleship Row where, on that ill-starred morning of December 7, our battleships lay two by two, sitting ducks for Japanese dive bombers. Inland stretched another sea of rustling green cane, slashed by brick-red clay roads, and beyond rose the green mountains, the eternal home of Hawaii's incredible rainbows.

Our quarters were neat bungalows located in trim lawns, where ageless, unidentifiable women from the Orient, typical of the racial admixture of the Islands, settled each morning like birds. They hid beneath huge, floppy hats to weed the lawns or prune the wayward hibiscus. Makalapa was laid out like a real estate development, with tennis courts and a swimming pool, and the streets were named after Pacific battles. When we captured an island, or fought a naval engagement, the name was given to a street and Makalapa became a residential history of the Pacific war. I lived on Makalapa Drive near Betio Street, named for the island where the battle of Tarawa was fought.

Dominating Makalapa was CINCPAC headquarters, a gray, four-story building with decks instead of floors, as the most junior ensign soon learned. Admiral Nimitz had a fondness for brisk walks, preferably uphill, and a passion for secrecy. This

Texan was a fine pistol shot—he practiced every morning on his private range outside CINCPAC, where a Marine stood on precautionary duty and a notice on the wall warned passersby that firing was in progress.

The Admiral's private ambition was to sink the six Japanese carriers that bombed Pearl Harbor. Four of the carriers were sunk by our Navy at the Battle of Midway but the *Shokaku* and *Zuikaku* were still afloat when I arrived at Pearl Harbor in the autumn of 1943.

"Holland," the Admiral once said to me, "the happiest day of my life will be the day when I reach my office to find a message on my desk reporting that we have sunk these two carriers." That happiness never came to Nimitz all at once but eventually —in June and October, 1944—the score was wiped off the slate.

Nimitz was godhead of the hierarchy at Makalapa and the Thrones, Dominations, Princedoms, Virtues and Powers of brass ranked through Vice Admirals down to the lowest myrmidons, who inhabited bachelor officers' quarters.

More naval brass was sheltered in this sanctuary than anywhere else in the world. God only knows what would have happened if the Japanese had learned of its existence and bombed Makalapa. The course of the war probably would have been changed but the strictest security shielded the settlement from this appalling eventuality. While Makalapa was the most brassbound community in the world it also was the most secret. It had no existence in communiques or press handouts. The mere whisper of the sacred name Makalapa made a censor blanch, and Honolulu taxidrivers bluntly refused to go into the district under the mistaken impression that they would be arrested immediately by MP's.

Less awed by the esoteric existence imposed upon the community by security authorities were the newspaper correspondents who, with alliterative irreverence, called us "The Mad Monks of Makalapa."

I mentioned penetrating the inner defenses of Makalapa because it was difficult for a Marine to get beyond them. When I arrived at Pearl Harbor to command the V Amphibious Corps,

Rear Admiral Turner met me at the airport and took me out to Makalapa where, to my astonishment, I was conducted to quarters in the section at the foot of the hill reserved for junior lieutenants. I was a senior Major General, senior to all Rear Admirals at Pearl Harbor with one exception, but with the habitual disregard of the Navy for the Marines it was decided that any old place would do for a Marine General.

If there is one thing I have fought consistently over the years, it is this non-recognition by the Navy of the status of the Marine Corps. So I went into action and I didn't stay long in those foot-of-the-hill quarters.

I protested and after the usual explanation of a billeting officer's error I was moved up the hill. Two doors away lived Vice Admiral Charles A. Lockwood and across the street were Vice Admiral Raymond A. Spruance and Vice Admiral William L. Calhoun, which put me in a better frame of mind, although I never was able to acclimatize myself to the prevailing social conditions.

For one thing, I had no white uniforms. It never occurred to me to bring them, since I was on my way to the combat area. To my surprise, war had failed to take the starch out of Honolulu's shirt front and many civilians never appeared to take the war seriously. In this they were aided and abetted by ranking Army and Navy officers, who circled around the Big Five, the commercial and social apex of life in the Hawaiian Islands, enjoying lavish hospitality. Dances at the Outrigger, overlooking the beach at Waikiki, brought out as many white uniforms as a peacetime ship inspection.

At first I was stubborn; I stuck to my khaki uniforms and earned the reputation of being a cranky individualist who believed that in war we should dress like soldiers. I hate to admit it but polite jeers at my habits of dress finally wore me down and on my first trip back to the Coast I decided to dig out my white uniforms and avoid embarrassment by wearing them. Once or twice I did surrender to current social standards, but not cheerfully.

Going formal in the middle of a war was part of the queer

detachment that civilians in Hawaii, working on the vanity of the services, were able to maintain. I never understood exactly how they managed it. This dressiness always impressed Marines back from the foxholes more than any other phase of Honolulu's wartime front. However, I am sure that the main endeavor of the inhabitants of Makalapa was to bring the war to a speedy and successful conclusion.

After the Gilberts, the staff of the V Amphibious Corps plunged into the next phase of the Central Pacific offensive, the capture of the Marshall Islands. During our planning of this operation, General Marshall, Army Chief of Staff, visited Pearl Harbor and addressed a conference of Army, Navy and Marine chiefs in the area.

His discussion of certain aspects of the use of machine guns and rockets from small landing boats—along experimental lines we had tried and abandoned—was an indication of his unfamiliarity (like most Army officers) with amphibious technique. It is difficult at best to hang on in a small boat plunging and wallowing among reefs, shallow waters, surf and a running tide. I felt that Marshall's intention was to belittle the Marine effort instead of giving us a helpful analysis, which a soldier of his unquestioned caliber could have done; and once again I recalled his anti-Marine role in the Iceland Command controversy.

Lieutenant General Richardson sat there, eating it up. It was plain that he had not abandoned the hope that command of the offensive eventually would fall into the Army's lap and Marshall's criticism fed that hope.

Thinking over Marshall's talk that night, I began to wonder if it could be possible that the Joint Chiefs of Staff were working in the dark back in Washington. Apparently they were receiving incomplete information on the actions in the Pacific, which would account for Marshall's ill-formed opinions. For instance, Nimitz was not forwarding all information to Washington. Like MacArthur, ruling at the other side of the Pacific, the Admiral exercised a proprietary interest in his own theater of operations, to the exclusion of the Joint Chiefs.

Confirmation of this news starvation came in a letter from Admiral King, COMINCH, passed on to me for reference. I gave an interview after Tarawa and some of my remarks were badly garbled because of Navy censorship and public reaction to our losses.

King deplored the "bad press" Tarawa had received and explained that, although volumes of newspaper stories had been published on the battle, no official account had reached Washington. Apparently the Joint Chiefs had to read the newspapers or turn on the radio for news of the Pacific because Nimitz was not keeping them informed.

The letter of the Commander-in-Chief, dated December 16, 1943, nearly a month after Tarawa, demanded plaintively:

> Prompt information to this Headquarters of important details of each landing operation. This may be accomplished either in a report or by sending to Washington an officer familiar with the operation.
>
> Prompt information of detailed plans to this Headquarters. The Commander-in-Chief, United States Fleet, does not demand that these be sent in advance of an operation, but he should not be left in the dark indefinitely as to what it was planned to do.

I would not go so far as to say that the Joint Chiefs did not know what was happening once they had drawn the broad lines of policy but judging by this letter their information was, to say the least, incomplete.

Planning for the Marshalls began long before I arrived in the Pacific and before we captured the Gilberts. Certain basic decisions were approved by President Roosevelt in Washington in May, 1943, and CINCPAC submitted detailed plans for the Marshalls operations to the Joint Chiefs as early as July 1, 1943. These plans, however, involved a number of uncertain factors: lack of intelligence, ignorance of the type of defense the Japanese would adopt, absence of air photographs, and only a theoretical knowledge of the ability of amphibious vehicles to cross reefs under fire.

Kelly Turner and I did not begin actual planning on the basis of information available and on tests of amphibious equipment until the first week in October, and two weeks later Nimitz issued his operations plan establishing the task organization for the capture of the Marshalls but leaving the precise objectives to be designated later.

The ground forces allocated as assault troops were the Fourth Marine Division, fresh from amphibious training at Camp Pendleton, and the Seventh Army Division, veterans of Attu, with the 106th Infantry from the Twenty-seventh Army Division, and the 22nd Marines as Corps reserves. I immediately ordered the Fourth Marines into further amphibious training at Maalaea Bay on the island of Maui, with specific attention to maneuvers for atoll warfare and also the use of supporting artillery, which was to be a feature of our tactical plan. I asked for the Seventh Division to be turned over to me for similar training but this was not immediately possible.

Our thrust into the Marshalls involved considerable revision of early plans before we were able to decide upon detailed objectives. Lying 2,400 miles west of Hawaii and almost midway between Hawaii and the Philippines, the Marshalls had been in Japanese hands since World War I, when the enemy took them from the Germans. They were mandated to Japan in 1920 by the League of Nations. From north to south, they stretch 700 miles and consist of some 30 large atolls, all following the general coral pattern of a ring of small islands encircling a central lagoon. The islands barely rise above the blue water and those which attained 20 feet above sea level were considered topographically "mountainous."

In the center of the group is Kwajalein, the largest atoll in the world, running 60 miles from north to south and 20 miles from east to west. Northwest of the great atoll, in the loneliest stretches of the ocean, are Eniwetok and Bikini atolls, which since the war have been converted into our atomic experimentation bases in the Pacific.

When we decided to invade the Marshalls the Japanese had

fortified six atolls: Eniwetok, Jaluit, Kwajalein, Maloelap, Mille, and Wotje. Their total garrison was 25,000 men. Our original plan called for the capture of Kwajalein, Maloelap, and Wotje, the development of bases on the main islands of these atolls, and the neutralization of Mille and Jaluit in order to insure our control of the Marshalls. D-day for the attack on the first atoll was set for January 1, 1944. In my estimate of the situation, I expressed the view that we should take Maloelap and Wotje first, and then move on to Kwajalein.

The intervention of the Gilberts operation diverted my personal attention temporarily from the Marshalls, but Bobby Erskine and part of my staff remained behind at Pearl Harbor to work on the plans based on the original Nimitz directive.

When I returned from Tarawa, armed with practical experience in atoll warfare, plus a knowledge of Japanese defense tactics and our own limitations, I could see plainly that the Marshalls plan was too ambitious. To undertake an operation of the extent contemplated, we would need at least another division of troops, in addition to the two divisions assigned, and even then I was doubtful that we could gain our objectives.

On December 6 I recommended that we abandon the idea of taking the three objectives selected in the Marshalls and concentrate on one. Kelly Turner, also with Tarawa in mind, supported me. On the selection of the single preferred target, however, the top echelons differed and the conference room at CINCPAC echoed with dissent. Nimitz and his planning officer, Rear Admiral Sherman, favored striking directly at the heart of the Marshalls, by-passing other atolls. Spruance and Kelly Turner were opposed to this course, basing their objections upon the fear of air attack from Jaluit, Maloelap and Mille, lying across our route through the group. My own view was that a bold blow at Kwajalein was not only feasible but the most practical way of reducing the entire group. I favored the Nimitz-Sherman proposal.

We finally decided upon the capture of Kwajalein Atoll, plus an additional unnamed atoll with a good anchorage, needed as an advanced base for the Pacific Fleet. The additional target selected later was Majuro, an atoll the Germans once intended to make their advanced Pacific base. The Japanese developed at Majuro barracks, a railroad and an airfield. These they abandoned; we found only one Japanese on Majuro. He was a shipwrecked petty officer, who built himself a pillbox on the beach and armed it with machine guns taken from an American plane that crashed on the island. The Majuro anchorage fulfilled all naval expectations.

In the light of our Tarawa experience it was apparent that the assault troops needed more training and required additional equipment, especially amphibious vehicles. This meant postponing D-day in the Marshalls until January 31, by which time I felt the troops would be at the top of their efficiency.

Meanwhile, I was having personal difficulties with the Navy command, which once again attempted to usurp my functions as V Amphibious Corps Commander. Kelly Turner, who always had suppressed ambitions to be a General, wanted to take detailed charge of the training of land forces, which was my responsibility, and I had to be very firm in opposing this usurpation because I realized that if the Navy ever got a footing in the sphere of troop training, the Marines would have the devil's own time regaining proper authority.

Once more naval tactics were following the course of my pre-Gilberts experience. The Navy command attempted to deprive the Corps of all tactical responsibility and relegate us to the realm of planning and training only. A week before the expedition sailed from Pearl Harbor for the Marshalls the directive from Nimitz again omitted my name from command. After planning the operation and training the troops, I was to be left behind at Pearl Harbor, with the Navy assuming operational and tactical control. And once again I went to bat with the higher brass. Spruance saw that the final directive was changed to include me and my staff.

For the first time in the Pacific the Navy and Marine commands were accommodated in one of the new AGC's specially designed command ships, which had received first use in the Mediterranean. This was to be our floating headquarters until shore headquarters were established. In the *USS Pennsylvania*, flagship at Makin, only a small office on the flag bridge was available for my staff, and living quarters were limited. The new AGC's of the *Appalachian* class were 12,000-ton ships, good for 16 knots, with ample accommodation for task force and expeditionary force commanders and their staffs. The *Rocky Mount*, Kelly Turner's flagship, had good living quarters; office space was cramped, but communications facilities were excellent. I was allowed to take with me a larger staff than before, though I still did not have as many officers as the operation warranted.

With our naval gunfire inadequacies at Tarawa as a powerful argument, I had stressed as prerequisites for our assault on Kwajalein the importance of greater volume and more effective gunfire and air bombardment, as well as a wider and more prolonged range of neutralizing attacks. At Tarawa, the Japanese had fortified Betio for a year and a half. The enemy had been in the Marshalls for 25 years and we could only guess what they had accomplished in that period. I also insisted upon naval bombardment and carrier and land-based airplane strikes at every base the Japanese might use to send air attacks against us. I recommended that these strikes be continued for at least ten days before we landed.

In preparation for the Marshalls, the Navy supported us fully. Every enemy base from Eniwetok in the northern Marshalls to Nauru in the Gilberts was attacked repeatedly. Spruance commanded four carrier task forces and at least 15 battleships in the greatest naval assembly ever seen up to that time. Our Navy was expanding rapidly, with new ships coming out to the combat zone almost daily. Co-operating with the Navy was the Seventh Air Force, whose planes dropped hundreds of tons of bombs on Japanese positions. Not for a single day was there any let-up.

The necessity for overwhelming firepower, both in preparation and during the beach assault itself, was a Marine Corps tenet of amphibious doctrine. We who knew the Navy intimately could gauge and harness the terrific residual firepower of the Fleet for employment against shore targets. The technical achievement of adapting naval batteries to this mission—together with much of the two-way selling job required to create enthusiasm and confidence for the new technique on the part of both Navy and Marines—was to a great extent the result of the drive and ingenuity of a single officer, Lieutenant Colonel (now Colonel) Donald M. Weller, USMC. Few officers contributed so much, by singlehanded effort, to the winning of the war, as did Don Weller, Naval Academy graduate, veteran field artilleryman and Marine. A member of my staff from the prewar Atlantic Amphibious Corps days to the end of the war (with the exception of a "respite" in command of an artillery battalion in two of the Third Marine Division's hard-fought operations), Don Weller was, in his medium, that of naval gunfire support, truly an architect of victory.

The magnitude of the Kwajalein bombardment was historic. Prior to our landing we dropped 15,000 tons of naval and land artillery shells and bombs on the objective islands. In two days, the Navy used 5,270 tons of ammunition on Kwajalein, an island three miles long and 700 yards across at its widest point, and 4,580 tons on the twin northern islands of Roi and Namur, less than two square miles in area. Army artillery, operating from a nearby island, Enubuj, poured 600 tons of ammunition and Army planes dropped 27 two-thousand pound bombs on one Kwajalein beach. Marine artillery likewise operated on Roi-Namur in the north.

Lieutenant Colonel E. G. Van Orman, in Weller's absence the naval gunfire specialist on my staff, worked out the bombardment to equal the firing of 326,700 seventy-five millimeter shells, or nearly two tons of explosive for every Japanese.

Referring to the bombardment, which surpassed anything in any war, a cynic on board the *Rocky Mount* paraphrased Winston Churchill and his remark made the rounds: "Never in the history of human conflict has so much been thrown by so many at so few."

Kelly Turner had the answer to that charge and to the fact that we needed two divisions to capture islands which conceivably could have been taken by considerably fewer men.

"Perhaps we did bring along too many men, too many ships and use too much effort," he said in an interview. "That is what people might say but it must not be regarded in that light. We determined that not a single life should be lost unnecessarily, and that the operation must be completely possible. The scale wasn't too great. It was just an indication of what we can do and will do. It is evidence of the power we are going to use against the Japs."

Considering the difficulties I had experienced in putting over my views on naval gunfire, this statement sounded very reassuring. I was happy that at Kwajalein we had "sent a man to do a boy's work." The superabundance at Kwajalein was the direct result of the insufficiency at Tarawa, although with more discriminating and effective use comparable results could have been obtained with less ammunition. In my report, however, I did not minimize the gunfire results. Knowing that targets would get tougher as we moved westward toward the Japanese homeland, I pleaded for even more intensified naval and air preparation and stressed the importance of better fire control. But, sad to relate, we never again got that concentrated amount of gunfire and air bombardment.

Operation FLINTLOCK (Kwajalein) was distinguished by the magnitude of the planning, the celerity of the Marines and the cooperation of the Army. Turner commanded the Southern Attack Force working on Kwajalein Island and Rear Admiral Richard L. "Close In" Conolly the Northern Attack Force.

Conolly justified his name by taking his battle-wagons so close (2,000 yards) that his guns almost poked their muzzles into Japanese positions. Admiral Conolly occupied a warm spot in the heart of every Marine. They admired his boldness and appreciated the way he came to their assistance, even if his action wasn't outlined in the operational plan.

The pattern for the capture of the two objectives at Kwajalein was unvaried. In the northern part of the atoll, the Fourth Division Scout Company and the 25th Regiment (Colonel Samuel C. Cumming), under the overall command of Brigadier General J. L. Underhill, seized a number of small islands flanking Roi and Namur and we got our artillery ashore and brought it to bear on the two enemy islands. For this phase of the operation the Seventh Division used DUKW's, the pneumatic-tired amphibious truck developed by the Army. DUKW's had never before been used in any numbers in the Pacific and they proved very successful. In the southern sector of the atoll, the Seventh Division Reconnaissance Troop and the 17th Infantry, following the same plan, seized a number of adjacent islands and landed artillery. In this way powerful artillery support was available for the main landings on the northern and southern objectives.

The 23rd Marines (Colonel Louis R. Jones) landed on Roi, originally believed the "toughest" objective, and secured it in a few hours. Roi had a three-runway airfield and was connected with Namur by a causeway. The 24th Marines (Colonel Franklin A. Hart) were assigned to Namur, a stronger position and, although facing greater opposition, secured it in 25 hours.

The 184th and the 32nd Infantry landed on Kwajalein and it took them five days to capture the island. I fretted considerably at the slowness of the Army advance. I could see no reason why this division, with ample forces ashore, well covered by land-based artillery and receiving tremendous naval and air support, could not take the island quicker. Every hour the transports and other ships of the fleet had to remain in the vicinity of the action the greater was the danger from enemy air and submarine attack. We had not yet smashed the Japanese Combined Fleet; we hadn't been able to find it.

The Fourth Marine Division at Kwajalein was, as the British say, "blooded." Afterward they were no longer green and untried. Their landings, in the execution of an extremely complex and intricate scheme of maneuver, were less than perfect, due to communications failures and insufficient numbers of amphibian tractors—not to speak of more than equal greenness and similar failures in the Navy's organization. In addition, like most new troops, the Fourth Division had fallen prey to a trigger-happiness only exceeded by what I had seen on Makin. Nevertheless, the division as a whole had acquitted itself well, manifesting the dash and offensive spirit which I regard as essential and characteristic in Marine Corps units, and which enabled both Roi and Namur to become ours in the shortest possible time with a minimum of casualties. Assuming that an adequate beachhead could be gained in short order, I had directed Major General Harry Schmidt, Commander of the Fourth Division, to land on Roi and Namur at the earliest possible opportunity.

"Harry," I told him, "the minute you set foot on that beach I want you to assume command ashore." He was ashore early and I was very pleased with the dash displayed by the division in capturing its objectives.

After Roi and Namur fell, Brigadier General Underhill, using the 25th Marines, captured the remaining islands in North Kwajalein, and the 17th Infantry cleaned up the islands in South Kwajalein, with the result that in a little over a week we controlled the whole of the atoll and not a single one of our ships had been hit in enemy naval or air action.

After the terrific barrage, Kwajalein proved a significant victory because of its relatively low cost in lives, time and equipment. The Army and the Marines lost 356, killed and missing, and accounted for approximately 8,500 Japanese.

From a military point of view, Kwajalein suggested certain important improvements in our amphibious technique, which had progressed from the field of pure theory to the hard reality of battle.

We needed more coordinated planning to tie up the loose ends of our assaults and more advance information on targets to facilitate training. Our amphibian tractors proved effective but they lacked speed in the water, needed more efficient radio equipment and additional armor. These defects were remedied in future designs and a stern ramp was added to some models. We also needed repair facilities afloat before we got them established ashore, and our control and employment of amtracks was capable of improvement. What was even more important, I realized in surveying our amphibious progress, was the need for special units to remove beach obstacles and mines and give us a better picture of beach conditions. The answer to this was the underwater demolition teams, which were first tried out at Kwajalein, but did not begin to perform miracles of intelligence-gathering until later operations.

After we secured Kwajalein the place became a regular tourist haunt. The big Army and Navy brass from Pearl Harbor descended on us like flies. They came up the lagoon from Kwajalein to Roi and Namur by destroyer in such numbers that we had to drop Marine drivers and let the brass drive their own jeeps. My Marines got a shock when they saw a General playing chauffeur. It always amused me to see the boys from Pearl coming visiting after the battle was over. The photographers had a gala day snapping pictures against the background of shelled buildings while visiting brass hunted for samurai swords and other souvenirs.

The closing chapter of our occupation of the Marshalls was the capture of Eniwetok, northwest of Kwajalein. Of all the atolls in and around the Marshalls, Eniwetok ranked only after Kwajalein in strength and importance. The northern island, Engebi, had an airfield through which all Japanese planes from bases farther west were channeled. It also possessed minor naval facilities. During our planning of the Marshalls operation, I became convinced that Kwajalein might prove to be an easy objective and, although I had the 22nd Marines and the 106th Regiment from the Twenty-seventh Army Division in reserve, it was more than possible these troops would never be needed. The two divisions we took along were quite sufficient at Kwajalein.

On November 16 these two regiments were organized into a subordinate tactical group under the command of Brigadier General Thomas E. Watson and group landing maneuvers were practiced on Maui. Some time before the Joint Expeditionary Force left Pearl Harbor for Kwajalein a joint study by the CINCPAC staff indicated that the next operation should be Eniwetok and a

148

provisional date was fixed for May 1, although Spruance recommended that the operation could be undertaken early in April.

While CINCPAC was contemplating this distant study, the idea occurred to me that Kwajalein might be so easy that we could go directly from that atoll to Eniwetok without the laborious, time-wasting procedure of returning to Pearl Harbor after Kwajalein had been captured. My staff started planning along these lines, preparing estimates and concepts and we were soon convinced of the feasibility of the idea.

I did not mention the plan to Spruance or Turner, or to any of the top Navy echelons at Pearl Harbor. My reason for this secrecy lay in the fear that Navy conservatism would kill the idea at birth because, from the Navy viewpoint, it was inconceivable to proceed from one operation to another without returning to base to refuel, reprovision and rearm the ships. Any argument that these preparations could be made in the forward areas always met with a monumental list of difficulties and objections which the Navy had little difficulty in evoking.

En route to Kwajalein, we completed our Eniwetok concept, which I tucked away and waited for a favorable opportunity to produce. As soon as it became apparent that we would not need the Corps reserve, Kelly Turner mentioned the possibility of going ahead and taking Eniwetok. I agreed that this action was possible and added that I had already discussed the suggestion with Bobby Erskine, my Chief of Staff. While Kelly Turner delved into generalities about the operation, I put my hand in the drawer of my desk and pulled out the plan.

Kelly Turner is an aggressive fighter. I knew that if I waited for the right moment in the forward areas to produce my plan he would be less hampered by the innate conservatism of the higher Navy echelons, and much more likely to accept it. That is precisely what happened. The plan appealed to him and he approved. Spruance added his approval. Nimitz later concurred and we set to work on the details. The 22nd Marines and the 106th Infantry, less its 2nd Battalion, which was at Majuro, were assigned the task of taking Eniwetok.

Speed was the essence of our efforts. The more time we spent planning and preparing, the longer the Japanese, warned by Kwajalein, would have to strengthen their defenses, and the more costly would be our victory. If we could strike before their defenses were completed, we could save many lives. In advocating this approach, I was following my old policy of speed and my favorite theory: "When you get hold of the Jap, never turn him loose. Keep the pressure on him and he can't take it."

Harry Hill was called from Majuro on board the USS *Cambria* to take command of Operation CATCHPOLE, and I wanted to go along with the expeditionary troops but Kelly Turner insisted that Tommy Watson should do the job.

The main Japanese positions at Eniwetok had received a good going over from our carriers and, to prevent any interference from other Japanese bases, Spruance took all the fast battleships he could muster, plus Rear Admiral Marc A. Mitscher and his fast carriers—afterwards known as the famous Task Force 58. In the middle of February he struck at Truk, the Japanese headquarters farther west, and Ponape and Kusaie in the Carolines, while Army planes from Midway hit Wake. Bypassed islands in the Marshalls were kept under control by cruiser patrols.

Hill and Watson took the two regiments to Eniwetok and were blessed with good luck from the start. Although our intelligence was meager, we had the good fortune at Kwajalein to capture a secret Japanese chart showing the main channel to the lagoon and all the soundings. In fact, we captured so many of these charts that we were able to distribute a Japanese original to every ship. The main elements of our force steamed directly into the lagoon and anchored off the beaches. This greatly helped landing operations because we had no surf to contend with, and enemy defenses were weakest on the lagoon side of the islands.

In less than half a day we captured Engebi, in the north, and in five days took Eniwetok and Parry, in the south, completing the conquest of the atoll on the evening of February 22, 1944, Washington's Birthday. Had we waited another three months in accordance with the CINCPAC plan, the Japanese would have had time to fortify Eniwetok and the cost would have been much higher. As it was, our losses were small and by capturing Eniwetok we won control of the entire Marshalls group.

CHAPTER VIII

O
UR SWIFT seizure of the Marshalls gave us in the
Central Pacific a momentum we never lost. The time saved enabled us to revise our strategical concept of the situation and
advance our timetable six months. The attack on the next group
of islands blocking our way to Tokyo, the Marianas, originally
was contemplated as the concluding phase of the 1944 program.
But it became possible in the summer of that year, and addition-
ally, in the fall, we were able to undertake the important Palau
operation and wipe out Japanese resistance in the Western
Carolines.

In the overall plan for the year (GRANITE Plan), issued by
CINCPAC in January, 1944, the mid-summer target was Truk, the
naval and air base in the Central Carolines, guarding the southern
and eastern approaches to Japan. Through its supposed strength,
Truk had always been a nightmare, compelling us to build all
our plans around this base. We considered Truk's capture necessary to protect our flank in the Marianas campaign.

By the middle of February, the target date of June 15 was
set for the assault on Truk but by the middle of March the Truk
plans were abandoned. In a series of powerful carrier strikes, the
Navy exposed the vulnerability of this base by destroying Japanese air strength based there and by sinking a harborful of
cargo ships.

Following our policy of bypassing all but essential strong
holds, General MacArthur meanwhile advanced up the coast of
New Guinea, establishing bases at Aitape and Hollandia. At the
same time, Army and Navy forces seized the Admiralties and

Emirau, providing us with a chain of bases to ring Rabaul and put us safely within long-range bombing distance of Truk. The bogey vanished forever.

Hence the Marianas supplanted Truk as our next objective and we started planning the capture of Saipan and Tinian, the main Japanese islands in the group, and the recapture of the American island of Guam. By the end of March we received the final joint staff study from Admiral Nimitz and from then on planning proceeded rapidly at headquarters. This was the greatest opportunity the Marine Corps had been offered.

For the task of recapturing the Marianas, Operation FOR-AGER, Nimitz designated the III Marine Amphibious Corps, comprising the Third Division and the 1st Provisional Brigade, and the V Marine Amphibious Corps, comprising the Second Division and the Fourth Division, with the Twenty-seventh Army Division attached as reserve and the Seventy-seventh Army Division alerted in Hawaii as area reserve. Command of all expeditionary troops was given to me.

I cannot describe the exultation that swept through Marine ranks when it became known that for the first time we were to operate in the field as organic units instead of a joint command. We were a Marine field army, commanded by a Marine General, going into action independently against the Japanese, and the opportunity to enhance the prestige of the Marine Corps was so great that it stirred every man in my command. No more of that odious "secondary force" talk at the Naval War College. The Marine Corps had come of age.

Another development increased this feeling of pride. After Tarawa and the Marshalls, Spruance was promoted to Admiral and Turner to Vice Admiral but no recognition was made of the part played by the Marines. This omission stung our officers and enlisted men, who considered with some reason that they had done as much as the Navy to capture these islands, and that their action merited recognition.

Lieutenant General Vandegrift, who succeeded General Holcomb as Commandant of the Marine Corps, felt that his Corps had won the respect and admiration of the American people and was entitled to a three-star General to lead the Marines in the Pacific.

My promotion to Lieutenant General had been recommended to Secretary of the Navy Knox by General Holcomb, but Admiral King, COMINCH, replied that he was not prepared at that time to promote me. On assuming office as Commandant, Archer Vandegrift pressed the point and bolstered his arguments by citing the promotions of Spruance and Kelly Turner. Events were following the usual line. After the feast, the crumbs were given to the Marines—if there were any crumbs. King countered that Nimitz had not recommended me for promotion, but Vandegrift induced him to query the Admiral and find out what he thought. A dispatch came back with the recommendation.

In the meantime, I had written to the Commandant pointing out that the work of the Corps in the Pacific should be recognized by the promotion of a Marine General to the rank of Lieutenant General. I added that if King refused to promote me he should promote somebody else, and I would accede to my relief and return home. My idea was that a Marine Major General should be promoted, and I did not care who it was, provided the promotion was made and the Marine Corps accorded deserved recognition.

I do not know whether the Commandant forwarded this suggestion to King, but I did receive the promotion, and a personal letter from Secretary Knox, dated March 15, 1944, stated:

> I want to be the first to congratulate you on your promotion to Lieutenant General. I have to be the first to know, because I have just signed your commission.
> I am very proud of you and the way you have handled yourself in this war. You have certainly lived up in fine fashion to the highest traditions of the Marine Corps. This new promotion is a richly deserved recognition of the services you have rendered in a critically important combat area. I know that you are going on to further triumphs in the future.

Nobody can accuse the Marine Corps of being topheavy with brass. My promotion made only two Lieutenant Generals in the Corps, the other being the Commandant, who was promoted in the South Pacific after Guadalcanal. Later, Vandegrift, was made a full general, and on retirement Harry Schmidt, Turnage and I received four stars. By Congressional action, the same rank was conferred posthumously on General Geiger. From now on, Commandants of the Corps also will rank as full Generals.

At the end of March, Major General Geiger, who commanded the III Amphibious Corps, flew up from Guadalcanal to Pearl Harbor and stayed with me at Makalapa. Roy Geiger was a heavyset, bear-like and totally fearless man. He was someone who could only have happened in the Marine Corps. One of the pioneers from the box-kite days of Naval Aviation, he had flown and commanded almost every kind of aircraft or aviation unit that ever existed. Like all Marine officers, however, he had always kept his feet on the ground.

The outset of active operations in the Solomons found him in command of our air effort on Guadalcanal, directing and occasionally flying the strikes which broke the back of Japanese air in the Southern Solomons. Promoted after Guadalcanal, he was given one of the most important tactical group commands in the Marine Corps, namely, the III Amphibious Corps, and thus became my counterpart in the South Pacific. In this capacity he was to command the Bougainville, Peleliu and Guam operations (not to speak of leading his corps on Okinawa, and succeeding, after General Buckner's death, to command of the entire Okinawa battle). I imagine I am correct in asserting that no military aviator since the Wright brothers has ever exercised, quite interchangeably, such major air and ground commands, all in one war—nor is it likely to happen again, unless the Marine Corps and its aviation are allowed to continue unimpeded by inter-Service vendettas.

The ten days of Geiger's visit enabled us to work out with our joint staffs the important problems of the forthcoming operation, as well as the personal aspect of Marine participation. I emphasized the opportunity that lay before the Corps and cautioned Geiger to assume command ashore at Guam as soon as possible after the landing, in order to keep things moving.

For Operation FORAGER the troops were divided into two

groups, the Northern under the V Amphibious Corps, which I commanded, and the Southern under the III Amphibious Corps, commanded by Geiger. My targets were Saipan and Tinian. Geiger's was Guam.

I held the dual position of commanding all the expeditionary troops and also the subordinate Northern group. In addition to holding these two jobs, I had to provide two staffs. This ambiguity was straightened out later when the Fleet Marine Force, Pacific, was formed and I was made Commanding General. Major General Harry Schmidt succeeded me as commander of the V Amphibious Corps.

Kelly Turner also served in a dual capacity. Under Spruance, who was overall boss of the operation as Fifth Fleet Commander, Turner was not only joint amphibious force commander but also director of the subordinate Northern attack force at Saipan and Tinian. Rear Admiral Conolly was his deputy at Guam. It was a tribute to the cooperative spirit among the top echelons that this complicated organization ran so smoothly.

The weeks before we sailed for the Marianas were consumed by planning and training. The V Corps held amphibious exercises in the Hawaiian area, culminating in a full-scale dress rehearsal. Down at Guadalcanal, Roy Geiger conducted similar exercises. Because of the limited time and the necessity for intensive training, preparation of orders proceeded simultaneously instead of through the normal chain of command, starting from CINCPAC and working down to the lowest echelon, so occasionally the first order was the last and the last was the first, but we avoided confusion by frequent conferences.

By this time the atmosphere at CINCPAC headquarters was brighter and more confident. The gloom that used to hang over the building and stalk the decks had begun to lift. Nimitz himself reflected the change. He had begun to realize that the Marines could take any island and take it quickly. He had only to name the target and he could cross it off the big map on the wall of his conference room.

After Tarawa, I could never understand the constant apprehension the Admiral displayed regarding the Pacific situation.

Never an exuberant man, he could work up, in his quiet way, an extremely pessimistic mood. Nimitz had no reason to be alarmed. He was a lucky man. He had Bull Halsey and Ray Spruance, two of the greatest admirals in the world, commanding the Third and Fifth Fleets (actually the same fleet but changing designation with different commanders); he had Kelly Turner, a brilliant leader of amphibious forces afloat; he had Harry Hill, Spike Blandy, Dick Conolly and Ping Wilkinson, amphibious Admirals; he had Pete Mitscher, Slew McCain, Arthur Radford and a dozen other carrier Admirals, who could strike anywhere; he had Charlie Lockwood, whose submarines were sinking hundreds of thousands of tons of enemy shipping and crippling the Japanese fleet; and he had many excellent transport commanders.

In addition, he had four Marine divisions of the best amphibious troops in the world, all battle tested and of the highest morale, as well as a fifth division in the process of organization. The Japanese were on the run. Nimitz couldn't lose. He knew the Marines would win. If we didn't, he would probably be yanked out of his job and perhaps the Army would be in command. Admiral Nimitz was riding to fame on the shoulders of the Marines, so what did he have to worry about? But he did worry.

There were a number of reasons for our acquisition of the Marianas. Nimitz needed an advance naval base for the Fifth Fleet to attack and destroy Japanese sea communications and gain control of the sea in the Central Pacific. We needed air bases, from which we could isolate and neutralize enemy-held islands in the Central Carolines. And we needed bases, in official language, to "initiate very long-range air attacks on Japan." By this we meant, speaking very guardedly at the time, bases for B-29 raids. I saw my first B-29 at Hickham Field before we left Hawaii for Saipan.

These giant, long-range bombers were coming off the production line in large quantities. They were our new "secret weapon." All that we needed to use them against the enemy was airfields within their effective bombing range. The Marianas provided the answer because the nearest of the three main islands—Guam, Saipan and Tinian—was only 1,250 nautical miles from the shores of Japan.

The target date for Saipan, our first objective in the Marianas, was set for June 15. I left Pearl Harbor on Kelly Turner's command ship, the USS *Rocky Mount*, on May 29, with the major elements of the Northern group. Slower groups had sailed a few days earlier and the majority of reserve troops left two days later.

A few days before I sailed an explosion blew up one of our ships, an LST, and damaged six others, destroying a considerable amount of equipment. At first we suspected sabotage by enemy agents among Hawaii's predominantly Japanese population but investigation entirely disproved this theory. The explosion was an accident and the losses were quickly replaced.

Roy Geiger's Southern group left Guadalcanal on May 5 for Kwajalein which, with Eniwetok, was the staging base for the operation. This spreadover of dates was dictated by the magnitude of the task. FORAGER was by far the largest operation we had yet undertaken and involved great problems of troop assembly and logistics. For Saipan alone we had to transport 78,000 men and 100,000 tons of supplies from Hawaii. The Fifth Fleet, commanded by Spruance, was the largest ever assembled in the Pacific. More than 550 ships were used to transport, land, cover and support the expeditionary troops.

Equipping the expedition was a mammoth task. Supplies necessary to support the two Corps had to be transported from Pearl Harbor and from the United States. Ships had to be loaded so that equipment and supplies were available when needed for combat, and garrison equipment had to be stored meticulously so that base development could proceed once the island was captured. We had developed combat loading to an exact science since Tarawa.

Saipan was smoking when we arrived off the island at dawn on June 15. For three and a half days, Task Force 58 had subjected not only Saipan but Guam, Tinian, and two smaller islands, Rota and Pagan, to an intensive carrier and surface bombardment, followed by a specific bombardment of the landing beaches and installations on the southwest coast of Saipan. Minesweepers cleared the waters in the vicinity and the newly organized demolition teams went into action, removing beach obstacles in preparation for the landing.

By attacking the Northern Marianas we gained strategical and, to a lesser degree, tactical surprise. Even our pre-landing bombardment did not convey our real purpose to the Japanese immediately. They believed the shelling to be routine, similar to previous visitations of the Navy. According to information obtained by our G-2, the Japanese General Staff were convinced that the Palau Islands or the Philippines would be the next American objective after the Marshalls. Proceeding on this assumption, defenses in these areas were strengthened at the expense of the Marianas.

Although the Japanese had occupied Saipan for thirty years, very little in the way of fortifications had been built. When war started in the Pacific, an elaborate plan of fortifications was drawn up for Saipan but Tokyo brushed it aside in favor of other priorities. Such supplies as were shipped there were largely lost through American submarine and carrier action and when it was decided to rush through a six-month intensive program to make the island "impregnable"—the Japanese were very fond of this word—it was too late.

Captured documents showed the Japanese chief of staff on Saipan complained to Tokyo as recently as two weeks before we landed about the lack of matériel that kept his men "standing around with their arms folded." Not more than twenty-five percent of their program was completed at the time of our attack. We found coastal defense guns up to 200 mm. crated, or uncrated and not installed, and large quantities of equipment and matériel waiting to be used.

From a military point of view, the problem we faced at Saipan was different from that of any other island. It was a conquest of what is known technically as a "limited land mass," which means that we had to make an amphibious landing to secure a beachhead and then fight a land campaign of uncertain duration.

Saipan is twelve miles long and six miles wide. It is a coral island, distorted by volcanic action into a series of high ridges and deep ravines running from the 1,554-foot Mount Tapotchau in the center and levelling out into a wooded plateau at the northern end and into lowlands in the south.

What the Japanese lacked in planned fortifications they made up by cleverly exploiting the natural features of the island. At points of advantage on the central mountains and the ridges they emplaced well defiladed artillery and mortars, which bore upon the landing beaches. They resisted our advance from every cliff, cave and cranny in which they could hide with a rifle, a machine gun or, in some cases, field pieces which they dragged in and out of their caves. Obviously, what we had learned at Guadalcanal, Tarawa and the Marshalls was little use here, and no classic principles of land warfare could be applied. Saipan could only mean one thing: a savage battle of annihilation.

Our landing was the most advanced mechanical demonstration we had ever made in the Pacific. We had 800 amphibious vehicles (LVT's)—troop-carrying tractors, tanks armed with 75 mm. howitzers and 37 mm. guns, and the new LVT (4)'s, a model with a back-dropping ramp that unloaded our artillery directly ashore. We had enough of these vehicles to land 8,000 men in twenty minutes from LST's (Landing Ship, Tank), standing at the reef. In addition, we had a battalion of Army DUKW's.

Alternative landing plans had been prepared but the beaches lending themselves best to our purposes lay north and south of Charan-Kanoa, a sugar refinery village on the edge of the west coast canefields. A fleet of small gunboats, armed with 20 and 40 mm. guns, delivered close support fire on the beaches, aided by the new rocket gunboats, which shot out projectiles like whole batteries of five-inch guns fired at once.

Spearheaded by armored amphibian tractors, which gave the Japanese their first sight of these new machines, the Marines hit the beach at 0843 on June 15, the Fourth Division (Major General Harry Schmidt) on the right and the Second Division (Major General Thomas E. Watson), on the left. The first three waves in amtracks got ashore with little opposition but the following waves ran into the full force of Japanese resistance.

The Japanese held their fire until this moment and then poured a terrific volume on the reef and on the beach, inflicting heavy casualties, knocking out tractors and causing much confusion. Fire from the ridges behind the village was sustained and accurate, registering on target flags fixed on the reef. Casualties among the key personnel of some outfits were particularly high. One Second Division battalion had four commanding officers in the first few hours. In the confusion, or to avoid the concentration of fire, companies were landed on other beaches and amtracks made round trips, carrying in troops and bringing back wounded. The best we could do was to get a toehold and hang on. And this is exactly what we did, just hang on for the first critical day.

The Japanese never before had displayed the type of mobile defense they employed at Saipan. Lessons learned previously were of no value against the improvised defenses they had installed here, as I could see even from the *Rocky Mount*. Naval and air bombardment, aided by very good air reconnaissance, had knocked out most of the big coastal guns, pillboxes and permanent installations but enemy resistance was not effectively diminished.

Saipan, with its 29,662 troops, was the most heavily garrisoned island in the Marianas. We faced an unusually confident enemy, who derived considerable strength from the belief that he could hold the island against invasion and need only fight a delaying action until the Japanese Fleet came to the rescue. That we would undertake an invasion on such a scale without adequate naval forces to offset any threat by the enemy fleet did not appear to enter his mind. This was a great fallacy, but this brand of morale-building propaganda was pumped into the garrison until almost the very end. They were plagued by no doubts on this point.

We faced the heaviest and most diversified assembly of weapons and the best developed system of terrain defenses we had encountered. From the ridges behind Charan-Kanoa and from the foothills of Mount Tapotchau, fire was heavy and deadly. In addition to anti-boat guns and 75's, the Japanese had howitzers up to 150 mm. and eight-inch mortars, the most vicious piece of artillery they developed during the war. The initial mistake we made at Saipan was this: we did not soften up the enemy sufficiently before we landed.

For Saipan we could use no preliminary artillery bombardment from neighboring islands, as we had done at Kwajalein. There was no continuous naval and air preparation, a fault we remedied later at Guam and Tinian. Three and a half days of surface and air bombardment were not enough to neutralize an enemy of the strength we found on Saipan.

A more significant reason for the partially ineffective Saipan bombardment is one which I have never seen in the operation reports, and that is the fact that most of the pre-landing shelling was delivered by the new battleships and cruisers of Task Force 58, the mighty carrier task force which was always on the march in the Western Pacific.

At this point, perhaps I should explain that the technique of delivering effective naval gunfire against shore targets is not only inherently complex, but also considerably different from the normal methods used by warships in firing on other ships or against aircraft. Furthermore, the Navy gunnery officer, accustomed to "seeing" well-defined targets either by radar, or optically, is entirely at a loss to find, or to evaluate, targets which are artfully camouflaged and hidden on the land. Realizing these unavoidable handicaps, we had proposed—and Nimitz had approved—establishment of a naval gunfire shore bombardment range at Kahoolawe Island in the Hawaiian area, where every one of the older battleships and cruisers normally used for bombardment was required to undergo concentrated training at the hands of Marine Corps shore fire control experts.

Through no fault of their own, however, the Task Force 58 ships, which were almost always at sea, covering the carrier sweeps and bringing the war to Hirohito's front door, had little if any opportunity to go through our Kahoolawe workout. As a result, when confronted with the Saipan bombardment mission, they were far less experienced than the Marine-trained older ships in finding, hitting and evaluating the critical and less obvious targets.

We encountered very few Japanese on D-day. Enemy troops were well hidden and we experienced only the power of their weapons as we fought for a beachhead. We saw few Japanese bodies, because the enemy had learned to remove the dead behind his lines, thus robbing us of valuable intelligence material. However, despite the opposition and the heavy casualties to our Marine infantry, we got four battalions of artillery ashore, two 75 mm. pack howitzers and two 105 mm. howitzers, and two companies of tanks. Our artillery suffered heavily at first because we lacked observation but when it did get into action it provided powerful counter-battery fire against hidden Japanese guns.

With tanks the Japanese counterattacked from Garapan, the island capital, but their force was scattered by our naval guns. During the night of D-day, a small party counterattacked through Charan-Kanoa and reached the beach, where the two Marine divisions had not yet been able to effect a junction, but this attack also was broken up.

Japanese fire on the reef and on the beach was equally intense the next morning, in spite of the considerable naval and air support we were receiving, and we were unable to load further equipment or supplies until that afternoon, when the flow ashore became smoother. Our casualties for the first twenty-four hours on Saipan exceeded 2,500 and created a serious hospitalization problem because our hospital ships did not arrive until June 18 and the wounded had to be distributed throughout the transport fleet.

That Saipan was going to be a long job, much longer than we had anticipated, and would affect the plan for the entire Marianas operation, was apparent. Therefore, after a command conference, we decided to postpone indefinitely the invasion of Guam, which had been set for three days after D-day on Saipan, June 18, and prepare for a three week's campaign on this major Marianas island.

On D-day I put in the reserves of both Marine divisions and the next day committed elements of the Twenty-seventh

Army Division, which was afloat in reserve. After we postponed the Guam assault, I transferred the 1st Provisional Brigade to reserve afloat and the rest of the Guam expeditionary troops went back to Eniwetok.

Although the struggle ashore on Saipan was bitter and costly, I had no doubt of the outcome. My policy regarding reserves is that it always is better to get them on the beach rather than have them sitting out at sea on ships. That is why I put in all the Marine reserves as soon as possible and then ordered the Twenty-seventh ashore. The 165th Infantry first was attached to the Fourth Marine Division and when the full Army division was employed, command was handed over to Major General Ralph Smith.

Forty-eight hours had now elapsed and we were firmly dug in but not for another three days could it be said that we had "secured" our beachhead. We were under terrific pressure all the time. All Corps artillery, including our 155's, was ashore, enabling the Fourth to attack Aslito Airfield under cover of our own artillery, aided by naval and air support, and make an advance of 1,200 yards. When the line was reorganized, the airfield was placed within the zone of action of the Twenty-seventh Division, which captured it, releasing the Fourth for their push eastward across the island.

Such was the June 18 picture of the situation when I was ashore on Saipan. We held a 10,000-yard strip of beach against a weakening enemy, whose casualties must have been high since our offensive was supported by the full force of our artillery. We had all our equipment ashore and were beginning to thrust inland.

Fighting with our backs to the sea, protected by the power of the Navy, our attention had been concentrated on our yard-by-yard advance inland—once our beachhead was only a dozen yards deep at one point—when suddenly the scene of action switched to the sea.

Our submarines reported sighting a powerful Japanese task force leaving Philippine waters and heading for the Marianas. The rescue fleet which the Japanese on Saipan expected was on its way. In face of this threat Spruance, who had alerted the Fifth

Fleet to such an emergency, arrived in the transport area on his flagship, the USS *Indianapolis*, to confer with Kelly Turner on board the *Rocky Mount*.

After the conference, Spruance announced that he was leaving immediately to intercept the Japanese. Amplifying the submarine report, he said that two Japanese task forces had been sighted. A second group of enemy ships was moving northeast and the two forces were expected to rendezvous at midnight. Their total strength was four battleships, six aircraft carriers and a large number of cruisers and destroyers.

When I wished Spruance good luck on the *Rocky Mount* before his barge left for the *Indianapolis*, I asked him, "Do you think the Japs will turn tail and run?"

"No," he replied, "not now. They are out after big game. If they had wanted an easy victory, they could have disposed of the relatively small force covering MacArthur's operation at Biak (New Guinea). But the attack on the Marianas is too great a challenge for the Japanese Navy to ignore."

Ray Spruance is a highly competent but cautious sailor, with an awareness of all angles of the task before him. With typical caution, he told me it was too sanguine to hope he would destroy the enemy fleet but that he did hope to inflict sufficient damage to put it out of action for the rest of the war. If he could do this, he added, he not only would dispose of the threat to the Marianas but would facilitate subsequent operations by removing permanently the menace of the Japanese Navy, always a potential danger to the amphibious operations we were undertaking at increasing distances from our bases.

After Spruance left, Kelly Turner told me that as a precaution he was taking the entire transport fleet and its naval units out to sea. He believed it was the Japanese intention to reinforce nearby bases like Rota and Guam with planes flown off the carriers and then attack the transport fleet. Already we had had two Japanese air raids, which did little damage, but the prospect of large-scale raids was ominous. Kelly Turner said he could not afford to risk the safety of the transports while Spruance dealt with the Japanese Fleet.

With the invasion forces ashore on Saipan for only three days, this was a grave decision but I realized that it was essential and that we must hang on like good Marines until the fate of the Japanese Fleet was decided. The USS *Cambria,* flagship of Harry Hill, a few destroyers, gunboats and one or two essential transports constituted the only naval units left in support of the operation.

It must have been amazing and cheering to the Japanese to see the American fleet disappear over the horizon. One day hundreds of ships of all sizes and purposes filled miles and miles of anchorage and the next they were gone, leaving the invasion troops hanging on to a thin beach strip, unprotected from the sea. The Japanese must have heard the news of their fleet's approach by radio and rejoiced, but any chorus of *banzais* was muted by the pressure we put on them.

Admittedly, it wasn't pleasant to see our fleet leave. I had 78,000 men ashore and we were left to our own devices. Except for a few planes from the now operable Aslito Field and a few naval units, we had nothing but our own equipment and resources on the island. The departure of the fleet deprived us of supporting naval gunfire and, since Spruance had to take along his carriers, we were robbed of the powerful air support which had helped us to keep our footing.

Even more serious was the logistics problem. Only a few transports with essential supplies were left behind and when conditions grew desperate three or four other ships were detached from the fleet circling out at sea and sent back to relieve our needs. We were indeed orphans of the Japanese storm.

I had told Admiral Nimitz that Marines die for their country as willingly as the Japanese. There may be Marine annihilation, I had said to him, but there never will be a Marine defeat. My Marines will die to the last man; they never will be taken prisoners.

If that time comes, I emphasized to my divisional officers, there will be no one left alive to tell the tale. And I'll be with you. I meant those words. I had no intention of being taken prisoner and I drilled this code into the minds of my officers.

The Japanese knew, or were able to guess, how we stood. It needed no master mind to appreciate the situation on Saipan after the fleet left. The only unknown and highly significant factor was time: how long would it last? The answer to this question was Spruance's success with the Japanese fleet.

Our position ashore was not too bad. When I went ashore I had not the slightest apprehension. We had landed all our artillery and this partially compensated for the lack of naval gunfire. I had two magnificent Marine divisions, commanded by men of the highest caliber, Watson and Schmidt, and Corps artillery, Army and Marine, commanded by Brigadier General A. M. Harper, U. S. Army, whom I would have been proud to call a Marine.

The Marine has a winning philosophy. He feels that once he gets on the beach with his weapons, he can't be pushed off. And we were all too busy to worry a great deal about the departure of the fleet. We were keeping the Japanese worried. We knew the sailing of the fleet would bolster enemy morale and that the Japanese would exploit this fact, but we never gave them a chance. We never relaxed pressure on them: instead, we stepped it up. The Japanese never got a minute's peace or a yard's leeway. Given an opportunity, now they were faltering, they would try to reorganize and drive us off the island. But they never got that opportunity. We incessantly pushed them off balance.

On June 21 our fleet returned from the Battle of the Philippine Sea, in which Spruance engaged the Japanese and sank three aircraft carriers, the *Shokaku*, the *Taiho*, and the *Hitaka*, one destroyer and one fleet tanker and destroyed 403 combat aircraft. In addition, three more carriers, one battleship, three cruisers and three fleet tankers sustained varying degrees of major damage. This American naval victory definitely disposed of any possible Japanese relief of Saipan.

Tremendously reassuring to us was the sight of the hundreds of ships back at their anchorage off Saipan. In addition to the stimulating naval victory, which cheered us, the return of the fleet brought back the transports we badly needed. It also brought to our assistance the naval gunfire and the air support necessary for the second phase of the operation, which was opening now that we were ready to push beyond our beachhead in full strength.

By June 19, the Fourth Division had driven across the island to the east coast. The southern portion of Saipan, with the exception of a pocket at cavernous Nafutan Point on the southern tip, was in possession of the Twenty-seventh. The Second Division was firmly anchored south of Garapan and we planned a pivotal movement, based upon the Second Division and sweeping across the island, for the capture of Mount Tapotchau, the main Japanese line of defense. On the east, the Fourth Division was at Magicienne Bay, already driving north, and I decided to pass the Twenty-seventh Division through the left of the Fourth so that I could employ three divisions abreast against the enemy.

This phase of the attack opened on June 22. I put the Twenty-seventh in the center of the line. As a precautionary measure, I formed two temporary Marine battalions, one from Corps headquarters and the other from the shore party. At that time my headquarters in Charan-Kanoa was protected by a company of 120 men of the V Amphibious Corps Reconnaissance Company, in command of Captain James L. Jones, whose Pacific island reconnaissance exploits are unique. These troops I ordered to reconnoiter assigned battle positions in the rear because I felt that, if the Japanese counterattacked, I would have two battalions to cover any unfavorable development.

After my experience with the Twenty-seventh at Makin and Eniwetok, I was reluctant to use them again in the Marianas, but when the operation was planned they were the only troops available in Hawaii and I had to take them.

The trouble with the Twenty-seventh Division was, if I may coin a word, "militia-itis." As originally mobilized, the division had come entirely from the New York National Guard, with a good record and tradition from World War I. Much of its leadership, as was the case throughout the New York Guard, stemmed from a gentlemen's club known as the Seventh Regiment, traditionally New York's "silk stocking" outfit, and likewise a worthy unit, *per se*, with an impeccable reputation for annual balls, banquets and shipshape summer camps. Any division, however, springing from such sources and maintained intact after mobilization, contains the entangled roots of home town loyalties, ambitions and intrigues. Employer-noncommissioned officers in the Twenty-seventh were sometimes commanded, if that is the word, by employee-officers; there was sometimes a gentlemanly reluctance on the part of officers to offend Old Seventh messmates through harsh criticism or rigorous measures; in the eyes of many, especially the ambitious, there were reputations— New York reputations—to be made or broken; and behind all there was Albany, where the State Adjutant General's office allocated peacetime plums.

A machine like the National Guard is an admirable and a truly constitutional machine for peacetime training. It is in a position to capitalize on all the values of local allegiance, but after mobilization these same allegiances become barnacles on the hull. The War Department must have realized this, especially in so clear-cut a case as that of the Twenty-seventh, which had been posing "political" problems to Washington ever since mobilization. These were, if anything, intensified by the fact that some of the higher-ups in the War Department were important in the Militia. Congressman "Jim" Wadsworth, who incidentally spurred on the anti-Marine Corps faction during the merger drives of 1946 and 1947, was an influential New Yorker of much military background and firm National Guard connections.

In such an atmosphere there could have been only one square-cut solution for the War Department: to disband the division after mobilization, or at the very least, to transfer its original personnel far and wide, and replace them with anyone on earth but former members of the New York Guard. What is more, such a widespread transfer would probably have benefited the entire Army, because, man for man, the New York National Guard enjoys an excellent reputation for individual peacetime training.

That such a shakeup was never made—especially after the showings of the Twenty-seventh Division regiments at Makin and Eniwetok—reflects broadly upon the War Department, and more particularly on its senior Pacific representative, Richardson, who, had he been willing to open his eyes and swallow inter-Service stiff-neckedness, could have broken up a military combination which could do only harm to the traditions of the Army and to those of a fine state.

A lot has been written about the differences between Army and Marine methods in action. The two services use the same weapons and the same tactical manual and, therefore, I do not propose to enter into an unprofitable discussion here, but only to summarize the facts of the case concerning the Twenty-seventh Division on Saipan.

On the first day of the Tapotchau attack, the Second Division advanced 1,000 yards and the Fourth 2,000 yards. The Twenty-seventh was directed to pass through the Fourth and join a coordinated continuation of the attack on the morning of June 23. The Second and the Fourth, on the flanks, jumped off according to schedule.

The attack by the Twenty-seventh was late starting. According to reports to me, one battalion moved 50 minutes late, other elements moved even later and the 106th Infantry was unable to start forward until three hours and fifteen minutes after H-hour. I considered the two Marine divisions on the flank were jeopardized by the sagging in the center of the line and I plugged the gaps between them and the Twenty-seventh. We made little headway that day. By nightfall my map showed our lines as a deep U, with the Twenty-seventh very little ahead of its departure point and still occupying the bottom of the U, and the two Marine divisions holding the flanks.

Furthermore, the 2nd Battalion, 105th Infantry, a Twenty-seventh Division unit, assisted by tanks, had been given the mission of cleaning up Nafutan Point, a broken peninsula jutting out of the southeast corner of Saipan, which was now in our rear. In order that our attack northward could progress with safety, I wanted this cleanup done as aggressively and rapidly as possible. The area contained 500 to 600 Japanese troops, plus battlefield jetsam of civilian refugees and a good many wounded, who had holed up to die in the caves. It has since been claimed that more than 1,200 enemy troops were on Nafutan, but a captured Japanese operation order which came to our headquarters later showed that, as of June 26, there were only 500 effective, unwounded personnel, and the 1,200 count comes unsubstantiated from one who was a party in interest to the subsequent controversy over this little operation.

The battalion from the 105th Infantry (which was subsequently awarded the Army's Distinguished Unit Citation for its performance on Saipan) failed to show the aggressiveness which its mission demanded, and it even permitted, on the night of June 26, a column of some 500 well-armed and organized Japanese, the last such on the Point, to march, *in column of twos*, right through its lines with hardly a shot fired. All these Japanese had to be killed before daybreak by Marine cannoneers and riflemen from the 14th and 25th Marines. The alibi for this performance claims that the frontage assigned this battalion (some 2,000 yards, according to the contemporary periodic reports) was excessive. What is not taken into consideration, however, is that, due to the taper of Nafutan Point, a single advance of less than 200 yards on the battalion's left would have shortened the total frontage by almost a thousand yards.

As Major General George W. Griner, USA, who later came into command of the Twenty-seventh Division, officially reported to me concerning the Nafutan Point operations about this time, ". . . a faint-hearted attack was made. The means were available for complete success, had a determined attack been made." Griner, incidentally, eventually had this battalion commander relieved.

It was in this context of all-round poor performance by the Twenty-seventh that, on the afternoon of June 23, I sought the help of Major General Sanderford Jarman, who was to assume the post of Island Commander when we captured Saipan. I asked him to see Ralph Smith and appeal to him, as one Army man to another, on the grounds that the reputation of the Army was suffering through a lack of offensive spirit. Before Ralph Smith went into the line, I had impressed upon him the need for strong, offensive action on Saipan. The Japanese were on the run, I told him, and in order to lick them we had to keep them moving. As my admonition had failed, I hoped that Jarman could influence him.

Shortly afterward, Jarman returned and reported that Ralph Smith had promised to do better the next day. Jarman also reported that Ralph Smith said if he did not do better he deserved to be relieved.

In a communication to Richardson, produced at the subsequent Army investigation by the Buckner Board—named after Lieutenant General Simon Bolivar Buckner, who presided— Jarman reported that, on June 23:

> I found that General (Ralph) Smith had been up to the front lines all afternoon and was thoroughly familiar with the situation. I talked to General Smith and explained the situation as I saw it and that I felt from reports from the Corps Commander that his division was not carrying its full share. He immediately replied that such was true; that he was in no way satisfied with what his regimental commanders had done during the day and that he had been with them and had pointed out to them the situation. He further indicated to me that he was going to be present tomorrow, June 24, with this division when it made its jump-off and he would personally see to it that the division went forward. I explained my interest in the matter was that I was senior Army commander present and was anxious to see that the Army did its job as it should be done.

There was no improvement the next day. What had promised to be a swift, effective movement degenerated into a laggard action that almost came to a standstill. The two Marine flanks had to advance slowly to prevent the widening of the gaps between themselves and the Twenty-seventh in the center.

I took my map and went on board the *Rocky Mount* to discuss the situation with Kelly Turner. We both went on board the *Indianapolis* to see Spruance, who was in overall command of the operation. I told him the facts and said that the situation demanded a change in command. He asked me what should be done.

"Ralph Smith has shown that he lacks aggressive spirit," I replied, "and his division is slowing down our advance. He should be relieved." I suggested that Jarman take over the Twenty-seventh Division as a supplementary duty until another commanding officer was appointed. Turner supported me and Spruance agreed.

On June 24, the following message was despatched from Spruance as Commander, Fifth Fleet, to me as Commander, Northern Troops and Landing Force, and circulated to others concerned for information:

> You are authorized and directed to relieve Major General Ralph Smith from command of the Twenty-seventh Division, U. S. Army, and place Major General Jarman in command of this division. This action is taken in order that the offensive on Saipan may proceed in accordance with the plans and orders of the Commander, Northern Troops and Landing Force.

Accordingly, Ralph Smith was relieved and returned to Honolulu and Jarman succeeded him. Relieving Ralph Smith was one of the most disagreeable tasks I have ever been forced to perform. Personally, I always regarded Ralph Smith as a likable and professionally knowledgeable man. However, there are times in battle when the responsibility of the commander to his country and to his troops requires hard measures. Smith's division was not fighting as it should, and its failure to perform was endangering American lives. As Napoleon has said, "There are no bad regiments, only bad colonels," and the basic remedy for the defective performance of the Twenty-seventh Division was to find a leader who could make it toe the mark. Ralph Smith had been only too conscious of what was wrong, as he was the first to admit to Jarman, but he had been incapable of strong and necessary action. I realized at the time, as I in turn said to Jarman, that the relief of Smith would stir up a hornet's nest because of its inter-Service implications, and because I knew how Richardson would make capital of such a situation; but in the face of the enemy, I felt that we were all Americans, and that victory was more important than any Service's prestige.

One of Jarman's first acts was to relieve one of the Army's three regimental commanders.

Referring to this officer's conduct at Saipan, Jarman wrote to Richardson on June 30:

> Frankly, ——— appeared to be muddled. The mountainous terrain and rough going was too much for him. Based on my observation of the Twenty-seventh Division for a few days, I have noted certain things which give me some concern. They are, first, a lack of offensive spirit on the part of the troops. A battalion will run into one machine gun and be held up for several hours. When they get any kind of minor resistance they immediately open up with everything they have that can fire in the general direction from which they are being fired upon. Second, at night if a patrol comes around their bivouac area they immediately telephone in and state they are under a counterattack and want to fall back to some other position. Third, I found that troops would work all day to capture well-earned terrain and at night would fall back a distance varying from 400 to 800 yards and sometimes 1,000 yards to organize a perimeter defense.
>
> I had, in the brief time I was in command of the Twenty-seventh Division, to issue an order that ground gained would not be given up, that the perimeter of defense was to be formed on the ground captured, and troops in the rear could be brought up.

A few days later, Major General Griner, formerly in command of the Ninety-eighth Division in the Hawaiian Islands, was appointed to relieve Jarman. Griner's orders, which were signed by Lieutenant General Robert C. Richardson, Jr., commanding Army troops in the Pacific Ocean Area, did not direct him to report to the Corps Commander. In other words, Richardson completely ignored me in sending a new division commander to me.

However, Griner realized the anomaly of such a situation and reported to me officially. I gave him a full account of the action of the Twenty-seventh and expressed the hope that he would reorganize the division and develop among the men a better fighting spirit.

Continuous pressure exerted by the Second Division on the left and the Fourth Division on the right enabled the Twenty-seventh to clean up their sector. Finally, the line was straightened out until the Second was pinched out at Garapan and the line across Saipan was held by the Twenty-seventh on the left and the Fourth on the right.

Army protagonists, swayed by a mistaken sense of loyalty to their own branch of the Service, have magnified this incident into an importance out of all proportion to its proper place in the history of the war. Other Army generals were relieved in the South Pacific, France and Germany, with nothing like the acrimonious reactions which marked the relief of Major General Ralph Smith. Perhaps the fact that I was a Marine General offended their sensibilities.

My attitude was that I was responsible for the capture of Saipan and that it was my duty to see that every officer and every man fought to the best of his ability. In my judgment, the conduct of the Twenty-seventh Division under Ralph Smith's command was unsatisfactory and I acted accordingly. Admiral Spruance, as Commander, Fifth Fleet, fully approved, although his official Saipan report, regarding the unsatisfactory work of the Twenty-seventh, was actually censored, at Nimitz's recommendation. There was no question of animus against an Army General. I would have relieved a Marine General under the same circumstances, only sooner.

The Twenty-seventh could have no quarrel with the Marines. On June 19, a few days before my best judgment compelled me to relieve him, Ralph Smith, in a disc made for radio transmission, now on file in the Library of Congress, stated:

It irritates me a little to read these stories back home—because a soldier and a Marine get in a fight in a saloon the relations be-

175

tween the services are at cross-purposes. Nothing could be further from the truth out here in the field. In this landing we came in behind the Marines. Because of the conditions under which we are landing . . . we've been using largely water, rations and ammunition that the Marines have helped us get ashore and furnished to us. Some of our casualties have been evacuated to Marine hospital ships . . . For the first part of the operation we were entirely dependent upon the Marines and I want to take this opportunity to stress the very cordial feeling that exists between the outfits. One of the 165th's officers remarked to me this morning that Saipan has sealed the "blood brotherhood" between the services.

The whole incident might well have ended there but for the uninvited visit by Richardson to Saipan after the island had been declared secure, but while we were still mopping up. He arrived on July 12 and hardly had he set foot ashore, where I was in command, than he began making trouble. In flagrant violation of the oldest service customs, he began taking testimony for the Buckner Board, which he had convened at his headquarters on Oahu, known throughout the Pacific as the "Pineapple Pentagon." His purpose was to pass on my actions in relieving Ralph Smith.

Not content with this, he began issuing orders to the Twenty-seventh Division and he paused to issue some decorations, although the division was still serving under me. Finally, he had the effrontery to berate the entire Marine Corps, and me in particular, in the most amazing conversation that I have ever had with a United States general officer. Fortunately, Major General Harry Schmidt, commanding the Fourth Marine Division, was with me at the time and was able to confirm the truth of Richardson's unbelievable behavior.

Richardson called upon me while I was entertaining Admiral Spruance, who was making a trip ashore. Therefore he paid his official call upon both of us. I returned his call and took Harry Schmidt with me. En route to his headquarters, I was surprised to find Richardson holding a parade of Army troops under my command and presenting decorations. This ceremony, without my knowledge or consent, held within a hundred yards of my command post, was contrary to all principles of command relationships.

I waited until the ceremony had concluded and then went to Richardson's quarters with him. Harry Schmidt and I had barely seated ourselves when Richardson opened up with some sharp remarks on the conduct of the Saipan operation.

"You had no right to relieve Ralph Smith," he told me. "The Twenty-seventh is one of the best trained divisions in the Pacific. I trained it myself. You discriminated against the Army in favor of the Marines. I want you to know that you can't push the Army around the way you've been doing."

It was as much as I could do to contain myself as he continued with the old, familiar line.

"You and your Corps commanders aren't as well qualified to lead large bodies of troops as general officers in the Army," he continued. "We've had more experience in handling troops than you've had and yet you dare," he almost screamed, "remove one of my Generals."

He next accused me of faulty technical decisions and indiscriminate sacrifice of lives. Apart from the fact that he was wrong, I was astounded by his impropriety in making such statements. A military command in battle carries with it the authority to conduct tactical operations according to the judgment of the commander. Results are the touchstone and success bears an automatic seal of approval. As long as you keep on fighting and winning, no one, not even a superior in the chain of command, is authorized to interfere. An officer outside the chain of command, such as Richardson, never possesses the right to meddle.

For a man with my explosive reputation, I must confess that I conducted myself with admirable restraint under this barrage when he said, "You Marines are nothing but a bunch of beach runners, anyway. What do you know about land warfare?"

As events turned out, it was probably just as well I held my tongue because Spruance, prior to Richardson's arrival, had extracted a promise from me to suffer in silence while Richardson was on the island. I gave this promise because Spruance made it a personal request.

Spruance had not, however, reckoned with Kelly Turner. When Richardson presented himself aboard Turner's flagship, the latter gave him the rough side of a very rough tongue after Richardson had declined to admit himself in any way accountable, while in the Marianas, even to Turner, Commander of the Joint Expeditionary Force then engaged in conquering those islands. Thus, to my official report of this entire episode, which was certified to in writing by Harry Schmidt, Kelly Turner added a scorcher of his own in which he reported Richardson for "unwarranted assumption of command authority" and "irregular interference" with me in the performance of my duties. After Turner had reminded Richardson of a few things I was too speechless to say, Spruance also had a word with Richardson and referred the entire business to Nimitz, with the remark that Richardson had no authority to exercise command functions in the Saipan area without specific permission therefor from the high command.

Nimitz, who had verbally approved Richardson's visit, simply passed all the correspondence to the latter with a polite invitation for his comments; but if anything ever happened to Richardson as a result, it was certainly not apparent.

Nimitz knew very well that Spruance had authorized and directed Ralph Smith's relief, with Turner emphatically concurring, but this was one occasion on which the Navy was more than glad to yield all command responsibility to the Marine; and I was left alone to face the torrent of Army censure and National Guard umbrage which followed as soon as an Army representative could "leak" their version of the story to the San Francisco press.

Repercussions followed close on Richardson's heels. Prior to departing from Saipan, he had convened his Buckner Board and when he returned to Oahu, he had with him a wad of carefully culled certificates and affidavits to present to his *ex parte* board. Of course, since the board had Army jurisdiction only, it possessed neither authority nor inclination to hear what Turner, Spruance or I might have to say, nor to include in its proceedings any Navy or Marine documents except for a few odds and ends. The witnesses were such as could be scraped up in the Army casual camps, rest homes and hospitals of the Hawaiian Islands, and these presented what "evidence" seemed needed. To do Ralph Smith credit, I must say that his testimony was the most fair-minded of the lot. He repeatedly warned his inquisitors that he had few if any records and was forced to rely on memory, and, despite repeated openings offered him in Richardson's Star Chamber, he never once launched into a diatribe or a sob story. Adversity, I think, became him well.

The findings could be foreseen without any crystal ball. Buckner and his learned colleagues concluded that although I had possessed all the authority necessary to relieve Ralph Smith, my action in doing so had been unwarranted by the "facts" of the situation. Furthermore, despite their precept's limitation of the inquiry to the relief of Smith, they took it upon themselves to consider the whole conduct of the Saipan battle, including events as late as July 8, and to place on record a harangue against me by Major General Griner while still under my command.

For the time being, this concluded the controversy with Nimitz asking me to comment on the board's findings, which I did as ordered. Before autumn, however, an Army representative had touched off a full-dress public discussion and many guesswork versions of the Saipan affair. Two months after the battle, Bob Sherrod, of *Time* Magazine, who had probably made more assault landings in the early waves than most Marine officers, ventured to write an accurate report of what had happened and you would have thought the skies were falling. The truth hurt, so Richardson immediately demanded the revocation of Sherrod's press credentials and Nimitz, always inclined to compromise, passed the Richardson buck along, although he was fully aware of this correspondent's integrity.

This brought the entire matter officially to Washington for decision on the Sherrod case, and it was there that Admiral

King had the last word. Richardson, stated King to General Marshall, had deliberately launched into inter-Service matters of high command outside his proper bailiwick, and had indulged in intemperate personal attacks on my character and professional standing. This action, done wilfully and knowingly, had brought real harm to Service relationships, the wartime COMINCH concluded. Marshall never attempted to refute this; Sherrod's credentials were not revoked; and there the matter was destined to rest until it was reopened in 1947 by a select group of former Twenty-seventh personnel close to the War Department.

I have always deplored this incident as far too typical of the amount of top echelon time and effort expended in the Pacific on matters not pertaining to the winning of the war. Inter-Service disputes, given unmerited prominence, can grow into the greatest enemy of victory when they take priority over all other interests in the minds of Generals and Admirals. Equally deplorable is the effect upon the men who carry into peacetime the animosity thus engendered in wartime.

CHAPTER IX

~~~~~~

I HAVE always considered Saipan the decisive battle of the Pacific offensive. Creasy, establishing the criterion for his *Battles,* defined decisive as an event which varied the world drama in all its subsequent scenes. Saipan was decisive because it varied the Pacific drama in all its subsequent scenes.

Iwo Jima and Okinawa were costlier battles and carried us closer to Japan, but their capture was made possible only by our earlier success at Saipan, which breached Japan's inner defense line, destroyed the main bastions and opened the way to the home islands.

Complemented by the capture of Guam and Tinian, before finality sealed the victory in the Marianas, Saipan was the death of Japan's hope of resisting our advance. The defense of Saipan reached classic heights of fanaticism, with the sacrifice of the island's commanding general and almost the entire garrison.

Equally severe as the blow to military prestige was the psychological tremor that caused a cabinet shake-up in Tokyo and forced the government's unprecedented admission to the Japanese people that the Americans were perilously close to their homeland. We acquired advance naval and air bases which decreased our dependence on Pearl Harbor and enabled us to isolate Japan from the sea. The grand climax came later, when fleets of B-29's started bombing Tokyo and every important Japanese city came within destructive range of the bases we had captured in the Marianas.

The importance of Saipan lay in its relation to the entire scheme of Japanese defense in the Central Pacific. Saipan was Japan's administrative Pearl Harbor, without Pearl Harbor's massive permanent naval and military installations. It was the naval and military heart and brain of Japanese defense strategy. In itself it was a fortified island of considerable strength.

Japan's Central Pacific Fleet Headquarters, under Vice Admiral Chuichi Nagumo, was located here. Nagumo was the man who led the Japanese attack on Pearl Harbor, as well as the Japanese striking force in the Battle of Midway. The 31st Army Headquarters, comprising all Central Pacific army troops, under Lieutenant General Hideyoshi Obata, was there. Saipan also was headquarters of the Northern Marianas Defense Force, under Lieutenant General Yoshijo Saito. This command included his Forty-third Infantry Division and all Army troops from Tokyo Bay to Aguijan Island in the Northern Marianas. Saipan was headquarters of the 5th Naval Base Force, under Rear Admiral Tsujimura.

Obata was absent, probably on an inspection tour, when we attacked and the defense of Saipan fell upon the aging shoulders of Saito. None of these high echelon officers, with the exception of Obata, escaped the holocaust that followed our final drive to the northernmost tip of the island. If the Japanese, after sinking our fleet at Pearl Harbor, had landed and taken Oahu, destroying the garrison and causing the death of Admiral Nimitz and top Army and Marine commanders, the loss would have been somewhat parallel.

I went ashore at Charan-Kanoa on the afternoon of June 17, after Kelly Turner had announced that he was taking the transport fleet to sea.

Charan-Kanoa had been badly damaged by our shelling and bombing. The sugar mill was in ruins and the yards of the narrow-gauge railway, which ran along the west coast of Saipan, were wrecked. Houses in the village, formerly tenanted by Japanese employees of the sugar mill, were in good shape. For some unknown reason, they had escaped the full effect of our attack.

Normally, Saipan is a pleasant island, with calming patches of bright green vegetation and brilliant flame trees, but under the milling of thousands of feet and hundreds of heavy-tracked vehicles, the dirt roads had disintegrated into fine, penetrating dust. A passing jeep could put up a smoke screen more effective than our chemical services could produce and blot out the sun like a Biblical plague. When it rained, jeeps became amphibians caught in quagmires that had been roads a few hours before.

Harry Schmidt's Command Post was near the beach, south of the mill. Headquarters troops were building him a sand-bagged shelter when I arrived to confer with him. Schmidt told me that the Fourth had suffered heavy casualties from artillery and mortar fire but that the line was moving slowly ahead.

The first night we occupied whatever quarters we could find and later retired to foxholes. One of my aides, digging in for shelter, uncovered a complete human skeleton and we discovered that the Command Post was actually an old cemetery that had been churned up by shells. The Japanese made the first of their many nightly nuisance raids that night, flying planes from Guam or Rota, but did little damage. The last tracers from our anti-aircraft batteries streaking across the sky at the disappearing planes were the signal for a heavy downpour, which flooded our foxholes and made life miserable for everyone.

At daybreak we moved off to V Corps Headquarters, which had been established at Charan-Kanoa. This village was laid out in rectangular blocks with small, bungalow-type houses built of plaster, wooden slats and concrete, with roofs of corrugated iron. Except for broken windows, some of these houses were habitable. In backyard quadrangles stood large concrete cisterns for catching rainwater, fed by pipes from the roofs. Each house had its air raid shelter.

The one selected for me had a well in the backyard and also, most unfortunately, the carcase of a carabao, lying near a shell crater. The first thing Asbill and Sergeant Bradley had to do on Saipan was to bury that loathesome animal, which must have weighed a ton. They told me that the interment of a body that size and odor was no easy task with an ordinary shovel. They had need for a bulldozer. After the two of them had cleaned up, they went foraging and came back with furniture and a cot with springs, which was indeed a luxury after a non-resilient foxhole.

My quarters were next to the combined office and quarters of my Chief of Staff, Brigadier General Graves B. Erskine, located at the other side of the house we shared. All I had to do to keep in touch with the situation was to walk the few steps to his office or call to him through the thin wooden partition.

Erskine was the neck of the funnel of information. He was continually in personal or telephonic contact with the General Staff and the Special Staff sections and members of his staff kept him informed of the progress of the battle, phase by phase. His office buzzed with activity and his only regret was that he could not get away more frequently to visit the front. For nearly two weeks, his personal knowledge of Saipan was limited to the area immediately adjacent to our quarters. Duty tied him to his desk.

In Erskine's desire to see for himself what was happening, there was no ego. A brilliant staff officer, he knew from long experience that frequently the only way to obtain information in battle is to go and see for yourself. He drilled this fact into his staff. If an officer complained of lack of information from subordinate units, he knew the first question Erskine would ask would be, "Have you been there to find out for yourself?" If the staff officer was unable to give an affirmative answer, it was hard going because Bobby Erskine could indulge in biting comment.

Equally competent officers on my Northern Landing Force (Saipan-Tinian) staff formed a great Headquarters group. My G-1 (Administration) was Lieutenant Colonel Albert F. Metz and my G-3 (Operations Officer) was Colonel Robert E. Hogaboom, who helped me train Army troops for the Aleutians campaign.

An answer to the criticism that I discriminated against the Army was the fact that, in addition to having an Army officer, Brigadier General Harper, commanding the XXIV Corps Artillery, as my artillery officer, I had numerous excellent Army officers on my staff.

My G-2 (Intelligence Officer) was Lieutenant Colonel Thomas R. Yancy, AUS, of the Army's General Staff Corps, who had been with me since the early days of the Amphibious Corps, Pacific, in San Diego. Running the G-4 Section was Lieutenant Colonel Joseph Anderson, a West Pointer, who did a Herculean job maintaining a steady flow of supplies and equipment. Colonel A. V. Wilson, Corps Engineer, also was an Army officer.

Two or three times daily, staff conferences were held. We discussed every phase of the situation—casualties, enemy strength, enemy weapons, our lines and dispositions, our supply problems. Special staff officers filled in the picture with additional details. Questions by the staff were encouraged. Erskine summed up the situation at the end of the session. These conferences were excellent examples of inter-staff cooperation.

With such staff support and loyalty it would have been possible for me to sit back and take things easy. I was 62 when we attacked Saipan, and many times during that month I felt like a tired old man under the strain of directing a campaign which required so much nervous and physical energy.

I was determined to take Saipan and take it quickly. Upon the outcome of this operation rested the first proof of the ability of the Marine Corps to do a big job well. The problems confronting us were never out of my mind and when the pressure was on, when the issue at stake was critical, all my weariness vanished. I never felt better in my life than when I faced this challenge.

After the relief of Ralph Smith from the Twenty-seventh Division, the assault on the Mount Tapotchau line commenced. Dealing with the diverse elements of my command was no easy matter, but I claim I dealt with them all fairly.

Here I think I will turn over the record to Asbill, my aide. He says of me:

His methods of controlling the divisions were skillfully varied to suit the personalities and situations involved. He used threats, exhortations, sound advice, sympathy: he cursed, demanded, cajoled, urged and praised. Invariably, his method was the right one.

When the Fourth Division executed its pivotal movement and

began its rapid march to the north, he frequently called Harry Schmidt on the phone to encourage him and to let him know that the performance of his troops was appreciated. From General Smith's end the conversation would run something like this: "Hello, son, where are your front lines? Wait a minute now. Let me check my map. Are you all the way up there? Boy, you'd better slow 'em down or you won't be able to find your men. I think we'll take that '4' off your Division patch and put on a race horse instead. Well, how about the left flank? Do you have enough troops to fill up the gap? If you don't, I'll give you a battalion. You're doing a fine job, son. Keep it up. I'll be up there pretty soon to see you."

A conversation of quite a different tone occurred when the 2nd Battalion, 105th Infantry, which was directly under Corps control, was being held up, day after day, at the neck of Nafutan Point, on the far side of Aslito Airfield. Staff observers had returned with the information that, though the terrain was rugged, practically no Japanese had been encountered.

General Smith called the battalion commander, "Colonel, this is General Smith. What's holding you up down there? Sure, the ground's rough but it's rough all over this island. That's no excuse. How many Japs are in front of you?

"Well, if there aren't any Japs, how the hell could you be held up?" Then the conversation changed to a monologue, "Now listen, Colonel. I want you to push ahead with your battalion and clean up that damned place. If you don't, the Japs will break through and be all over the airfield. Now move out and take it. Do you understand?"

Shortly afterward, the Japanese on Nafutan Point did break through, exactly as the General had warned. A party of 500, who had been hiding in caves, broke through the 105th Infantry, attacked Aslito Airfield, where they damaged a number of planes, and nearly reached Hill 500, some 3,000 yards north of the field, before they were cleaned up by the 14th and the 25th Marines after the artillerymen had taken a heavy toll.

The Japanese break-through at Nafutan Point, referred to in the previous chapter, posed a peculiar psychological problem, which was to develop throughout the campaign. It was here that the Japanese pledged as a slogan and a password, "Seven Lives To Repay Our Country." This phrase, meaning that each Japanese was to kill seven Americans before he died, was in the battalion order issued before they emerged from their caves and marched to the airfield. It became a rallying cry, forlorn but sustained, for the whole campaign, but we saw to it that this ambition was not fulfilled at Nafutan Point or anywhere else on Saipan. The 14th and 25th Marines took care of Nafutan. Elsewhere my Marines were equally alert to enemy attack.

For once the Japanese had more tanks than we had estimated but their sardine-can variety proved no match for our guns or our bazookas, which ripped them apart as though they were the clockwork toys from Japan that used to flood the stores before the war.

Naval gunfire scattered the first tank attack from Garapan down the coast soon after our landing, but early on the morning of June 17 the enemy counterattacked in strength from the vicinity of Lake Susupe, in reality nothing but a marsh behind Charan-Kanoa. There was a spectacular bravado about this attack. A Japanese officer, standing in the turret of the lead vehicle, waved his sword in the manner of a cavalryman charging, while a bugler sounded the call.

The attack was met by staunch Marines of the Second Division, who achieved our first major tank victory in the Central Pacific war by destroying 31 enemy machines. The Second used half-tracks (semi-tractor and truck), 75-mm. guns, infantry anti-tank weapons, and bazookas. One of our half-tracks got in the middle of the attacking force and destroyed four enemy tanks singlehanded while bazookas and artillery fire tore the others to pieces. The Japanese tanks were so flimsy that a number were put out by hand grenades fixed in their tracks as the vehicles passed over the foxholes of individual Marines.

This victory was an achievement in coral island warfare but as we advanced northward up the island to seize the Tapotchau line we ran into several more tank attacks. The day before the 8th Marines, Second Division, captured the mountain, we destroyed 30 more tanks in three different attacks on various parts of the line.

When we captured Tapotchau, the tactical position on the island changed radically. Mount Tapotchau, the highest point of the range, is approached by a slope on the west side, up which wound a pilgrims' path to a little shrine, and falls away down a steep precipice to the east. The surrounding terrain is a series of steep cliffs and deep ravines, pitted with caves from which the Japanese fought our advance. The mountain provided them with excellent observation facilities, which were denied to us on the lower ground. While they held Tapotchau, they looked down the muzzles of their guns at us; when we took it, we looked down the muzzles of ours at them.

The capture of Tapotchau was a magnificent piece of work by the Second Marines. The Sixth Marines prepared the way by capturing Tipo Pale, the commanding hill, and the Eighth Marines fought their way up the slopes of the mountain to the summit after heavy mortar and artillery preparation.

Strangely enough, the Japanese on the summit showed little resistance, considering this was the key to the island, and we were able to establish observation posts on top almost immediately, adding to the effectiveness of our artillery, which played a large part in supporting our advance.

The pressure we kept on the Japanese was telling fearfully. To maintain this pressure, we followed a policy of by-passing strong points of resistance, leaving them to be mopped up by reserve troops, so that we could press the attack and prevent the enemy from using the terrain to our disadvantage. Kept on the move and deprived of their armor, the defending forces fell apart.

Although they resisted from caves and hideouts in the ridges, and tried to harass us at night from by-passed pockets, we dug them out and smoked them out in hand-to-hand combat. With flame throwers and hand grenades, the Marines ferreted the Japanese out of their holes and killed them. Patrols covered the terrain yard by yard, combing thick vegetation and rocky fastnesses for snipers. It was war such as nobody had fought before: a subterranean campaign in which men climbed, crawled, clubbed, shot, burned and bayonetted each other to death.

Bayonet fighting sounds out of place on a coral island but the Marines at times used bayonets at Saipan. This little-used weapon is part of the hand-to-hand combat training which makes the Marine such a superb in-fighter in such an emergency. Bayonet training was emphasized and advocated in the Corps by the late Colonel Anthony Drexel Biddle, USMCR, when I was Quartermaster at Philadelphia.

Biddle convinced the Marines that they could meet the enemy and kill him with the bayonet. He had studied bayonet fighting in England, France and Switzerland, and wrote a pamphlet on the subject, "Do or Die," which he distributed to the troops at his own expense. He thought this type of training would be useful in the future, when the Marines met the Japanese.

"How do you get a bayonet out of a Jap, once you've got it in?" I asked Tony one day.

"Shoot it out," he told me. And that's what the Marines did at Saipan and Guadalcanal on the rare occasions that they used bayonets.

Tapotchau had fascinated me ever since I first set eyes on the mountain which rose above the smoke of our D-day bombardment. Immediately after we captured it, the pilgrim's path was widened for jeep traffic and I rode up Tapotchau several times.

Looking down on the island from the former vantage point of the Japanese, it was easy to see why enemy fire had been so accurate. From the summit of this 1,554-foot mountain, the observer had a Pisgah-sight of Saipan. Practically the entire island stretched visibly before him, like a huge aerial photograph. With the aid of a map and a powerful Japanese telescope we found there, I could study the progress of the battle in detail, with the 72 square miles of terrain reduced to the proportions of a football field.

I ordered Major Generals Schmidt and Griner to go to the top of Tapotchau. My reason was two-fold. I wanted the Generals to have the opportunity of watching their own troops in action and of observing the rear areas held by the enemy. I also wanted to impress upon the two officers the accomplishment of the Second Marine Division in capturing the mountain. In comparison with Tapotchau, the terrain that was proving so difficult for the Twenty-seventh was as smooth as a table top.

One of my trips up Tapotchau was nearly my last. I was there with Major General Tommy Watson of the Second Division when the Japanese, noting unusual activity, which usually accompanied brass hats in the front lines, began to drop mortar shells around us with disconcerting accuracy. One shell fell 20 feet from my jeep, and Watson and I dived into the nearest foxhole until the firing stopped. When it ceased we were able to get down the mountain in comparative safety.

Preoccupied as we were with the battle for Saipan, we still had to face the other phase of Operation FORAGER, namely, the capture of Guam and Tinian. The latter island, three miles south of Saipan, had been subjected to considerable neutralizing fire, not only from the Navy but also from our own artillery. Driving northwards up Saipan, we had been annoyed by fire from Tinian, to our rear. Our 155 mm. batteries had to handle the double job of shooting across Tinian Strait at enemy guns on that island and of supporting our advance on Saipan. Naval and air units took over the bulk of the Tinian task, after the fleet returned from sea, but our excellent Army and Marine artillery kept up its systematic job of pounding Tinian while still engaged in its primary role of supporting us on Saipan.

On June 28, Task Force 58 commenced the first of a series of strikes on Guam and on the nearby island of Rota, in order to neutralize enemy airfields before the intensive bombardment would prepare for our assault on Guam three weeks later. On June 29, Rear Admiral "Close-in" Conolly and Major General Roy Geiger, commanding the Southern Attack Force and the Southern Landing Force, respectively, arrived with their staffs at Saipan to confer with Spruance, Turner and myself. Later, Major General A. D. Bruce, AUS, commanding the Seventy-seventh Infantry Division, flew out from Pearl Harbor to Saipan.

The purpose of the conference was to re-draft the plan for Guam so that it would encompass the battle experience we had gained on Saipan. A number of alterations had to be made in the light of tactical experience and the latest intelligence. We all felt there was room for improvement in our approach to the Guam problem, especially in respect to intensive and more sustained preparation of the objective before we landed. Task Force 58 started the process three weeks ahead of time, as a result of my suggestion that three days at Saipan had not been sufficient.

Roy Geiger toured Saipan, and under my guidance he studied terrain features and enemy tactics, so that the lessons of Saipan could be applied to Guam. With Geiger was Brigadier General P. A. del Valle, a Marine artillery veteran from Guadalcanal, who commanded the III Amphibious Corps Artillery. Our employment of artillery on Saipan was one of the major factors in our success; never before in the Pacific had Marines gone into action with so much armament, ranging from 75's to 155's. In addition, we had new rocket-launching trucks that thickened bombardment like a Pacific typhoon. The three of us saw as much of the island as possible, visiting division areas and conferring with unit commanders. When Geiger and del Valle left, I was certain that the study they made at Saipan would have a profound influence on the course of the Guam campaign, which it did, with a consequent saving of both effort and lives.

Another visitor to my Saipan headquarters was Spruance, who was always eager to learn first-hand what was happening. The Admiral caused me many anxious moments. He refused to wear a steel helmet or green dungarees. Instead, he came ashore in a conspicuous khaki uniform which made him a first-class target for a Japanese sniper. He coolly disregarded measures for his safety by exposing himself in the forward areas, which he generally visited unarmed, accompanied only by an aide.

I finally had to call him down for his recklessness. "Admiral," I said, "you are in command of this entire operation, but I am in command ashore. I cannot let you come onto the beach unless you follow the routes I prescribe and let me send an armed escort with you." Being above all a reasonable man, Spruance agreed, and his keen interest in the landing forces and his inspection trips provided him with a much more accurate and comprehensive picture of the battle than he would have had otherwise.

Spruance repaid his visits ashore by a princely largesse of ice cream, which was a cause for celebration at Corps Headquarters. The Admiral would send a Filipino mess steward ashore with a five-gallon drum of ice cream as a present for me. Naturally I gave it to the enlisted men. A General should eat like his men, and I always ate as my men ate. When we had "K" rations ashore, I had "K" rations. When we had "C" rations, I had "C" rations. When supplies improved to "Ten-in-One" and "B" rations, I had the same and ate captured Japanese rations if they were needed as a supplement.

When ice cream arrived, I took station at the front window of my well-perforated house in Charan-Kanoa, with the Filipino steward and the five-gallon drum, and would sing out to a passing Marine, "Hey, boy, come over here." He came at the double, thinking that I had important business or important trouble for him. When he reached my window, I would tell him to get out his canteen cup and have some ice cream.

In the sticky heat of Saipan, ice cream was something men dreamed about, and within a few minutes the word got around about the treat down at the Commanding General's house. Soon there was a line of Marines two blocks long, holding canteen cups, Japanese rice bowls, cracked teacups, anything they could pick up quickly. I managed to stretch out the ice cream to an amazing length by doling it out carefully, advised by the smiling little Filipino.

Admiral King and Admiral Nimitz also paid me a visit at Saipan, in great secrecy, but with plenty of censored publicity and excitement. They flew into Aslito Airfield—renamed Isely Field, after the naval airman killed during preliminary strikes on the island—and I took them on a jeep tour of the entire perimeter while fighting was still in progress. Our cavalcade came dangerously near sniper haunts several times, but the two visitors were too absorbed in the general picture of the battle to worry about the personal equation and nobody has ever accused Ernie King or Chester Nimitz of lack of guts or equilibrium.

I was so impressed by the combat ability of my Marines on

Saipin that I said to King, "Give me three Marine divisions, and I'll take Luzon."

The Admiral looked down his nose at me and growled, "What kind of meat have you been eating?"

"The same kind you've been eating for the last forty years," I replied.

King told Vandegrift later, "The trouble with Holland Smith is that he's like Stilwell in China. All he wants to do is fight."

The battle of Saipan had not long to run. Contained in the northern end of the island, the remnants of the Japanese garrison were trapped. Abandoned by and cut off from Tokyo, they fell back to a narrow strip of territory, fighting savagely in their disorderly retreat.

All signs pointed to an early end of the battle. From their desperate plight emerged the same psychological reaction we had observed after the breakthrough at Nafutan Point, where the rallying cry had been, "Seven Lives To Repay Our Country." It was clear, from my observations at Attu and from my study of the Saipan situation, that the garrison was building up for the final act, a wild *banzai* attack in which every man would seek destruction.

We had noted this feeling of abandonment among the prisoners. On other islands, following the code of no surrender, very few prisoners fell into our hands. Through July 27 on Saipan, we took 1,734 Japanese prisoners, including 17 officers. Among these were many wounded. We were transferring 50 of the most serious cases—blind, legless, broken-backed—to Honolulu, because of the shortage of hospital personnel in the forward area. A Japanese warrant medical officer asked me why we were sending these enemy wounded to the United States to become a charge on the American Government. They were useless, he said bluntly.

I asked him what the Japanese would do in this case. "Very easy in the Japanese Army," he said. "We would leave them a hand grenade apiece, and if they didn't use the grenades, it would be a simple matter to slit their jugular veins."

I had more than a hunch that the *banzai* attack was imminent. There also was an inkling of such an event in some of our prisoner intelligence, and air reconnaissance showed that the Japanese were concentrating north of Tanapag, in front of the sector held by the Twenty-seventh. The terrain in that part of the island lent itself to such action despite the fact that our air and naval gunfire were pounding these assembled reserves on Tanapag Plain.

My conclusion was that the charge would come down the coastal road, paralleling the narrow-guage railway on the west coast. In fact, before we left Pearl Harbor I had put my finger on this corridor for a *banzai* attack on Saipan if the Japanese decided upon one. With this thought hard in my mind I had issued a special Corps order on July 2, warning all units to take special precautions against nocturnal mass attacks and to button up their lines each night by physical contact.

Moreover, on the afternoon of July 6, accompanied by Major General Watson and Asbill, I visited the Twenty-seventh's Command Post and warned Griner, now in command of the Army Division, that a *banzai* attack probably would come down Tanapag Plain late that night or early the next morning. I cautioned him to make sure that his battalions were physically tied in. The line had been established well before sunset that evening by the 1st, 2nd and 3rd Battalions of the 105th Infantry, the 2nd Battalion holding the left flank running down to the sea.

I told Griner that my study of the terrain indicated that, if the attack came, it would be in his zone. As a matter of fact, when Watson was advancing up the west coast with the Second Division, I also cautioned him to keep his left strong, because I was sure that was where an attack would come. Griner assured me that his battalions were buttoned up and that his division was prepared for just such a Japanese move.

I left the Command Post satisfied that I had done all that was possible for a general to do. In rear of the Twenty-seventh was the 3rd Battalion, 10th Marines (Artillery), moved up into good position areas for supporting the advance of the Fourth Division on the higher ground.

It was apparent that the Twenty-seventh had profited little by the change in command. In addition to my warning, Colonel Yancey, of the Army, my Corps G-2, had cautioned all divisions that a prisoner had reported his unit alerted for an all-out attack that night, and that any man alive by the next afternoon must commit *hara-kiri*. An hour later the Army division informed Yancey, very skeptically, that the prisoner's story was considered "tricky" and further interrogation was necessary.

At dawn our line across Saipan was practically continuous, except, we learned later, for a 300-yard gap between the 1st and 3rd Battalions of the 106th Infantry. To make matters worse, this gap was not even covered by coordinated or planned fire, as is normal practice in even the most elementary offensive situation, let alone one as sensitive as this was. Shortly before 0500 the Japanese attacked down the coastal railroad, just as I had anticipated. It was a *banzai* attack insofar as the enemy was determined to fight to the end, but it was not composed of a disorderly foray of crazed men, although it was a motley force and included wounded and crippled, together with some well-armed troops and others carrying knives bound to poles. The attack had a semblance of organization; it was led by officers, and our troops experienced enemy machine gun, mortar and tank fire.

Thus between 1,500 and 3,000 Japanese took part, and the fanatical charge cut through our lines. Courageous machine gunners of the 105th Infantry, paying the price of faulty dispositions the night before, fired until enemy dead piled high in front of their weapons and blocked their field of fire, but the Japanese came on, charging over their own dead. The machine gunners fought until their ammunition was exhausted and their bodies mingled with the Japanese.

The gap between the battalions widened under the mad enemy rush, and the 1st and 2nd Battalions became disorganized, lacking ammunition to continue fighting. Some groups were cut off and isolated and others were driven to the beach. Four hundred and six American bodies were picked up in the general area after the counterattack. The 3rd Battalion also received glancing attack but repelled the enemy. While the other two bat-talions were being laced to pieces, the 3rd hardly moved beyond its pre-attack position to render any assistance. This failure later cost this battalion participation in the Army Distinguished Unit Citation awarded in 1948 by the War Department to the balance of the 105th Infantry.

Once through the gap, the momentum of the attack carried the Japanese through the two forward batteries of the 3rd Bat-talion, 10th Marines, a thousand yards behind the front. These artillerymen neverthelesss resolutely helped to check the in-vaders. Cutting their fuses to four-tenths of a second, which meant practically a muzzle-burst, Battery H., 10th Marines, fired point blank into the advancing mob until all their ammuni-tion was expended. But the surviving Japanese surged on and overran the batteries. The artillerymen removed the firing locks of their guns to make them inoperable, picked up their rifles and turned infantrymen, sustaining 136 casualties in the process. Thus they helped to stem the desperate enemy tide, falling back themselves until the Twenty-seventh Division's reserve regiment (the 106th Infantry) began to come up.

Four hours after they attacked, the Japanese momentum was spent, but in the general confusion it took us many hours to straighten out the picture. After learning the seriousness of the breakthrough, Griner had ordered the division reserve—the 1st and 2nd Battalions, 106th Infantry, together with all avail-able tanks—to counterattack. By mid-afternoon they succeeded, side by side with men of the 10th Marines, in recapturing the two battery positions overrun by the Japanese, and a solid line was established from the beach to the left of the Fourth Marine Division, just short of the area where remnants of the 105th Regiment were beleaguered.

Here again, however, even while isolated comrades were being slowly butchered, the 106th Infantry failed to press the attack. Only 300 yards short of scenes which have been com-pared by witnesses to those of Custer's stand, the Twenty-seventh Division's reserve regiment halted and consolidated because, as the Army commanding officer later explained to Griner, he was apprehensive of an attack on his rear from by-passed Japanese. Many of the 105th's infantrymen, stranded on the reef, were rescued by amtracks and DUKW's and evacuated to destroyers. The next day I removed the Twenty-seventh from the line and replaced them with the Second Marine Division, which liquidated the surviving Japanese.

It is easy to be wise after the event, but here was a case where we could have been wise before the event. It is extremely difficult to halt a *banzai* charge but, if you are alerted and prepared, such a charge, even so fierce as this one, can be contained before it does too much damage. The 1st and 2nd Battalions of the 105th Regiment, and the 3rd Battalion, 10th Marines, fought courageously but, as Admiral Spruance correctly pointed out in his report on Saipan to Admiral Nimitz, the gap between the two battalions could have been closed by swinging the 3rd Battalion forward or could, at the very least, have been covered by machine guns.

The 3rd Battalion, although not as heavily engaged as the other two, made no effort to go to their relief. More important to us, in view of the fact that I had warned Griner of the *banzai* attack, was Spruance's official finding that the front line units of the Twenty-seventh were alert to the imminence of the attack. When Richardson visited Saipan, he held an investigation of the *banzai* attack and, I was subsequently informed by Jarman, approximately 100 officers of the Twenty-seventh Division were slated to be relieved.

During the regimes of Jarman and Griner, which had followed close on the heels of Ralph Smith, two of the three infantry regimental commanders of the Twenty-seventh Division were relieved, the commander of the 106th Infantry, together with his executive officer, as already recounted; and the CO of the 105th Infantry, who had to be placed in the charge of a medical officer after a hysterical crying spell on July 5, by Griner. In confirmation of my original judgment on the leadership with which the Twenty-seventh Division had landed on Saipan, the only Twenty-seventh Division infantry regimental commander not relieved on Saipan promptly lost his regiment on Okinawa. This clean sweep of their leaders, together with the inevitable subordinate shakeup which went hand in hand with each, dramatizes as nothing else could the true state of that unhappy division.

If any advantage was gained from the fantastic Saipan breakthrough, we gained it, because the *banzai* attack undoubtedly expedited the course of the battle and was the prelude to the last act of the Saipan drama. When we cleaned up the area in front of the Twenty-seventh's sector and wiped out the scattered groups of Japanese resistance, we counted 4,311 enemy bodies, some of which were obviously long decomposed and could not have been killed during the *banzai* attack.

Another drama of Saipan was taking place behind the Japanese lines, where the remnants of the garrison of nearly 30,000 men, from Lieutenant General Saito downward, were committing suicide. On the morning of July 6, prior to the *banzai* charge, Saito issued his last message to the Imperial Army on Saipan, declaring:

Heaven has not given us an opportunity. We have been unable to utilize fully the terrain. We have fought in unison up to the present time, but now we have no materials with which to fight, and our artillery has been completely destroyed . . . Whether we attack or whether we stay where we are, there is only death. However, in death there is life. We must utilize this opportunity to exalt true Japanese manhood. I will advance with those who remain to deliver still another blow to the American devils. I will leave my bones on Saipan as a bulwark of the Pacific.

Saito, however, did not advance with his men in the final attack, nor did Vice Admiral Nagumo. Saito committed *harakiri* and he was accompanied in death by other high officers. A captured Japanese officer gave us a remarkable personal account of the last hours of Saito.

The General was ill and had been unable to eat or sleep for several days under the strain of the losing battle he was fighting without hope of relief from Tokyo. Despite his illness, aggravated by age, he hoped to reorganize his scattered forces and make a last stand on a new line in the northern part of the island. As we advanced, he continued to move northward and re-establish new headquarters. His sixth and final Command Post was in a cave in a valley which, according to our prisoner informant, became known among the enemy as the "Valley of Hell" because of the intensive naval gunfire and artillery we kept pouring into it.

This is what the Japanese officer told us:

Saito called his Chief of Staff and held a secret conference of his unit commanders. The details of that conference were never revealed to us but undoubtedly they aimed at taking final action in realizing the end in true Japanese Army fashion. This final decisive action had to be one of two courses:

First, to remain as we were and starve to death or, second, to make a last stand and fight to the finish. The Commanding General and the Chief of Staff chose the latter. . . . . The final order and instructions were written up and resulted in the order to carry out the aforementioned ceremonial action.

After issuing the order, the work of Headquarters was finished. Everybody put his personal belongings in order. By kindness of the Headquarters cook, a farewell feast for General Saito was prepared for the evening of July 5. This consisted of only *sake* and canned crabmeat.

Why did they hold this last farewell feast? Since General Saito, because of his age and exhausted condition, would not participate in the attack of July 7, and had decided to commit suicide in his cave, he was feted.

10 a.m., July 6. This time was set by the General himself as the final hour. I had to be up at the front that morning in a liasion capacity, so I was unable to witness the final hour.

I think that it happened in the following manner: Cleaning a spot on a rock, General Saito sat down. Facing the misty East, saying *"Tenno Haika! Banzai!"* he drew his own blood first with his own sword and then his Adjutant shot him in the head with a pistol. When I returned to Headquarters from my duties at 10 p.m. on July 6, they had already cremated the General's body.

Two days after the *banzai* attack, organized Japanese resistance ceased, and Saipan was secured. The Fourth Marine Division, advancing along the east coast of the island, captured

Marpi Airstrip and went on to take Marpi Point, the last enemy stronghold, on July 9, twenty-four days after we landed at Charan-Kanoa.

Saito's death was the signal for a wave of suicides, which made hard-boiled Marines shudder at Japanese savagery and regret their own helplessness to interfere when they saw hundreds of Japanese civilians, whose emotions had been worked upon by the military, join the mad rush for death. Men, women and children flung themselves over the cliffs or were pushed over by Japanese soldiers, who shot stragglers, and then followed their victims to death, either by jumping after them or destroying themselves with hand grenades.

Saipan was the supreme example of the futility of the Japanese military doctrine regarding a civilian population. Several thousand Japanese civilians had already surrendered to us in the Charan-Kanoa and Garapan areas and were segregated in camps until we could decide their future. They had stayed behind when the Japanese moved inland and thus escaped the full force of last-minute propaganda that death by horrible torture would be their fate if they were captured by the American Marines, and therefore death by their own hand was both preferable and honorable. Instead, they trusted us and lived to take their place again in the world as useful citizens.

The manner in which Admiral Nagumo met his death was never learned. Some obscure cave on Saipan must hold that secret. He, too, probably was cremated after committing suicide, because he was reported alive the night before the *banzai* attack. It was an ignominious end to the career of the man who sank our fleet at Pearl Harbor and by so doing brought us into the war and ended Japan's dream of empire.

CHAPTER X

IN war, as in every other phase of activity, there are enterprises so skilfully conceived and successfully executed that they become models of their kind. Our capture of Tinian, southern sister island of Saipan, belongs in this category. If such a tactical superlative can be used to describe a military maneuver, where the result brilliantly consummated the planning and performance, Tinian was the perfect amphibious operation in the Pacific war.

The assault on this island, planned in intervals snatched from preoccupation with the battle of Saipan, gave us the great B-29 base after only nine days' fighting, with a minimum of casualties and the highest ratio of enemy dead in any of our Central Pacific victories. This ratio worked out at 30 Japanese for every American killed, and we lost only 290 men. When Guam was regained, providing the Pacific Fleet with advance facilities second in importance only to Pearl Harbor, we controlled the whole of the Marianas, a series of powerful bases from which we could carry the war to Japan proper.

Before the end of the great Marianas battle, however, important changes had been made in the Marine Pacific command. Once Saipan, the key position, had been captured I was elevated to take over a newly created headquarters for all Marine Corps combat units in the Pacific. This was Headquarters, Fleet Marine Force, Pacific, or FMFPAC, as it was short-titled. The Fleet Marine Force had existed for many years under a number of command setups, but the new command enabled us to coordinate every one of our fighting units in one Fleet-type command, responsible directly to Admiral Nimitz.

My Marines, thus grouped together, were as much a part of this balanced land-sea-air fleet as were its aircraft carriers, submarines or battleships. The whole combination, which had spearheaded our relentless march toward Japan, constituted a striking demonstration of balanced naval power in its most effective and crushing sense.

Incident to my assumption of this new role, Major General Harry Schmidt was given my hard-hitting V Amphibious Corps and Major General Clifton B. Cates, now 19th Commandant of the Marine Corps, took over the Fourth Division from Schmidt. I left my entire staff with Harry Schmidt, with one exception. Bobby Erskine, my dynamic Chief of Staff, I insisted on retaining, which I did until he in turn was promoted to Major General and received a fine command, the Third Marine Division, which he led with distinction on Iwo Jima.

Nevertheless, I was not happy, for this change meant that my days of tactical command were nearing an end. Hitherto I had commanded troops in the field, which was to my liking. I had led them under a succession of varying designations from Amphibious Corps, Atlantic Fleet, to V Amphibious Corps, which was the oldest corps headquarters in point of continuous service in the U. S. armed forces. I feared that now I would become a highly paid administrator, coordinator and supervisor little better than Richardson, the Army's three star representative at Pearl Harbor. But balancing my personal preference for active service against the needs of the Corps, I realized that the expanding scope of our Pacific operations and the increasing employment of Marines made the change imperative.

The capture of Tinian was a foregone conclusion both to the Americans and the Japanese after we landed on Saipan. Tinian is approximately two-thirds the size of Saipan, from which it is separated by a three-mile strait. The central portion is a high plateau, with sheer cliffs running down to the sea. This green island rose like a billiard table to receive our B-29's, when mass air raids on industrial centers in Japan were launched from the Marianas.

Tinian had a garrison of 9,000, mostly veterans of the Manchurian campaign, under Colonel Kiyoshi Ogata, an Army officer not lacking in fighting spirit. Ogata was killed on D-day, leading his men into action, and they doggedly carried on without him. This garrison had better troops than other islands: they were fairly well armed and had an additional month in which to strengthen their defenses.

The Japanese on Tinian must have understood while the Saipan battle was in progress that their turn could come as soon as the nearby island was reasonably secured. They didn't have a chance, although they utilized their month's grace by developing their defenses to the utmost. We did not land until July 24, but as early as June 11 Pete Mitscher's Task Force 58 stood off Tinian and started its task of methodically reducing Japanese defenses as soon as they were discovered.

Fram Saipan, just across the narrow strait, our Corps artillery joined in this saturation of Tinian. Our 155's—Long Toms and howitzers—were able to range over more than half of the entire island, while smaller guns reached some targets. Starting with a single battalion, we increased the weight of our armament until the bombardment reached its crescendo with 13 battalions of 155's and 105's pounding Tinian from the south shore of Saipan.

The Japanese garrison tasted the bitterness of death before it overtook them. For six weeks not a day passed without a naval bombardment or an air strike, and for three weeks Corps artillery on Saipan was never silent. For the first time, we used a new secret weapon, the napalm-gasoline incendiary bomb, which destroyed canefields and the cover which hid defenses. These attacks were the basis of a painstaking, unhurried plan to knock out all observable targets and thus prepare Tinian for our landing as no other island had been prepared. We were resolved that there would be no repetition of our Tarawa or Saipan experiences, where we suffered from lack of preliminary preparation and lost heavily in consequence.

Our singular success at Tinian lay in the boldness of the landing. The Japanese outfoxed us at Kiska; we completely outfoxed them at Tinian and vindicated the soundness of the most unorthodox plan of assault ever attempted in the Pacific. We sneaked in the back door, uninvited and unexpected, while the Japanese waited for us at the front door. Surprise, fatal to Japanese mentality, threw them completely off balance.

The best—in fact, the only—beaches on the island lay along the southwest coast of Tinian, in the vicinity of its capital, Tinian Town. Here stretched several thousand yards of exactly the type of beach where an amphibious landing of any magnitude could be expected. No others along the coast offered such conditions. Therefore, it was here that the enemy concentrated his strength.

Hills and ridges around the town formed a natural amphitheater overlooking the sea and offered ideal terrain for defense. Colonel Ogata exploited these physical features by fortifying the hills and protecting the beaches with mines and underwater obstructions. Landing on such beaches and trying to force a way up the hills in the face of enemy fire would have been as futile as the charge of the Light Brigade.

Studying the problem from Saipan, we concluded it was feasible to land, not at Tinian Town, but directly across the strait on the northwest coast. This plan had numerous advantages. We could embark the assault forces, load equipment and supplies on Saipan, and cross the three mile strait like a river, without the complicated organization of an amphibious force. Instead of being a ship-to-shore operation in its initial phases, Tinian would thus become a shore-to-shore operation, like Normandy and many of those undertaken in the Mediterranean and the Southwest Pacific.

Even before I left Pearl Harbor for the Marianas, I had my eye on two small beaches on the northwest coast of Tinian. When I say "small," I mean infinitesimal in comparison with the wide areas we generally utilized. These beaches—named White Beach One and White Beach Two for the operation— were respectively 65 and 130 yards wide. To land one Marine division we normally required 4,000 yards, not 200, and at first the problem of channelling two divisions, the Fourth and the

Second, plus thousands of tons of equipment and supplies, through this narrow door seemed insoluble.

On closer inspection from Saipan the problem diminished. With only three miles of water to cross from our staging base, instead of the thousands of miles we generally travelled to our objectives, it seemed a workable plan to disregard the meagerness of the landing beaches and move swiftly ashore before the enemy was alerted. Firmly established, we would not be dislodged.

If these beaches could be used, I decided that the north was where we should land, and I staked my reputation on the results of reconnaissance. Captain James L. Jones, of our V Amphibious Corps Reconnaissance Battalion, took his men ashore in rubber boats on two after-dark missions and examined enemy positions and beach conditions at Tinian Town and at the two points I had suggested across the strait from Saipan. Abandoning their boats 400 yards from the beach, the men swam ashore undetected by Japanese working parties or patrols. Jones returned, with no casualties—as was surprisingly the usual case in these daring ventures—and reported that Tinian Town beach was heavily mined and strewn with underwater obstructions, and that the area was strongly fortified.

On the other hand, he reported, White Beach One and White Beach Two were suitable for a rapid landing in spite of their size and that they were only lightly defended. Lieutenant Commander Draper L. F. Kauffman, USNR, in command of our Underwater Demolition Team, confirmed this report after he and his men also had reconnoitered the beaches.

Before I relinquished command of the V Amphibious Corps, I submitted the White Beach One and White Beach Two landing plan to Kelly Turner and he dismissed it with the observation that it was impracticable. That summation touched off a chain of bitter argument on the subject, because I considered it eminently practicable, since it possessed the essential element of surprise and bypassed one of the most formidable beaches in the Pacific. Our session on board the *Rocky Mount* generated considerable unprintable language. In essence, Turner based his objections on the limited size of the beaches.

"You can't possibly land two divisions on those beaches," he insisted. "You need ten times that amount of room to get the men ashore. Let me tell you what will happen. The Japs will move in on you before you get all your men ashore and then you will be in a jam!

"Suppose the weather goes against you? And it looks like it will. What would you do then? The only feasible beaches are at Tinian Town, and that's where we are going to land."

Intelligence reports had described in detail the defense preparations the Japanese had stacked up in their fortified amphitheater at Tinian Town. If we attempted a landing there, as Kelly Turner insisted, it would be suicide.

"If we go ashore at Tinian Town," I told him, "we'll have another Tarawa. Sure as hell! The Japs will murder us. What's more, we probably will be repulsed, and that will upset our entire timetable. What do *you* say to *that?*"

He said a great deal, and we went on in this vein for hours, but I countered all his arguments against my chosen beaches. I pointed out that, while we would run into the full force of Japanese resistance at Tinian Town, we could land practically unopposed in the north, make a right sweep in the rear of the town, where enemy strength was concentrated, and gain sufficient maneuver ground for a quick—and bloodless—operation.

Finally I extracted from Kelly Turner a promise that decision on the beaches would be deferred until we had the results of our reconnaissance. Armed with this report on beach conditions, I went back to the *Rocky Mount* and, in the face of this incontrovertible evidence, Turner reluctantly withdrew his objections. I have always felt that Admiral Spruance, the final authority, recognized the inherent soundness of my plan, and that his support finally swung the decision. I handed over the general plan to Harry Schmidt and he worked out the details.

The bitter recriminations over this shortcut to success on Tinian left me reflecting on the persistence of naval intransigence. I had just captured Saipan and was faced with the further responsibility of capturing Tinian, yet my judgment in a largely military matter was subjected to naval expediency. Here was a concrete example of a military man of long and uniformly successful experience having his plans challenged by a naval officer who had never commanded troops ashore and failed to understand the principles of land warfare.

As it developed, through planning and not by happenstance, because we provided against all contingencies, including the weather, the landing exceeded expectations. To describe this unique shore-to-shore operation, which saved hundreds of American lives, I might use the simile of an inverted funnel. Through the narrow neck we poured the men, who emerged through the wide mouth and fanned out in the area beyond the beach. In this way we put ashore the entire Fourth Marine Division in nine hours, with only 15 killed. By nightfall on July 24, we held a front 4,000 yards long and 2,000 yards deep, strong enough to resist the Japanese counterattack and break the back of enemy power the very first night.

Altogether, we put 42,000 men with complete equipment, artillery, trucks, tanks and supplies, across these narrow beaches in the next few days. This was no mean feat, considering that the weather did turn against us.

The superiority of this shore-to-shore attack was that it largely dispensed with transports and the laborious, time-wasting process of loading and unloading. Landing craft carrying troops went directly from Saipan to Tinian. Amtracks and DUKW's loaded on Saipan, crossed the strait, and made for inland sites predesignated as dumps, thereby obviating unloading on the beach and reloading for transportation inland. To facilitate the movement of tanks, artillery and other heavy equipment up the steep beaches, the ingenious Seabees constructed pontoon causeways and special ramps, and when the heavy swell predicted by the Navy did appear, it made little difference to us.

This landing on such a narrow area might have been blocked if the Japanese has guessed our design. But nothing went wrong as we fed the men through the narrow funnel neck onto the beach. From an exhaustive study of the situation, I knew that the Japanese did not have sufficient troops to defend the western and northern beaches, and reconnaissance definitely showed that most of the garrison was immobilized in the rear of the Tinian Town area.

And besides, we took no chances. Rear Admiral Harry Hill, commanding the Navy support force, ostentatiously kept most of his ships off Tinian Town and concentrated fire on that area. To strengthen the illusion that we intended landing on the "logical" beaches, the Second Division staged a feint, which apparently was convincing to the enemy. Two runs were made within 400 yards of the beach and our landing craft received heavy fire before returning to the transports for re-embarkation. By this time the Japanese were certain that Tinian Town was our objective, and that our initial assault was a failure.

Meanwhile, we got ashore in force on the northern beaches, in circumstances extremely confusing to the Japanese. In addition to the powerful demonstration off Tinian Town, which indicated one thing to their puzzled minds, a heavy bombardment covered the northern area and disguised our real intention, which was something quite different. More than 200 planes were available to support the attack, and, added to our 13 battalions of artillery blasting away from Saipan, were three battleships, three heavy cruisers, three light cruisers, sixteen destroyers, and thirty gunboats.

The Japanese discovered our ruse too late. During the night of July 24, the garrison commander rushed up his troops to meet us in the north, but by that time we were well dug in and waiting for him. The battle that night and early the next morning sealed the fate of Tinian. The enemy attack was not a *banzai* charge. Is was a well coordinated movement, but our line was strong and integrated. This strong beachhead line was an essential feature of the plan.

Ogata's night attack was directed at several points in our line, and the Fourth Division was ready for everything. Troops with bazookas were stationed at likely tank crossings; 37 mm. guns were emplaced all along the line with cannister and antipersonnel shells; machine guns covered fire lanes and our artillery was alerted. The most serious threat came down a narrow-gauge railroad, led by six tanks, five of which we knocked out; the sixth escaped but was destroyed the next day.

The 24th Marines (Colonel Franklin A. Hart) bore the brunt of the night attack. Thrown back, the Japanese reorganized on higher ground at 0100 and struck at the juncture of the 25th and the 24th Regiments. Several hundred broke through and reformed in a swamp which was not covered by our machine guns. From the swamp they split into two parties, one of which aimed at our artillery positions, where artillerymen lowered their muzzles, fired pointblank and routed the frenzied mob, now stirred to *banzai* pitch.

For four hours, the 24th fought another group, wiping them out with mortar, machine gun and rifle fire in the light of flares, while artillery cut off their retreat. It was one of the fiercest nights in the Pacific war and also one of the most decisive. Twelve hundred Japanese bodies were counted along the Division front at daybreak and another 700 to 800 were estimated to have been carried away by their comrades. Nearly a quarter of the Japanese garrison was killed that night, thus deciding the ultimate result of the battle.

With our 4,000-yard beachhead secured, the Second Division landed and took over the eastern zone. The two divisions advanced abreast down the island, making from two to four miles' progress a day, over terrain admirably suited to the employment of tanks, artillery and infantry. There were excellent roads, along which heavy equipment could be moved, and the Second Division's capture of Airfield Number One, near Ushi Point, one of the three airfields we took, enabled planes from Isely Field, Saipan, to operate almost immediately.

Other factors likewise made our advance rapid. The Fourth and Second Divisions had just completed the capture of Saipan and were well trained, confident and eager to force a quick decision. The assault on Tinian took place two weeks after the capture of Saipan but those weeks were no rest period. Surcease, you might call it, but not rest.

It was a period devoted to reorganization, replenishment of equipment and training for the Tinian operation. We had the men on tip-toe all the time. They had to be kept up to battle pitch so that when they were thrown into action again they retained their zest and offensive spirit. One big problem in rehabilitating men back in Hawaii, after an operation involving weeks of idleness on shipboard, was to restore this offensive spirit, but at Tinian we had no such problem.

Another factor was intelligence. We knew practically everything there was to know about Tinian. No troops ever landed on a hostile shore knowing their objective as well as we did. From Saipan, we maintained daily air reconnaissance and studied terrain features and enemy defenses through powerful telescopes. Unit commanders were flown over the objective island to familiarize themselves with the details. Divisional commanders, general staff officers and on down to battalion commanders made frequent flights and supplemented our maps and the information we had gained from enemy documents captured on Saipan. This was a new procedure in amphibious war.

Tinian Town, originally strongly defended from the sea, was captured with only slight resistance after its garrison had been decimated and scattered during our advance to the south. A score of enemy strongpoints also fell into our hands with relative ease. A tank-led counterattack against the 24th Marines, on July 31, was the last show of strength. After that, enemy resistance dissipated, and the remnants of the garrison fled into the caves studding the formidable ridge and cliff south of the town.

Our last overwhelming demonstration of fire superiority involved that ridge and cliff. Nineteen warships, including two battleships, 112 planes and eleven battalions of artillery, shelled and bombed the rocky points before the infantry jumped off in the final attack against the remaining enemy, whom the Marines wiped out with flame throwers, demolition charges, rifles and machine guns. By August 1, the island was declared secured, and two days later the Stars and Stripes was raised officially.

Although we gained a military victory when we drove the few remaining soldiers into the southern caves, it was only then that the battle started for the lives of 13,000 civilians. Terrified men, women and children hid in the hundreds of caves with the soldiers, apparently waiting for death with oriental fatalism. We sent out a jeep, equipped with a loud speaker, and broadcast appeals urging the civilians to come down from the 200-foot cliff and we would give them water, food and medical attention. A handful emerged and entered our lines but thousands more did not budge.

Among the few who came to us were the superintendent of the sugar refinery at Tinian and his wife. He offered to speak to his people and, most unexpectedly for a shy Japanese woman, his wife followed his example. A few more civilians responded to this joint assurance that the Americans were keeping their promises, but even then our efforts were not substantially rewarded.

By one of those strange acts of fate, the Japanese soldiers themselves set off the final stampede that saved thousands of civilians from death. While we were calling to them to come down from the cliff, puffs of smoke and sounds of explosions in the caves told us that suicides had started again. Suddenly, one soldier marched to the edge of the cliff and jumped into the sea. Another followed . . . and another. The pattern was repeated for an hour while the Marines looked on helplessly, hoping that the unfortunate civilians would not be led to that horrible death by the fanaticism of so many samurai-stimulated Pied Pipers.

The tragedy that broke the evil spell occurred when a party of Japanese soldiers roped 40 or 50 civilians together and threw a hand grenade among them. Explosives buried in the ground blew the group to pieces. It was a barbaric performance, designed to terrorize the people into joining the death ceremony, but instead, they concluded that even the Americans, represented in Army propaganda as torturers of Japanese prisoners, could not be so cruel as their own people. The civilians ran for their lives, dragging their children and carrying their feeble old people.

By August 12, we were taking care of 13,000 civilians, half of whom were Japanese, the balance, Chamorro natives of the Marianas. Major General J. L. Underhill, USMC, was appointed Island Commander, and under him civil affairs progressed far better than at Saipan, where our lack of experience and personnel trained in handling alien civilian populations had created an unsatisfactory situation during the early days of the occupation.

Tinian, the perfect landing operation, continued on a high scale of civilian administration. Fortunately a number of houses were still habitable, for which the Japanese and "unclassified" men, women and children proved appreciative and cooperative. General Underhill assembled a competent staff to administer Camp Churo, where we established a school for 2,500 children. The internees had their own trade store and their own "live" theater, where a troupe from Okinawa, caught on Tinian on J-day, produced plays that belonged, for robust humor, with those of Elizabethan days. I am convinced that the civilians we saved and cared for on Tinian met the peace with a deep conviction that American democracy works.

Our assault on Tinian preceded the invasion of Guam by three days, and until Tinian was captured these two operations were fought simultaneously.

When I assumed the position of Commanding General, FMF, Pacific, and turned over command of the V Amphibious Corps and Northern attack troops to Harry Schmidt, I still retained command of the Expeditionary Troops in the Marianas, and in this capacity I commuted between Saipan and Guam. The new command gave me more freedom of action, and I no longer was restricted to one phase of a three-phase operation, as I was in the Gilberts. I could move as I chose and as circumstances required.

Historically, Guam was the most important operation we had undertaken because it was our first reconquest (except Attu) of American territory. Guam is the biggest island of the Marianas, 30 miles long and from 4 to 8 miles wide, and was the largest Central Pacific land mass we had invaded.

Guam became an American possession in 1898, after the Spanish-American War. Spain sold the other Marianas islands to Germany, and Japan's participation in World War I resulted in her seizure of these German holdings, which the League of Nations later awarded her under mandate. As our original interest in the Marianas was confined to Guam, we found ourselves isolated in a chain administered by the nation we in the Marine Corps felt would be our enemy.

The island's only prewar importance was as a minor naval station and coaling base en route to the Philippines. Never was Guam considered a distant outpost of American power. It was administered by the Navy, which appointed a Governor, and the Marine Corps provided a small garrison stationed at Sumay, a village on the Orote Peninsula overlooking Apra Harbor. More recently, Guam had become a station for Pan-American Airways' trans-Pacific planes. Beyond these factors our interest was academic, since Congress was never convinced that we should fortify the island. The only positive result of our acquisition of Guam was a growing sense of responsibility for the Guamanians, who thrived under our democratic system and, despite other Government Departments' criticism of Naval Administration, bravely demonstrated their loyalty when the Japanese seized the island after Pearl Harbor.

Contrasting with our pre-battle information about Tinian, our knowledge of our former possession was almost less than we knew of the most secret Japanese islands. Although the Navy had administered Guam for 40 years, scant information was available regarding military possibilities or terrain features. Little effort, except by a Marine reconnaissance officer in 1936, had been made to explore Guam from a military point of view in case we had to fight for it. Few attempts had been made to collect and record the data required for its defense. I believe our forces had similar difficulties when we re-entered the Philippines late in 1944.

Duty on Guam was somnolent retirement for Navy officers, overcome by the heat and far from the beaten track. The one energetic Navy commander who made his mark on Guam was a product of the Captain Bligh era, who confounded the carefree Guamanians by making it an offense, punishable by fine, to whistle in the streets of the capital, Agana.

Our only up-to-date first-hand information when we landed came from beach reconnaissance and air photographs, which was not too extensive because a large portion of Guam is covered by thick jungle.

Roy Geiger was entrusted with the recapture of Guam. His troops were the Third Marine Division, the First Provisional Marine Brigade and the Seventy-seventh Army Division. The Marine Brigade was particularly interesting, since it was a composite force of Marine units assembled before the Fifth Division was organized. Most of the men were veteran fighters of long service in the South Pacific. The Brigade included four former Raider battalions, who had landed on numerous South Pacific islands. Originally incorporated into the 1st Raider Regiment, these battalions were reorganized into the 4th Marines—designation of the famous China Marines, who had been captured on Corregidor in 1942. With the addition of the 22nd Marines, veterans of Eniwetok, they composed the 1st Provisional Brigade.

In reality, Guam was two independent campaigns. Apra Harbor, on the west coast, bounded on the north by the low Cabras Island and on the south by the rocky promontory, Orote Point, was the focal point of attack. The Third Division landed north of the harbor and the First Brigade and the Seventy-seventh Army Division south of the harbor, separated by a distance of about five miles. We planned a pincer movement, with the northern and southern arms enclosing the harbor area and Orote Peninsula, where the Japanese were positioned in considerable force.

The Japanese were no better organized on Guam than we had been. Their garrison was a polyglot force. Like our own administration, the Navy took control when the Japanese seized the island, but, with war on, the Tokyo General Staff started pouring in large numbers of Army troops, although Guam defenses were starved by our submarines and by the same priorities that crippled Saipan—the enemy's belief that after the Marshalls we would strike at the Palaus or the Philippines.

Captured documents revealed that the Japanese originally intended to garrison Guam with the Thirteenth Division from Manchuria. Forward echelons of these seasoned troops actually arrived, but eventually the Army troops assigned here were drawn

214

from the Twenty-ninth Division. We did not discover why the Thirteenth never arrived from Manchuria.

Our G-2 advanced the suggestion that the entire convoy transporting the division had been sunk by our submarines, but a sudden change in conditions in China or Manchuria probably caused the Japanese to alter their plans for the Thirteenth.

Guam's garrison was estimated at 18,000, headed by Lieutenant General Sho Takashima, a subordinate unit of Lieutenant General Saito, late commander of the 31st Army on Saipan. Most of these troops came from Manchuria and their scattered designations showed how hurriedly they had been shipped to Guam. Supporting the Twenty-ninth Division were elements of the Eleventh Division, under Major General Toyoshi Shigematsu.

Our two assault forces went ashore on July 21, after long and sustained preparation. An astronomical number of shells were dropped and most of the observed Japanese defenses were knocked out. "Close-in" Conolly, the Admiral who had prepared Roi-Namur so admirably for the Fourth Marine Division, had worked over Guam with the same thoroughness which had made Marines thank him in the Marshalls.

The Third Division, under Major General Allen H. Turnage, landed north of Apra Harbor, with the 3rd Marines on the left, the 21st in the center and the 9th on the right. Down the center of Guam runs a ridge with half a dozen peaks over 1,000 feet high, although the ridge is severed by passes. The 3rd ran into difficulties as soon as they landed. From the ridge, Chonito Cliff projected into the sea. This cliff was a dangerous enemy stronghold, supported by deadly fire from the reverse face of the ridge.

While the 21st moved inland with appreciable speed and the 9th, on the right flank, made rapid progress toward the southern end of the ridge and Piti Navy Yard, our prewar station on Apra Harbor, the 3rd made no progress whatsoever. Terrific mortar and machine gun fire from the ridge kept the men pinned down, and, although they lost no ground, our general position north of the harbor deteriorated because the 3rd was unable to advance.

On the southern front, below Apra Harbor, Brigadier General Lemuel C. Shepherd, Jr.'s Provisional Brigade landed against heavy opposition and moved deliberately northward across the neck of Orote Peninsula, to pen in and destroy the enemy garrison of 4,000 occupying this well fortified rocky finger, with a ready-made airfield waiting for us to seize and operate. Following the Marine Brigade, the Seventy-seventh Infantry Division (Major General Bruce, AUS), held as a floating reserve, moved in and started to cross Guam from the east.

The capture of Orote Peninsula was, in some respects, the outstanding accomplishment of the Guam campaign. Relying on their old theory of static defense, the Japanese had converted the long, tapering rock into a fortress. But it could not withstand the weight of naval and air bombardment and the pressure we put on as Shepherd's veteran fighters advanced over difficult terrain, through intricate defenses, doggedly routing out the Japanese and killing them.

Offshore stood Conolly's supporting fleet, which never missed an opportunity to give us gunfire whenever and wherever it was requested. Air strikes came as frequently as showers in April.

Had the Japanese elected to surrender Orote and concentrate their forces elsewhere, instead of diverting a quarter of their garrison to a fortified rock where we could concentrate the full force of our armament, the story of Guam might have been different. But they made their choice, and five days after we started the all-out attack on the peninsula Orote was ours.

While Shepherd was fighting for Orote, the Seventy-seventh, coming in behind the Marine Brigade, remained almost stationary instead of extending across the island on the right of the brigade, and the Third Division, with its left flank anchored at the foot of Chonito Cliff, was still trying to punch its way out of the Agat cul-de-sac. It was worrying me that the Third and the Seventy-seventh Divisions were not taking a more aggressive action.

At this time I was at Guam on board the *Rocky Mount* with Kelly Turner, although Dick Conolly directed the operation from his command ship, the USS *Appalachian*. I conferred with

Roy Geiger and then went over to the USS *Indianapolis* to discuss matters with Spruance, to whom I had revealed my dissatisfaction. On July 24, taking Mac Asbill with me, I went ashore to visit the Third Division's beachhead.

Accompanied by Turnage, I inspected the Division's front line, which was still being held a short distance inland from the beach. The 3rd Regiment was dug in but I could see no evidence of Japanese in front of them. Actually, the enemy was in very considerable force on the reverse side of the ridge, running beyond Agana. The situation did not please me.

As a result of postponements of W-day on Guam owing to the unexpected strength of the Saipan defenses, the troops had been kept for many weeks on board transports, doing nothing, just killing time and resenting the delay. The inactivity and close confinement on board ship probably had taken their toll of the men. A long period of such idleness can play hell with combat efficiency.

That night I returned to Tinian on the *Rocky Mount*, eager to see how the battle was going on the first day. To my delight, and exactly as I had anticipated, we had slipped in through the small northern beaches and were spreading all over the island, almost unopposed.

Reports from Guam continued to be worrisome. The situation on the left flank at Chonito Cliff still dragged. A week elapsed, and the Third Division had been unable to progress at that particular point, thus retarding any movement by the Seventy-seventh on the right. I sent a dispatch to Geiger directing him to take more offensive action. On July 28, I returned to Guam with Spruance on board the *Indianapolis* and again immediately went ashore, where Geiger had established his III Corps headquarters.

With Roy Geiger, I called on the commander of the Seventy-seventh, Major General Bruce, at his headquarters. This Division had landed without opposition in the rear of the First Marine Brigade and moved through rough country to a position on the right of the Third Division. I was very much impressed by Bruce and his men and I felt that they would give an excellent account of themselves when Geiger decided that the time was ripe to move forward. When the Seventy-seventh did move, it moved fast.

The Seventy-seventh was a raw division, with no previous combat experience, but it showed combat efficiency to a degree one would expect only of veteran troops. Its aggressive patrolling, its close coordination with other units, and its superior conduct of assigned missions gave evidence of a high order of training, fine leadership and high morale.

Back at III Corps headquarters, Geiger and I discussed the situation, and I told him frankly that, although I had no desire to interfere with his plan of action, I thought that the time had come for a general movement to capture the remainder of the island now that Orote Peninsula and Apra Harbor were in our possession.

Geiger replied that before he moved his troops forward across Guam in a general attack he wanted to make sure Shepherd had cleaned up Orote, which would give us the use of an airfield we badly needed and also release the First Brigade for further employment.

I definitely disagreed with this line of reasoning, but I was restrained from making an overruling objection because that would have been an undue interference in Geiger's command. However, I did express the opinion that, having contacted the enemy, we must keep after him, keep the pressure on hard and keep him on the run.

It was perfectly apparent to me that Shepherd and his magnificent Brigade would finish Orote without delay and that the Third and the Seventy-seventh Divisions should be directed to advance immediately. The company commanders I had interviewed all said that was exactly what they were waiting to do when the command was given.

The last contact with the enemy in strength—although we didn't know at the time how strong he was—had occurred two days previously. For some reason, the counterattack generally launched on the first night of a landing had not come. Minor attacks were made at various points in our line but no serious effort to push us off the island developed until the predawn hours of July 26.

The first indication that the Japanese were moving came from heavy mortar and artillery fire on our extreme left flank. Then the main body struck at our center, in the Third Division zone, held by the 21st Marines. We learned later that this was one of the best organized and strongest counterattacks the Japanese ever made. Several groups participated, covered by mortar and artillery fire. These groups filed down mountain trails and through ravines. The flares we threw up, once we were alerted, mingled with their own flares to create an eerie, floodlit scene, with smoke, shell-blasts and machine gun flashes stabbing the shadows. The leading attack party appeared on the cliff overlooking our artillery positions and rolled down explosives on the guns below.

It was a night of bitter, exhausting fighting because the enemy came out of the darkness from all sides, in apparently unending streams. A number infiltrated our lines and in a major breakthrough penetrated a gap between the 21st Regiment and the 9th, necessitating a determined counterattack to repair the damage to our position.

Japanese sneaked in by twos and threes and, gathering forces, started to attack a battalion Command Post, but were routed by cooks, bakers, and clerks, hurriedly transformed into combat troops. Another party crept up to the division hospital and was wiped out by MP's, headquarters clerks and Marine combat correspondents, aided by the wounded, who jumped out of their cots, snatched up carbines, and joined in the fighting. Those incidents, however, were mere sideshows to the main battle, in which our artillery blazed all night.

The invaders were loaded down with explosives, indicating they intended to break through our lines, force their way to the sea, and destroy our supply dumps on the beach. Two Japanese actually did reach Piti Navy Yard and were killed by patrols. This is as far as they ever did get.

When daylight came the attack had ended, and survivors were on the retreat along the paths they had come. Only then did we realize how strong the enemy had been and what carnage our artillery had spread. Thousands of Japanese bodies were scattered along the trails, in the undergrowth and over the hillsides. We discovered that, instead of a *banzai* charge, this had been a coordinated attack by at least six battalions, the largest number ever used by the Japanese in a single counterattack against us. Our losses were light and in the morning the men of the Third Marine Division stared at each other in amazement when they saw the slaughter of the night. Without knowing it at the time, the Third Division, veteran of just such jungle actions at Bougainville, had broken the back of the Japanese forces on Guam.

In retrospect, this stands out as the most important of all enemy counterattacks on Guam. None did a great deal of damage, and they actually shortened the campaign, because they enabled us to meet the enemy face to face instead of compelling us to dig him out of ravines and jungles. Of all the campaigns fought in the Central Pacific, Guam provided the Japanese with the thickest cover of impenetrability for, after the capture of rocky Orote, it was almost impossible to see them in the jungles unless they emerged in numbers bent on counterattack.

Orote was secured on July 31, and Geiger gave the command for a general advance. The picture changed rapidly. The long deadlock that gripped the left flank at Chonito was broken, and the Third and the Seventy-seventh Divisions abreast started a rapid march up the narrow neck of the island. Agana, the badly damaged but still partially habitable capital, was in our hands by August 2. This gave the Guamanian population a tremendous lift. They streamed happily into the streets by the thousands, the women wearing pathetic finery saved during the long, dark years of Japanese occupation for the day of liberation. The Brigade moved in on the left flank of the line, and our forces reached the northern cliffs on August 10.

Before the final advance, there was some doubt about the whereabouts of the Japanese. Had they gone south or north? Marine patrols probed the southern part of the island and returned with a negative report; therefore, we drove north. When the attack order was given, we lost contact with the enemy except for minor groups. Our troops raced so fast up the island that our divisional artillery was forced to displace position five times in two weeks, which, while nothing notable in a land mass battle, was something to talk about in the assault on an island.

It was tough driving through the rocky volcanic ridges and thick jungles at the speed we developed. The balance of the campaign was as much a bulldozer's as a fighter's job because we had to insure supplies and passage of tanks and artillery across country almost devoid of roads. Often, the bulldozer was well ahead of the combat troops, and developed a rugged personality all its own. The roar of the bulldozer as it tore up palm trees and dug out rocks was as familiar as the noise of gunfire. Chonito Cliff, the rock that held up the Third Marines for eight days, was levelled for road material, and in the development of Guam as a base the bulldozer became a symbol of American efficiency.

It was a proud day for me when, standing with Spruance, Turner, Geiger, Shepherd, Turnage, Erskine and other officers, I saw the Stars and Stripes raised over the site of the former Marine Barracks at Sumay, on Orote Peninsula. Only a heap of rubble remained of the old two-story building, but as the flag broke in the bright Guamanian sunshine our presence was a vindication by the Corps of its motto, "Semper Fidelis," that had brought Marines back to Guam to avenge the 150 men the Japanese had captured after Pearl Harbor.

The battle of Guam did not end when we drove the remnant of the enemy garrison over the northern cliffs. At Saipan, we killed 7,783 Japanese in the first month following the islands' capture. At Guam, we killed 6,276 Japanese in the first three months following our official declaration that the island was secured. Guam yielded a large number of prisoners who lived precariously in the jungle. Occasionally they ambushed small parties, raided our supply dumps, or pilfered from the Guamanians, until they finally were routed out by Marine patrols or responded to loud speaker appeals to surrender. Pleas by well fed, co-operative prisoner volunteers from the stockade in Agana brought in hundreds. Colonel Howard Stent, in charge of psychological warfare on Guam, was responsible for this campaign.

As recently as the summer of 1947, a Japanese major and a number of men he had kept intact as a force since the island fell three years before, was at liberty on Guam until a message over the loud speaker convinced him that Japan had surrendered and the war was over.

The capture of the Marianas had cost us 25,500 casualties, of which 4,678 were killed; but we in turn accounted for 56,000 Japanese. We provided the nation with bases which proved their value during the remainder of the war and will be a guarantee of our Pacific security in the future.

CHAPTER XI

I HAVE ALWAYS been proud of the relationship between the Marines and the Submariners. A link exists between them, much more intimate than the prefix suggests, and this link was forged in the heat of the Pacific war. Submarines play an important part in a highly technical undertaking like amphibious warfare and the Marines owe a large measure of the success achieved in our assault on the Japanese Empire to the help received from the Submarine Force, U. S. Pacific Fleet, commanded by Vice Admiral Charles A. Lockwood, Jr.

But the basis for this relationship was more solid than technical collaboration. Marines and Submariners shared the same characteristics and the bond between them was stronger than between any other two branches of the naval service. We were both volunteers; to a man, we deliberately chose the most hazardous type of service.

Danger was the bond. The Marine admired the Submariner, who cruised for months at a time in enemy waters, hundreds of miles from his base, alone and unprotected except for his own resourcefulness, and hunted relentlessly by enemy ships. In return, the Submariner admired the Marine, who landed on hostile beaches in the mouth of enemy cannon, stormed massive concrete and steel fortifications and halted only when he was dead.

From contacts made at Pearl Harbor and more advanced bases and on joint missions against Japanese strongholds, an *entente cordiale* sprang up between the Marines and the Submariners, founded on this mutual admiration for the other fellow's handling of tough assignments. I am sure this comradeship will become traditional between the two services and future developments in amphibious warfare will provide us with many more joint missions.

During the Pacific war, we were driven into each other's company by the similar role of very junior partners which was forced upon us. We were two smaller services standing out against the background of the greatest Navy in the world, with its 4,000,000 men, of which 13 percent were Marines and only 1.6 percent were Submariners. I felt that the top Navy brass turned equal frigidity on both branches.

It seemed to me, Charlie Lockwood and I sat together at the daily conference at Pearl Harbor, like two kids from the wrong side of the tracks, expected to know their place. We developed a sympathetic attitude towards each other's operations. Lockwood told me about the Submariners and I told him about the Marines and we shared each other's apprehensions and triumphs. We knew we were the tough boys and the Navy brass couldn't get along without us.

Very little was heard during the war about the lads of the submarine service. They did their fighting in the far reaches of the Pacific, not in the newspapers. Their operations, their losses and often their successes were cloaked in silence. There was a good reason for this reticence. Its imposition was necessary to prevent the Japanese from obtaining information upon which to build a pattern of submarine patrol areas and from discovering the endurance and radius of our submarines and the methods we used. It was also important at times to keep the enemy ignorant of the fate of his ships which failed to reach their destinations. This secrecy paid dividends in saving submarines and lives of Submariners.

But while this secrecy was not understood and was frequently resented by the public, the Marines understood its urgency. You will not find a single Marine who does not appreciate what the submarines did during the war. They were our advance ears and eyes, following enemy naval movements outside Japanese home ports; they were our first line of naval defense, obstructing enemy interference with landing operations and they sank more than five million tons of enemy shipping.

Starting the war with only 51 boats in the Pacific, the submarine force faced the terrific task of covering 8,000,000 square miles of ocean and clearing it of enemy shipping. The force expanded as fast as our shipyards could produce new craft, but never more than 200 submarines were employed in the Pacific. Although the Japanese claimed 480 were "sunk or probably sunk," our losses from all causes, including accidents, were 52. The force numbered 4,000 officers and 46,000 men, of whom only 16,000 actually manned the submarines. Yet their record of sinkings is impressive. Excluding vessels of less than 1,000 tons, submarines sank 1,750 steel-hulled Japanese ships and threw the Imperial Japanese Navy for the loss of one battleship, eight carriers, 15 cruisers, 42 destroyers, 26 submarines, and other naval auxiliaries, patrol craft and other vessels, totalling 201 men-of-war. After the war, the Japanese informed us that 276,000 soldiers, sailors and civilians lost their lives in our submarine sinkings.

The popular conception of the role of the submarine, and indeed its main purpose, is the sinking of ships. This role was of vital importance because the steady rate of ship destruction prevented the reinforcement of enemy bases with men and material that would make our task of capturing these bases more difficult. A blockade was thrown around islands marked for invasion and few enemy ships ever broke through our underwater cordon to supply doomed garrisons. The Submariners were fighting Marine battles long before we hit an island, disposing of the enemy before he had a chance to land, and destroying weapons and equipment we would have had to face.

As our amphibious operations progressed, Lockwood increased the density of his submarine patrols, tightening his stranglehold on the enemy's seaborne supplies. The final feat of the submarines came in 1945, when they ran under the extensive Japanese minefields in Tsushima Straits, separating Japan proper from Korea and Manchuria, and cut the enemy's last supply lines from the Asiatic mainland.

Submarine activities were closely coordinated with each new Marine invasion. The blockade was especially successful in the

Marianas. Saipan would have been a far tougher nut to crack had the Japanese been able to complete their fortifications. In addition to Tokyo's bad guess on our plans after the Marshalls which crippled Saipan by the diversion of priorities elsewhere, there was abundant evidence of material starvation because of the submarine blockade.

When Tokyo finally realized Saipan's plight and began rushing through a defense program, ship after ship carrying vital materials such as concrete, timber and steel, was sunk. The Saipan garrison command complained bitterly of idle hands and no supplies. Our losses at Saipan were heavy but they would have been much heavier if we had run into the fortifications Tokyo contemplated but was unable to finish before we attacked.

The submarines did us a good service at Iwo Jima. On this volcanic island, fortified to Gibraltar-like strength with every type of Japanese weapon we had encountered in the Pacific and a few more, such as 320-mm. mortars and "buzzbombs," the Marines ran into very little barbed wire. This lack of the most common method of obstruction, in the midst of such a mass of highly developed defenses, appeared strange until a prisoner enlightened us. He said supplies sent to the island were lost by submarine action.

Enemy survivors of torpedoed ships added their testimony to the effectiveness of the blockade. On almost every island in the Marianas, I found men from ships our submarines had sunk. They were remnants of divisions rushed to the Marianas as reinforcements, but who arrived there in lifeboats or by swimming ashore. The Marianas became islands of lost souls as far as the Japanese were concerned, since most of these survivors were more of a handicap than a help to the garrisons. They lost their weapons with their ships.

Our submarines tore great holes in convoys and attacked unremittingly, day after day, until they made their maximum kill. Elsewhere I have referred to the mystery of the missing Thirteenth Division from Manchuria, assigned to reinforce the Guam garrison. Although internal conditions in China and Manchuria probably caused the Japanese to change their minds about moving this division, there was nothing fantastic in the G-2 suggestion that the entire convoy might have been sunk. A few days before the invasion of Saipan, a wolf pack nearly annihilated a convoy of enemy transports bound for the island with a division of troops. Five out of seven transports were sunk by our submarines, which kept up the attack for three days. The USS *Pintado* and the USS *Shark* distinguished themselves in this action, which took place only nine days before we landed on Saipan on June 15.

Two thousand Japanese troops were drowned in this action, and the Saipan armory was unable to arm those who got ashore. How many lives of Americans in our amphibious force were saved by this action is difficult to estimate, but since the Marines would have borne the brunt of the reinforced Japanese strength on the island, we are grateful for our share of the lives saved.

While the submarines maintained this strict blockade and lightened our landing jobs, far out in the ocean other boats were keeping ceaseless vigil for retaliatory naval action by the Japanese, now that we were assailing their inner defenses. The challenge of an American attack on the Marianas was too serious to be ignored.

If the Japanese Fleet had caught us off Saipan, our first venture in the Marianas might have resulted in disaster, but we had perfect confidence that our advance submarine reconnaissance would warn us of any danger. This is precisely what our submarines did. First the *Flying Fish* (Commander Risser), then the *Sea Horse* (Commander Slade Cutter), then the *Cavalla* (Lieutenant Commander Herman J. Kossler) sighted the Japanese Fleet; and their reports gave a beautiful picture which enabled Admiral Lockwood to locate his submarines where he figured the two Jap forces would rendezvous, and Admiral Spruance went out and defeated the Japanese Fleet in the first battle of the Philippine Sea. This battle, resulting from the alertness of submarine captains, undoubtedly saved the Marine force ashore on Saipan from a serious threat. How these submarines operated is best described by a typical experience, that of the *Cavalla*.

On June 16, the day after we landed on Saipan, the *Cavalla* surfaced 700 miles west of the Marianas. On the horizon Commander Kossler saw a large group of warships. They couldn't be ours, because we had no ships in the area. Obviously they were Japanese. The ships were fifteen miles away when first sighted and as they came closer their recognition left no doubt. They were ships of the Japanese Fleet, heading east at about 19 knots. The submarine was making about the same speed and since the enemy ships were astern Kossler reversed his course and turned back to investigate.

"There was a carrier as big as the Empire State Building," he said, according to the account I heard later, "and I could make out about seven other ships, looking like battleships and cruisers, in two columns.

"I hadn't seen any report of a Jap task force in this area, but what a target! I could have got that carrier easy. You can imagine my mental struggle. The biggest bag I'd ever seen but I couldn't do a thing about it. I was on reconnaissance."

The Japanese Fleet was heading for Saipan and it was Kossler's primary duty to report its presence. If he attacked, Japanese destroyers would have held him down and he would have been unable to send his report.

As Kossler explained, "I decided to go down and submerged about 100 feet. Soon the Japanese ships began passing over my head. I started to count the screws and found there were far more than the original 15 ships I had guessed. It took over an hour for the procession to pass over me. Then I realized I had contacted the Imperial Japanese Fleet, or a large part of it.

"I couldn't get off my report immediately because two Jap destroyers astern of the fleet delayed me from surfacing. They kept crossing and weaving, as if they were covering the rear against possible submarines. But I don't think they spotted us. Anyway, they kept us down two hours but I eventually surfaced and got off my report."

This was the information that alerted Spruance's Fifth Fleet and helped score the first great victory of the Philippine Sea. Incidentally, Kossler was not robbed of his kill. Returning from this patrol, he encountered another of Japan's big carriers, the *Shokaku*, hit it with four torpedoes, sank it and escaped after counting 100 depth charges exploding around him from enemy destroyers, who were hunting him.

Such was the type of long-range reconnaissance that kept us informed of Japanese movements. Similar stalking of Japanese naval units provided advance information for the Battle of Leyte Gulf. Nearer to Marine objectives, however, another type of reconnaissance simplified our landing tasks.

It is difficult to put men and equipment ashore without prior knowledge of conditions on the beach you intend to use. All our island objectives were minutely photographed before an operation and all pertinent information regarding beaches and terrain was studied and classified before we moved. But air photographs can be deceptive. While they provide a map-like view of the objective, which can be enlarged many times to reveal enemy defenses and other details, they are flat pictures and do not indicate topography.

Until our Photographic Reconnaissance developed the technique of oblique pictures, submarine photographic reconnaissance was an essential preliminary to any landing. Submarines went close in to our planned objectives and made pictures of landing beaches through their periscopes. They were able to get in undetected and the pictures they provided gave what might be termed a Marine's eye view of the beach before he hit it. Periscope level, at which the pictures were taken, was just what the Marine would see from his amtrack or landing boat. Supplementing this, the submarines provided valuable tide and reef data.

We had excellent submarine photographs at Saipan, Guam and Tinian, taken two months before we landed by the USS *Greenling*. These proved unusually valuable because of the absence of low obliques from other sources, and technically they represented a great improvement over previous efforts. At Iwo Jima, we had photographic coverage made by the USS *Spearfish* three months earlier, but by this time aerial photography had been improved and supplanted the submarine photographs.

The submarines also stayed around to help the men who were softening up the objective with naval and air strikes preceding an operation. Many an airman owes his life to the rescue service operated by our submarines in enemy waters, a service carried to the very beaches of Japan. These undersea watchdogs followed the course of raids and a downed aviator, floating in the water, was not astonished when a submarine popped up nearby and took him on board. The airman knew he could count on this service and it was a great morale booster. Altogether, our submarines rescued 500 American and Allied airmen, often under heavy fire. During our joint surface and carrier strike on Truk on April 1, 1944, one submarine, the USS *Tang*, electrified the fleet by picking up 22 downed American aviators.

There were occasions when resource and quick thinking were necessary. During one of the Guam air strikes, an airman was shot down in shallow water and appeared to be a goner. He was close enough in shore to be a target for Japanese machine guns, and not far enough out for a rescue submarine, the USS *Stingray* (Commander S. C. Loomis), to surface and haul him on board.

This predicament did not daunt either the submarine captain or the airman. A telepathic liaison united them. The captain took his boat in as near to the beach as possible, until his periscope was showing. The airman saw it sticking out of the water and grabbed hold of it so that the submarine could tow him slowly out to sea where, in deep water, it surfaced and took him on board.

A picturesque chapter of the war involved the joint missions of the Marine Corps and the Submarine Force. When I was in the Caribbean before the war, we introduced submarines into one of the landing exercises to test the feasibility of landing scouts on hostile shores. In the graphically simulated conditions of the exercise, submarines put men ashore from rubber boats and the experiment indicated that this method could be employed in actual war.

In addition to the Marine Scouts, we formed Raider battalions, which did extremely useful work under hazardous conditions in the South Pacific. Selected men were specially trained and equipped for landing unobserved on enemy islands and performing all manner of tasks. These ranged from reconnaissance to surprise raids and attacks on enemy positions, demolition of installations and destruction of equipment.

The type of man chosen for this job had to be tough. Our four battalions of Marine Raiders, eventually incorporated into the 4th Marines, were the elite of toughness. A 20-mile march with a hundred pounds of equipment on their backs, followed by hand-to-hand combat with a knife, was sometimes their role. They were taught all the tricks of undercover combat, they could out-read a jungle-tracker and out-swim a fish.

The Raiders were a nightmare to the Japanese and engraved the name Marine on the memory of many a brown man. By the very nature of their organization, the Raiders were highly expendable.

In the South Pacific, they operated from nearby bases, or were put ashore in rubber boats from small craft that stole along the coast after dark. During the invasion of Attu, in the Aleutians, a company of Army Scouts was put ashore by the submarines *Nautilus* and *Narwhal*. These boats were available to us later in the Central Pacific.

These submarines have an interesting history. The *Nautilus* and the *Narwhal* were sister ships, and with the *Argonaut*, which we also used, were the largest submarines in the world, with the possible exception of a French boat and a few Japanese long-range boats used to supply their beleaguered bases in the South Pacific and take off important personnel after we bypassed and isolated these islands. The *Nautilus* and the *Narwhal*, 370 feet long, were built in 1930, when the navies of the world once again were getting lost in superlatives but the two submarines were never duplicated, principally because they were less maneuverable and less practical than smaller craft.

The *Argonaut* was a giant among submarines. Never has her like been seen, before or since, in our Navy. Three hundred and eighty feet long, she was built as a minelayer capable of carrying 60 mines. She was the last of the *Argonauts* pioneered by Simon

Lake, whose interest was attracted to underwater craft by Jules Verne's *Twenty Thousand Leagues Under the Sea*. Lake confessed that the French scientific romancer was "the director-general of my life," and the last *Argonaut* could have substituted for Verne's craft in size. She was commissioned in 1928 and came to her end in 1943, when she was reported missing in the Pacific.

Each of these three submarines had a complement of 80 men and were not only capacious undersea transports but were formidable ships, their armament including two six-inch guns, which could provide substantial fire cover for a landing.

The Marines first used submarines at Makin in the summer of 1942, on a raid which I deplored from the military viewpoint but which proved the value of underwater craft in an operation of this nature. This raid was made before I assumed command of the V Amphibious Corps at Pearl Harbor. Lieutenant Colonel Evans F. Carlson had organized the Marine Raiders into the 2nd Raider Battalion, with Major James Roosevelt as his second in command.

Carlson embarked two companies of Raiders at Pearl Harbor on the *Argonaut* and the *Nautilus* for the 2,000-mile trip to Makin. The raiding party was well armed, with 55 caliber anti-tank guns, radio and other equipment. The *Argonaut's* huge mine chamber provided space for storing this equipment and also for accommodating most of the troops. With the balance travelling on the *Nautilus*, the men reported a comfortable voyage.

Off Makin, the Raiders debarked in rubber boats and went ashore before dawn on August 17. The plan was to seize a few Japanese prisoners, destroy stores and installations and return to the waiting submarines. Essential surprise was achieved when these two underwater giants surfaced in the darkness and the men debarked. But after the Raiders got ashore without discovery a chance rifle shot disclosed their presence and the fighting started.

The two submarines gave them valuable support. With their six-inch guns, they shelled the lagoon and sank two Japanese ships. Ashore, Carlson's men were attacked by a truck convoy, which they destroyed with an anti-tank gun, and then converted it into an anti-aircraft gun when a flight of Japanese bombers appeared. One bomber landed in the lagoon beside a big Kawanashi flying boat, which is about the size of our PB4Y. When the Marines opened fire with their anti-tank gun, the bomber tried to take off but was shot down a few feet off the ground. The Kawanashi was a sitting duck in the lagoon and went up in flames.

The plan called for the Raiders to evacuate the island that night, but a high surf prevented all but a few of the rubber boats making the return trip to the submarines. We lost a lot of equipment and half the raiding party was left on the beach until Carlson could improvise means of getting his men back to their home craft.

Daylight brought more Japanese bombers, compelling the submarines to submerge, and disaster stared the expedition in the face. The Raiders had lost most of their weapons and food when their boats capsized in the high surf and they tried to swim home. They were virtually powerless but Carlson, with typical Marine resourcefulness, sent his men foraging and, since many of the Japanese garrison of 250 had been killed, they had little difficulty in destroying the enemy radio station and gasoline stores and also collecting food.

They also found a large outrigger canoe and that night Carlson lashed his few rubber boats to the native craft and embarked his men, including wounded. This curious armada made the entrance of the lagoon, where the waiting submarines picked them up and returned them to Pearl Harbor. Thus ended the longest submarine raiding expedition ever undertaken.

Makin echoed loudly at the war trials in the Pacific when the Japanese rear admiral in command of the island was hanged at Guam for the torture-murder of eight Marines unfortunately left behind after the Carlson raid.

We again resorted to underwater craft during the Gilberts operation and with greater success than in the spectacular but almost useless Makin raid. After the seizure of Tarawa and

233

Makin, the neighboring Apamama Atoll remained to be captured. In planning for the Gilberts, the idea occurred to me that we could land Scouts on the main island of the Apamama Atoll by submarine to reconnoiter enemy positions before committing any sizable force.

Marine Scouts from the V Corps Reconnaissance Company, under Captain James L. Jones, embarked on the *Nautilus* at Pearl Harbor for this operation. They had a tough trip down to the Gilberts because the *Nautilus* was attacked at night by our own task force, which put a shell hole in her main engine air induction line. The submarine was diving when she was hit and she went down to 300 feet before her commanding officer got her under control. Captain Jones told me later he would not be averse in the future to ride in a surface ship. The Scouts landed at night in rubber boats. The island was occupied by only a score or more Japanese, who held a strong machine gun position. Leaving a containing force to take care of this pocket until the main body of our men landed, the Scouts went on to seize the rest of the island and later the entire atoll at a cost of one killed and two wounded.

Apamama is probably the only atoll in history to be captured from a submarine. While the Scouts were ashore, the *Nautilus* stood off and shelled the main island with her six-inch guns, acting as a one-ship fire-support force. When Brigadier General Hermle landed with the 3rd Battalion, 6th Marines, the conquest had been completed because the Japanese in the machine gun pocket realized the hopelessness of any resistance and committed suicide.

Apamama was a brilliant sideshow, on a small scale but efficiently carried out by Marine and submarine teamwork. I have often thought that, in the war to come, when all our warships are nothing more than giant submersibles, forced down into the ocean depths to escape the power of atomic bombs and other missiles, all amphibious operations will follow the pattern of Apamama, with Marine assault forces submerging and landing on hostile shores from beneath the sea.

These joint missions of the Marines and the Submariners

gave the Corps a pretty good close-up of the men of the other service. The lads who manned the underwater craft were not supermen and possessed no supernatural qualities of heroism; they were top-notch American youths, well trained, well cared for and armed with superb weapons.

Charlie Lockwood was a neighbor of mine at Makalapa, the staff residential quarter at Pearl Harbor. Through my long friendship with this brusque and forthright submarine Admiral, who lived only for the gallant deeds of his Submariners, I came to understand their life of lonely heroism.

A remark of Lockwood's has become legendary in the Pacific. One of his best submarine commanders was detached for duty as an instructor at the Naval Academy. Before the officer left, Lockwood said to him, "Now don't teach those midshipmen that the Submariners won the war. We know there were other forces fighting there, too. But if they'd kept the surface forces and the fly-boys out of our patrol areas we would have won the war six months earlier."

Like Lockwood, I don't claim the Marines won the war. There were other forces there, too, but if we had had another division in 1941 we could have made certain the Submariners shortened the war by six months.

CHAPTER XII

M Y FINAL operation and the climactic event of my forty years in the Marine Corps was Iwo Jima, the last fortress barring our path to Tokyo. Okinawa still had to be captured before we possessed a staging area large enough to mount forces for the proposed invasion of Japan, but Iwo Jima was the seal placed on the complete and utter defeat of Japan, which started when we broke through the Marianas defense chain and seized Saipan.

When I look back at the Iwo Jima battle, fought on the barren, volcanic island only eight square miles in area, among caves, pillboxes, bunkers and blockhouses comprising the most ingenious, elaborate and indestructible system of underground fortifications ever devised, I ask myself the question many people have asked me: Did we have to take Iwo Jima?

Iwo Jima was the most savage and the most costly battle in the history of the Marine Corps. Indeed, it has few parallels in military annals. In the first five days we suffered casualties at an average of more than 1,200 a day. One out of every three Marines who set foot on the island was killed or wounded. In the first 50 hours, our casualties were more than 3,000, and in a campaign lasting 26 days, with many more days of mopping up, our total casualties were 21,558, of whom 5,521 were killed or died of wounds. Divisions ended the battle with less than 50 percent combat efficiency.

Yet my answer to the question, tremendous as was the price of victory, is definitely in the affirmative. In fighting a war to win, you cannot evaluate the attainment of an objective in terms of lives, or money, or material lost. I said "Yes" to this

236

question before we laid plans to take Iwo Jima, and I say "Yes" today.

Occupation of the island was a military necessity for several reasons, as I shall indicate. The conditions of its capture were dictated by the Japanese, not ourselves, and we took it the only possible way—by frontal attack, by interposing our own flesh and blood whenever armament did not suffice.

Japanese defense plans for Iwo Jima, using fortifications constructed in its black volcanic ash, among the ridges and cliffs and ravines, torn from Dürer engravings of the Inferno, were based upon a simple proposition. It was this: if the Marines ever landed on the island and attempted to take it, the enemy would exact every possible American life. He would compel us to use the utmost effort to gain our objective, and he would make victory a thing of frightening proportions, even if the entire Japanese garrison perished, which it did. This would be a manifestation of the Japanese will to die.

To accomplish our task on Iwo Jima, we had to produce men who were tougher than the Japanese, who could beat them at their own game, whose patriotism transcended that of the enemy, who also could reach the heights of *Bushido*, but in the American way, which is based on cool reason and methodical efficiency instead of blind obedience to the dictates of fanaticism.

The boys we took from the farm, the factory, the school, and the office became the best amphibious troops in the world. We put them ashore on an island where every yard of terrain was the front line and supplied them with the best weapons; we gave them all the naval and air support we could obtain. They landed to discover that eight months of intermittent bombardment, 72 days of daily land-based air raids, and three days of stepped-up shelling had hardly scratched the fortifications the Japanese had prepared against us.

So they took Iwo Jima the hard way, the Marine way, the way we had trained them to take it when everything else failed. The combination of Marine training and overwhelming matériel told. Even the Japanese realized that willingness to die for their

Emperor was not equal to better troops, superior firepower, and equipment. The little brown supermen proved a myth against our boys. Despite all the things we had read or learned about the physical endurance of the Japanese, they fell short in comparison with the Marines.

The Marines were trained amphibious troops, but it wasn't amphibious war that they fought on Iwo Jima. Nor was the island a Cannae or a Waterloo. The field was too small. Eighty thousand troops, American and Japanese, battled on eight square miles of island—10,000 men per square mile. Fighting among subterranean defenses, it was troglodyte war on a primitive level, with modern refinements that burned men to ashes, blasted through concrete masses, split the earth with seismic effect, and entombed thousands alive.

In my report I wrote: "The entire operation was fought on what was virtually the enemy's own terms." He paid the piper and called the tune. But we enjoyed a superiority derived from the experience of three years of successful campaigning, plus complete sea and air superiority. In the end, the roles were reversed. We called the tune for a macabre dance. A message left by four Japanese found dead in a cave on Iwo Jima read: "To the Americans: We have fortified this island for over a year, but we cannot win this war alone, with just the *Yamato* (warrior) spirit. We cannot match your superiority. There is no other road for us to follow but to die."

They voiced the recurrent theme of the operation and I stress it because without this background it is impossible to comprehend events on the island. Despite massive planning and preparation and the greatest display and employment of armed might the Pacific had seen, it was, reduced to its essence, the man on the beach with his rifle who won this island for us.

Although Iwo Jima was seldom mentioned on prewar maps, preparations for its conquest caused repercussions throughout the entire American global command. The expedition was mounted in the Central Pacific, at Hawaii and at our new Marianas bases, but nearly every theater was alerted and cooperated. Naval vessels were withdrawn from the European theater to support the operation: the Philippines and China commands provided support: as far away as India, American and Allied forces undertook air and anti-submarine missions integrated with the general plan.

From the United States came the most modern ships. Many of the vessels in the fleet of 800 that appeared off Iwo Jima at dawn on February 19, 1945, were being built or had not been commissioned six months before D-day. All but one of the transports that carried the Fourth and Fifth Divisions from Hawaii were brand new. Some of the smaller units were only in the blue print stage when we started our planning. For the reduction of this tiny, pear-shaped island, the call went out "Come the four corners of the world in arms," American arms, that is. And they came.

The Navy paid its first visit to Iwo Jima simultaneously with our landing on Saipan on June 15, 1944. In the great ocean-wide sweep to neutralize Japanese air and naval bases, Vice Admiral Mitscher took Task Force 58 and gave the Japanese a taste of what was coming to them, although at that time the Joint Chiefs of Staff had not definitely decided on the capture of the island. Even in June, 1944, Pete Mitscher commanded a great task force: seven battleships, 15 carriers, 21 cruisers, and 78 destroyers. In making a combined surface and air strike on Iwo Jima, our naval forces ventured closer to the shores of Japan than ever before that time.

With the Marianas in our possession, our strategy was oriented towards a direct assault on the home islands of Japan. We now had bases which brought the greater part of Japan within bombing range of our B-29's and the construction of big airfields, especially at Tinian, enabled us to carry the war to nearly every Japanese city. Up to the Marianas invasion, B-29's operated only from bases of the 20th Bomber Command in China and their range was restricted to the island of Kyushu, in Western Japan.

The initial study of Iwo Jima was made only in the light of its strategical importance, which far outranked its size. It is the main island in the Volcanos, part of the larger Bonin Islands, which in turn belong to a chain called Nanpo Shoto by the Japanese. These islands extend 700 miles in a north-south line from the entrance to Tokyo Bay almost to the Northern Marianas. The Japanese had fortified a number of them, principally in the southern part of the chain, and Iwo Jima, 670 miles from Tokyo, together with neighboring Chichi Jima, was the key to the entire defense system.

Any attempt to invade Japan would run afoul of this island, which had two excellent airfields, to which the Japanese ferried new planes as fast as we destroyed them, and a third field under construction. Iwo Jima lay there blocking our path. Its seizure was a necessary preliminary to any direct assault on Japan and it threatened our occupation of Okinawa, to the northwest, which, by 1945, was part of our grand strategy for closing in on Japan.

On November 24, 1944, B-29's from the newly established 21st Bomber Command in the Marianas made their first raid on Tokyo and, as the tempo of these raids increased, another conception developed regarding the importance of taking Iwo Jima. This island lay almost midway in the air path to Tokyo, and our flyers, on their long return missions to Japan, began to experience enemy interference from Iwo Jima. Planes from the island harassed them both coming and going, and radar on Iwo warned Tokyo in advance that the B-29's were coming.

It was a 16-hour round trip to Japan and, all things being equal, B-29's were able to make the flight comfortably. Despite their size and their gasoline capacity, if the B-29's carried a useful bomb load they had little margin of flight. Our losses from anti-aircraft and fighter interception began to mount and Iwo Jima became the thorn in the side of our flyers.

Crews of the B-29's, subjected to flights at very high altitudes, to long hours in the air, and to bad weather, began to crack under the strain. It was bad enough to escape enemy fighter attacks and anti-aircraft over the target, but the knowledge that having dropped their bombs and strained their fuel to the utmost, the enemy was waiting for them halfway back to their base, started to tell on our flyers. It was recognized that Army Air Force morale on Tinian and Saipan was sagging badly.

No organization can stand inordinate losses over a prolonged period, and these conditions threatened the success of our bombing program.

Accordingly, the capture of Iwo Jima assumed new importance. It was imperative for us to remove the threat to our B-29's, acquire an advance base from which we could operate fighter protection for our planes flying over Japan, and also emergency landing fields for crippled B-29's on their homeward flight. Hitherto, damaged planes or those suffering engine or fuel trouble had only one resort if they failed to make their base: ditch in the sea. Many flyers and planes were lost this way.

We met all these conditions when we captured Iwo Jima. We removed the obstacle to our capture of Okinawa and our advance on Japan. We destroyed the Iwo Jima garrison, taking only 217 prisoners, most of whom were badly wounded. We started building up the island as an air base from the day we captured the first of its three airfields. Two weeks after D-day, while we were fighting for our lives through the central belt of Japanese defenses, the first disabled B-29 landed on Motoyama Airfield Number One, which the Seabees had repaired and lengthened.

Before the fighting was over and while we were still killing Japanese in their caves at the northern end of the island, 40 B-29's had landed. According to Army figures, in a few months 1,449 B-29's with crews totalling 15,938 men, had fallen back on emergency facilities at Iwo. By the end of the war, Air Force estimates declared, more than 20,000 U. S. lives had been saved because Iwo was ours. Possession of this base meant another 5,000 pounds of weight per plane, which could be taken on in bomb load or fuel, but more valuable was the inestimable safety factor added to B-29 flights.

Simultaneously, Iwo Jima was developed as a fighter base. Long before the last shot was fired on the island Army P-51 Mustangs were based there and were flying escort missions, greatly improving the efficiency of our heavy bombers. Later, the Mustangs were making fighter sweeps over Japan. Iwo Jima was a base beyond compare in our gigantic raids that wrecked Japan's cities, knocked out her war potential, and helped bring the enemy to her knees. Twenty-one thousand dead and wounded Marines made these things possible.

Planning for the operation started on a top echelon plane early in October, 1944, before the first B-29 raid on Japan. Admiral Nimitz issued a directive again designating Admiral Spruance overall commander, with Kelly Turner as commander, Amphibious Force, and myself as commander of Expeditionary Troops. Under Major General Harry Schmidt, troops belonging to the V Amphibious Corps were assigned to the operation. These were the Fourth Division, under Major General Clifton B. Cates, and the Fifth Division, under Major General Keller E. Rockey. The Third Division, under Major General Graves B. Erskine, was to be held in reserve. The Iwo Jima operation was to be completely Naval in the assault phase, with the Marines turning over the island to the Army after its capture.

Immediately following the Nimitz directive, I received the Joint Staff study and on October 14, as Commanding General, Fleet Marine Force, I issued a directive to Harry Schmidt designating him Landing Force Commander and directing him to prepare plans. It was two months before they were completed, because alterations had to be made in the original Joint Staff study in the light of intelligence we were receiving from constant air reconnaissance of the objective.

One of the changes concerned the Third Division. It had been proposed to hold the division in reserve, alerted at Guam. On further study, I considered it much sounder for this division to arrive with the other troops in the target area on D-day, available as a floating reserve. This decision proved sound because we ran into a larger garrison and far stronger defenses than we had anticipated. Instead of 14,000 Japanese we then believed to be holding the island, the enemy garrison totalled 22,000.

Meanwhile, a softening-up process of unparalleled intensity was proceeding. Starting with Pete Mitscher's strike on June 15, naval units made frequent surface and air strikes. Our newly arrived B-29's made Iwo Jima their target long before they started work on Tokyo. From the Marianas, planes of the Seventh Air

Force and the Strategic Air Force furnished most of the final 72 days' bombing. Every type of bomber, escorted by fighters, made the daily journey to Iwo Jima. All Army air bases were alerted to the task. Sometimes two or three raids a day, plus harassing attacks at night, were made, and these were interspersed with surface and carrier attacks. When Navy guns and Navy and Army bombers finished their task, a Marine Air Group went in with rockets. The Japanese, who didn't have a minute's peace, day or night, nevertheless built while we bombed. At the beginning of the aerial "softening" we could count 450 major defensive installations on Iwo: three days before we landed there were 750.

Chichi Jima and Haha Jima, two neighboring islands converted into air bases by the Japanese, also were attacked, but the focal point was always Iwo Jima. In our first big raid on December 8, 82 B-29's, 102 B-24's (Liberators), and 28 P-38's (Lightnings) dropped 800 tons of bombs. The Seventh Air Force dropped 5,800 tons in 2,700 sorties. In one square mile of Iwo Jima, a photograph showed 5,000 bomb craters.

All this added up to a terrific total of destructive effort, which the uninitiated might expect to blast any island off the military map, level every defense, no matter how strong, and wipe out the garrison. But nothing of the kind happened. Like the worm which becomes stronger the more you cut it up, Iwo Jima thrived on our bombardment. The airfields were kept inactive by our attacks and some installations were destroyed but the main body of defenses not only remained practically intact but strengthened markedly.

The closer we got to D-day, the greater was the anti-aircraft coming from the island. It seemed impossible that our bombing and shelling could be having so little effect. But that is what happened. Colonel Dudley S. Brown, my Chief of Staff, observed in his report on the operation: "The prolonged aerial bombardment of Iwo Jima, which was a daily occurrence for over 70 days, had no appreciable effect in the reduction of the enemy's well prepared and heavily fortified defensive installations."

My own study of early air photographs indicated that a situation of an incredible nature existed on the island. It was plain that Iwo Jima had fortifications the like and extent of which we had never encountered. Mindful of Tarawa, where most of the fortifications were above ground and were still standing when the Marines landed, my opinion was that far more naval gunfire was needed on an island five times the size of Tarawa, with many more times the number of defenses, most of them deep underground.

I could not forget the sight of Marines floating in the lagoon or lying on the beaches at Tarawa, men who died assaulting defenses which should have been taken out by naval gunfire. At Iwo Jima, the problem was far more difficult. If naval guns could not knock out visible defenses, how could they smash invisible defenses except by sheer superabundance of fire?

My staff, my division commanders and I agreed unanimously that in spite of considerable naval and air preparation, an additional long period of intense naval gunfire was needed as a prerequisite to our landing at Iwo Jima. The original provision was for eight days' fire by a cruiser division, plus three days by old battleships. A request from Harry Schmidt, which I transmitted to Kelly Turner on October 24, was for ten days' bombardment by a cruiser division and three battleships. This, we had decided, would prepare the beaches adequately for our landing.

Turner replied that this was impossible because of "limitations on the availability of ships, difficulties of ammunition replacement, and the loss of surprise." By the last remark I inferred he meant that we would be giving the Japanese advance notice of our intentions. Turner also informed us that the original eight days' cruiser bombardment had been abandoned and, instead, the division would bombard Iwo Jima at irregular intervals, starting December 15, and we would receive only three days' bombardment by heavy ships.

On November 8, I forwarded to Turner another proposal from Schmidt that the Navy should provide nine days' bombardment. Two weeks later he replied, not only completely rejecting our request but definitely confirming that there would be only three days. However, he promised that the bombardment would be the best possible, taking into account factors of ammunition supply, time and subsequent fire requirements.

We appeared to have run up against an irrevocable decision. Three days were totally inadequate but the decision was out of our hands, although we had presented all conceivable evidence, backed by photographic evidence of the island's defenses. The lack of naval gunfire, so vital to the success of a landing, struck at the very heart of our enterprise. Therefore, we made one last effort to alleviate a shocking situation. We had to haggle like horse traders, balancing irreplaceable lives against replaceable ammunition. I was never so depressed in my life.

On November 24, Harry Schmidt asked for just one more day's bombardment, making four instead of three. I favorably endorsed his request and forwarded the letter to Turner, who approved to a limited degree, and forwarded the letter to Spruance. Turner favored the new suggestion, provided there was no objection based on the general strategical situation.

Spruance rejected this plea on these very grounds. Part of the overall plan was a fast carrier strike by Task Force 58 on the Tokyo area, to coincide with the three days' bombardment of Iwo Jima, and Spruance had set his heart on making this strike the most impressive naval effort of the war. After the strike, Task Force 58 was to return to Iwo Jima to provide support for our landing and then leave for another strike at Japan, to neutralize any enemy air interference that might have developed.

The reasons adduced by Spruance for his rejection were:

That the initial surface bombardment must be simultaneous with the initial carrier attack on the Tokyo area, and that, if continuation of the carrier strikes beyond two days were neither desirable nor necessary, the enemy could then recover early enough to initiate threatening air attacks at the objectives on D-day.

That the shore-based air attack to be provided could be considered at least as effective as the recommended additional day of surface ship bombardment.

That there would be no opportunity for replacement of naval ammunition, and that there was therefore a limit to the amount of ammunition that could be made available for preliminary bombardment, allowing sufficient ammunition for D-day.

To me, naval insistence upon the priority of the strike against Japan at the cost of fire support for our assault on Iwo Jima was incomprehensible. To take the better part of the fleet away ignored the principal aims of our mission. It simply weakened the power we could use at Iwo Jima. To my way of thinking—and I am sure I was right—the operation was planned for the capture of Iwo Jima, but Spruance permitted the attack on Japan to overshadow the real objective.

While danger from the air did exist, there was no Japanese naval threat great enough to require him to send so many heavy ships with Task Force 58. The naval threat, which was so vivid when we started planning for Iwo Jima, vanished before we exchanged messages dealing with more gunfire. The Japanese Fleet was practically destroyed in the Battle of Leyte Gulf fought from October 23 to 26.

Limited, against our better judgment, to only three days' preliminary bombardment there seemed nothing to do but make the best of the situation. However, in a final effort to utilize the proffered gunfire to the best advantage, Harry Schmidt forwarded to me a final proposal based on a careful study of the bombardment plan. Dated January 2, 1945, it stated that he believed the preliminary gunfire to be inadequate for destroying targets flanking and at the rear of the landing beaches. He suggested that either the time for preliminary bombardment be increased or that fire be concentrated on the main landing beaches, generally ignoring the other parts of the island.

In other words, if he couldn't have all the fire power he wanted, he preferred it in the place where he needed it most. Fire poured on the landing beaches and on the airfield behind (Motoyama Number One) would be the most efficient way of using the limited amount allowed for our landing.

In his reply, Turner reiterated Spruance's reasons for disapproving of Schmidt's proposal. He said that he did not consider concentration of fire on the landing beaches a sound plan because other areas would receive too light fire coverage.

Thus were we defeated—a group of trained and experienced land fighters, our full realization of the necessity for naval gunfire based on many previous island operations—again overridden by the naval mind. Finding ourselves in this dilemma, we had tried our best to enlighten the high command, feeling that our judgment would be respected, but naval expediency won again.

Our troubles were not at an end. Due to a change of plans by Spruance, the ships allocated to the pre-D-day bombardment were unavailable and substitutions were made. We also were robbed of the services of the USS Washington and the USS North Carolina, two of our 16-inch-gun ships originally assigned to the niggardly allotment of fire but withdrawn at the last minute to join Task Force 58 and provide anti-aircraft fire. These two battleships were to have supplied one day's pre-landing fire with their powerful guns.

Turner protested to his chief regarding this sudden change. He pointed out to Spruance that fire support already had been seriously diminished and would be reduced dangerously without these two ships. They were much more valuable prior to D-day than later, because only a small amount of battleship fire would be needed after the landing.

Spruance was apologetic for this disruption, but he insisted that the importance of the strike was so great that he must give Task Force 58 all possible assistance to insure a successful outcome.

The Admiral stated he had informed Rear Admiral William H. P. Blandy, commanding the Amphibious Support Force entrusted with the bombardment, that our landing might be deferred if, on the evening prior to D-day, the required reduction of targets on Iwo Jima had not been accomplished. Spruance added, "I regret this confusion caused in your carefully laid plans, but I know you and your people will get away with it."

We appreciated his confidence in our ability to "get away with it" but this pat on the back was cold comfort against the loss of great modern ships, with 16-inch guns we knew could rip apart Japanese pillboxes and tear the heart out of concrete bunkers. I reflected ruefully that naval thinking had not changed in the 25 years since I was at the Naval War College.

Nine days before we landed, the situation produced the

following observation by my Chief of Staff, Colonel Brown, who wrote me:

> In view of the fact that the ships . . . are not now available for the pre-D-day support of the landing force, it is the opinion of the undersigned that the naval gunfire support has been so weakened as to jeopardize the success of the operation. Certainly, under the present plan of support, assuming that the initial landings are successful, the cost in Marines killed will be far greater than under the plan agreed upon before our departure from Pearl Harbor.

Brown's assessment was correct: we did lose more men than we had anticipated and one of the reasons was that sufficient neutralizing effect had not been achieved on the island.

My Chief of Staff recommended that D-day be postponed to allow the maximum expenditure of ammunition from the bombarding ships. This postponement also had the approval of Spruance, who passed on the final decision to Blandy. But we could delay no longer. The operation already had suffered two postponements. Originally, the target date was set for January 20. Then it was moved to February 3, because General MacArthur would not release the naval ships we required, which had been supporting his Luzon operation. The General-Admiral clung to the ships, delaying the Iwo Jima operation despite the fact that his campaign was almost completed and the Japanese Combined Fleet no longer existed to harass him.

MacArthur's withholding of these ships and the two postponements of D-day threatened to retard our offensive against Japan. The invasion of Okinawa had been set for March or, at the very latest, April. It was a race against time to reduce Iwo Jima. In fact, Kelly Turner, who was to command the Amphibious Force at Okinawa, left Iwo Jima before the island was secured in order to complete final plans for the next objective. Eventually, one ship did arrive from MacArthur's theater to join in the bombardment of Iwo Jima somewhere around D-day but that is the only one I can recall.

Therefore, it was imperative that we should not deviate from the final target date of February 19, with or without our desired gunfire support. On the eve of D-day, a study of photographs and reports indicated that the main defenses on and around the eastern beaches, where we were to land, had been destroyed or heavily damaged. Blandy, upon whom Spruance had thrust the responsibility of deciding, informed Kelly Turner that he believed a successful landing could be made the next morning, as planned. Ironically, he admitted that the bad weather had prevented him from expending his full allowance of ammunition and with an additional day of bombardment he could find and destroy many more enemy defenses. But the die was cast and the Marines went ashore.

The forces I commanded in the assault on Iwo Jima were the best equipped hitherto employed in the Pacific. Nothing was lacking in arms, mechanical equipment and supplies, and we were supported—somewhat less than we desired—by the most powerful navy force that ever sailed the seas. All of the latest developments in guns, tanks, amphibious craft and boats were reflected in the operation. We used 650,000 tons of supplies at Iwo Jima and 600 planes were available.

Excluding Task Force 58, which swept the seas, raided the Japanese homeland, and later supported us at Iwo Jima, 485 assault and garrison ships were employed. Altogether 110,000 men, of whom 70,000 were Marine assault troops, were transported to the island from points as far distant as Hawaii, 3,700 miles away. The Third and Fourth Divisions were veterans of many actions in the Central and South Pacific, and the newly organized Fifth Division, from Camp Pendleton, California, was built around veterans of the South Pacific. No troops in any previous operation had been so well rehearsed as these three Marine Divisions, which trained and rehearsed at their Pacific bases, and rehearsed again en route to the target, to make sure that every detail was completely understood.

I sailed from Pearl Harbor on the USS *Eldorado*, Turner's new command ship, which replaced the less modern *Rocky Mount*, full of confidence in the force I commanded but acutely aware of the difficulties of the mission. Latest intelligence told of the strength of the island's defenses, which remained somewhat obscure because our flyers reported few visible targets and few visible Japanese. When flyers did catch a sight of the enemy, he disappeared in the ground like a gopher, indicating that a network of subterranean fortifications existed in the volcanic rock.

My eagerness to come to grips again with the enemy, after the long interval since the Marianas, buoyed up my spirits. During this interval the Palau operation had been conducted successfully against bitter opposition and again it was proved that the Japanese were no match for the Marines. A short time before I sailed for Iwo Jima, I went into the hospital at Base 8, Pearl Harbor. A slight hernia was troubling me and the doctors said that a brief hospitalization would put me back in good physical shape for the work ahead.

My stay in the hospital was brightened by a romance, in which I played a part. One of the nurses—an attractive, brown-eyed girl—told me that she was going to marry a Marine officer the following Saturday. I congratulated her and she gave me the officer's name and his outfit. My heart sank. It was Wednesday and I knew that the Marine's outfit was under secret orders to sail for Guam on Friday. The officer obviously had not known that when he made arrangements for the wedding.

Stretched in my bed, watching the ships in the harbor below, I mulled over the problem and decided that the war would go along just the same if that Marine and his nurse were married on Saturday. So I called up the Operations Officer and told him to take the young man's name off the sailing list. "Ops" was a trifle surprised when I called. He probably didn't understand that the Commanding General was at the other end of the line and pointed out that since the young Marine was under orders to go, go he must. I finally convinced the Operations Officer of my identity and the name was taken off the sailing list. On Saturday morning, I gave the bride away at the wedding ceremony. It made me feel so good that the doctors were astonished by my rapid recovery.

At Saipan, the *Eldorado* took on board a distinguished passenger. Secretary of the Navy James Forrestal was in the Pacific at the time and he decided to accompany the expedition to Iwo

Jima to see the Marines in action and get first-hand knowledge of combined operations. I believe this was the first time in the history of the Marine Corps that a Secretary of the Navy went to war with his amphibious troops and, after my experience with Secretary Forrestal, I hoped that other civilian members of our Government would see the services under actual wartime conditions, instead of sitting back in Washington, relying upon official dispatches and their service aides to enlighten them. How much sense of reality is lost between a battleground and a glistening Washington desk!

The Secretary's presence was an inspiration to the Navy and the Marines. At first, the news of his arrival among us was not believed. On board ship he wore khaki like a Navy officer and the fact that he had no insignia did not make him conspicuous. Civilian war correspondents on board dressed similarly and the Secretary might have been taken for one of them. When he went ashore, we outfitted him in Marine utility greens—which I inherited when he left. We were proud to have him wear the uniform of the Marine Corps.

Although Mr. Forrestal showed keen interest in all phases of our work, he never intruded. Rather, he quietly fitted himself into ship routine and operation organization, studying details and absorbing information. His four years as Under Secretary and a year as Secretary had given him mastery of the multifarious ramifications of the Navy he controlled. He astonished me with his knowledge of combined operations and his grasp of technical matters.

During the voyage, the Secretary often came to my cabin to discuss some new angle that appealed to him and we talked for hours on end. Sometimes this discussion which, on the basis of knowledge and understanding, progressed on a level of equality rather than from the standpoint of a veteran Marine officer and amphibious expert trying to instruct a civilian Cabinet officer, took place as we walked the *Eldorado's* decks. From his conversation, it was evident the Secretary had delved deeply into the theory and practice of combined operations.

In discussions in my cabin concerning landing movements,

Mr. Forrestal revealed a perfect comprehension of the value of timing, the spacing of assault waves, and the importance of naval gunfire in the coordinated scheme. He examined with a keen eye the Marine staff lay-out and was constantly in and out of the operations room, reading the action reports after the Iwo Jima battle started. He was fascinated with the communications setup on the *Eldorado* which, with its radio, teletypes and other equipment, was indeed wondrous to behold.

"Mr. Secretary," I said to him one day, "you missed your calling. You should have been a Marine. You would have had a great career."

"Holland," he replied, "I did once consider that but banking caught me first. Anyhow, thanks for the compliment."

CHAPTER XIII

T HE EVE OF D-DAY at Iwo Jima found me unable
to suppress a deep emotional surge. The imminence of action
and the responsibility for the most appalling operation we had
yet undertaken weighed heavily. I was charged with the capture
of an island whose possession was indispensable to our assault
on Japan, and it was my last command.

Marines were to be employed at Okinawa but I knew this
would be an Army operation, owing to the preponderance of
Army troops. The invasion of Japan would be spearheaded by
Marines, but there, too, the Army would be numerically domi-
nant, under General MacArthur. There would be no more
strictly Marine combat commands in the Pacific. Furthermore,
I was approaching my 63rd birthday and I was the first to realize
I should move aside for younger men. Hence, victory at Iwo
Jima would be the climax, emotionally and militarily speaking,
to my four decades as a servant of the Government of the United
States.

The gravity of the coming battle filled me with apprehension. The man in the front line is blessed with a sense of im-
mediacy. He knows only the danger directly in front of him. The
general, however, knows far in advance what is to come and the
picture is always there, spread before him. He goes into battle
with the price of victory already calculated in human lives. This
knowledge is a terrible burden, never to be shaken off, night or
day. There is no escape.

I felt çertain we would lose 15,000 men at Iwo Jima. This
number was the absolute minimum calculated in our plans made
at Pearl Harbor, although some of my officers wistfully predicted

a lower figure. So far as the Marines were concerned, we had made every preparation humanly possible to capture the island as expeditiously and as economically as possible. We were to land 60,000 assault troops, and the estimate that one in every four would be dead or wounded never left my mind.

I was not afraid of the outcome of the battle. I knew we would win. We always had. But contemplation of the cost in lives caused me many sleepless nights. My only source of comfort was in reading of the tribulations of leaders described in the Bible. Never before had I realized the spiritual uplift and solace a man on the eve of a great trial receives from the pages of that book.

I prayed to God that night. I am a Methodist, but I have always been able to find comfort in the literature of the Roman Catholic Church. I read a passage from Father Joseph F. Stedman's *Daily Readings,* and it calmed me.

To the Marine, there is a universality of religion transcending sect and schism. It is based on comradeship in arms. I have seen Protestants at Catholic mass and Jewish chaplains ministering to Gentiles. For many years, I have worn around my neck certain Catholic medals, including a Saint Christopher blessed by Pope Pius X and given to me by a priest in San Francisco. He took the medal from his own neck to hang it around mine, praying that it would guard me against all the dangers and perils of the unknown.

The day before D-day was Sunday. Choked up as they were on the eve of their Gethsemane, the Marines on board the *Eldorado* were deeply moved by a little blue card distributed by the ship's Chaplain, Curt Junker. It contained the words of the following prayer by Sir Thomas Astlie, one of Cromwell's generals, written in 1645 before he went into battle:

Lord I shall be verie busy this day:
I may forget Thee, but doe not Thou forget me.

The task force arrival was timed for just before dawn in order that the transports in our column could take up their assigned stations in time to launch the waves according to schedule.

Iwo's commander was Lieutenant Colonel Tadamichi Kuribayashi, who headed the Ogasawara Forces, as the Japanese units
were called in the Volcano Islands. Major General Sadasu Senda
commanded the Second Mixed Brigade, 109th Division. The
naval defense force and a naval air force were under Rear Admiral Toshinosuke Ichimaru.

Of all our adversaries in the Pacific, Kuribayashi was the
most redoubtable. Some Japanese island commanders were just
names to us and disappeared into the anonymity of enemy
corpses left for burial parties. Kuribayashi's personality was
written deep in the underground defenses he devised for Iwo
Jima. He held us at arm's length until we cornered him and the
remnants of his force in the caves of Kitano Point. Iwo Jima was
notable in that organized resistance did not collapse after the
first few days, but continued to the end.

As one of my officers fervently remarked, "Let's hope the
Japs don't have any more like him."

Before he came to die on Iwo Jima, Kuribayashi had been
a cavalryman who broadened his training to include a knowledge
of all arms. Although I never saw him, and a minute search of
the caves where he made his last stand failed to produce his body,
we got his biography from Radio Tokyo. A short, paunchy
man in his middle fifties, he had commanded a cavalry
regiment at Lake Nomanhon, on the Manchurian border,
during the indecisive "undeclared" Russo-Japanese War of
1938–39.

Then Kuribayashi commanded the elite Imperial Guard in
Tokyo, which gained him an audience with Emperor Hirohito.
Under the Japanese scheme of command, Iwo Jima came within
the Tokyo defense limits and he started to fortify the island
formidably when we invaded Saipan. He took with him to the
island a number of cave specialists and they created the intricate
scheme of underground fortifications which our bombardment
could not reach.

Kuribayashi's strictly business qualities were reflected in
other matters besides his defenses. He must have been a martinet.
When we sailed from Pearl Harbor, we took with us rations for

the 1,500 civilians we expected to find on Iwo Jima. These rations were unnecessary. Months before we attacked, Kuribayashi evacuated to Japan all civilians from the sulphur fields and the garrison. He wanted no civilian hindrance. To him, Iwo Jima was solely a military base.

He permitted none of the pleasures of Japanese camp life to undermine the morale of his men. No women were found on the island. Although he pledged his men to a typical Japanese oath—to die for their Emperor and take ten Americans with them in death—he permitted no mad charges inspired by the *saké* bottle. We found no large stocks of liquor on Iwo Jima, as on Guam and Saipan. As a matter of fact, I fail to recall that anyone picked up a single bottle on the island.

Off Iwo Jima that cold February morning I examined again the air photographs which showed the island literally pockmarked by bomb and shell holes. Many big gun emplacements had been taken out but I was not surprised at the Japanese batteries shooting up a heavy cruiser as well as a dozen of our gunboats prior to our landing. If anybody had learned anything from our bombardment it was the enemy, who had gone underground so far that he was secure from 2,000-pound bombs. Some of my divisional generals thought that I was too pessimistic that morning, but they realized later that my fears had not been exaggerated.

Dawn broke for us favorably on D-day. The weather, after several stormy days, was clear; the rough seas subsided; surf conditions were as good as could be expected on an exposed rock. Iwo Jima had only two beaches, one east and the other west of the narrow isthmus connecting Mount Suribachi with the broader part of the island. Both beaches—coarse, black volcanic ash, like gravel—made for poor landing conditions but we made the best of two bad choices when we selected the eastern.

As the Marines debarked from transports and prepared to land at 0900, the main batteries of the battleships and heavy ships crashed on the island in a two hours' bombardment that blotted out all light "like a hurricane eclipse of the sun." Task Force 58 had returned from the Tokyo strike and joined the brazen chorus at least briefly. On the *Eldorado*, we were almost deafened by the roar, and under the fire of so many guns the island smoked as though the dormant Suribachi had sprung into life against us. Gunboats went close in and delivered a rocket barrage on the landing beach; this was followed by an air strike on the flanks. Heavy bombers from the Marianas were scheduled to bomb the island, but only a third of the assigned planes arrived; the rest, they told us, were held up by bad weather at their base.

Half an hour before the Marines hit the beach in their amphibious tanks and tractors, naval gunfire was resumed and for the first time in the Pacific we employed a rolling naval barrage. Starting at the edge of the beach, naval guns placed their fire 200 yards inland, and as the Marines began to land the fire was lifted in 200-yard jumps ahead of the men. This scheme proved highly successful.

The Japanese lay stunned under the terrific explosive shock of our naval gunfire, and in contrast to Tarawa and Saipan our first waves got ashore with little opposition until they advanced 350 yards inland. However, it wasn't long before the enemy recovered and when our barrage lifted, his artillery, mortar and small-arms fire began to fall among the boat waves. This fire came from Suribachi on the left and from higher ground on the right, well registered and pre-sited. A once strong line of pillboxes, some of which were still standing despite the weight of metal dropped on them, took a heavy toll of Marines on their way up the incline to the airfield, and when our tanks made the top they ran into extensive minefields, which caused many wrecks.

The nature of the Iwo Jima terrain was as obstructive as the Japanese. A series of terraces leading to the airfield made exceptionally hard going. Marine field shoes sank deep in the volcanic ash and men floundered their way to the top. Supply-laden amtracks and DUKW's bogged down. Tanks were mired in the ash, unable to move, thus becoming sitting ducks for the Japanese. Until we got wire mats down and bulldozers ashore to make a semblance of a road system, the only practicable vehicle was the light amphibian tractor known as the "Weasel." All our heavy equipment was under fire by the Japanese and in two days thirty percent of our tanks were out of action.

After D-day a rising surf played the devil with our boats. To hold our LSM's and LST's, we had to anchor them to tractors and tanks. The Higgins boats, smaller and more vulnerable in the angry ocean, got caught in the surf up the black beach, and were swamped by the powerful ebb. And as soon as one ship nosed into the ash, it came under enemy fire. Our losses of equipment were frightening; the beach soon looked like a row of frame houses in a tornado.

Despite the increasing volume of enemy fire which poured on the beach from every point, in an hour and a half we got eight battalions of troops ashore, with a large number of tanks. By mid-afternoon, the tank battalions of two divisions, though depleted by losses, were ashore; elements of two artillery battalions followed. Japanese fire mounted in intensity as the day wore on, but a few guns of our artillery were in action by the late afternoon.

By nightfall we had secured our beachhead, expecting to land the rest of the equipment the next day. From an unloading point of view, D-day was fortunate because the relatively light surf was in our favor. But the next day, and on succeeding days, the weather changed and unloading conditions on the beach were dreadful. It became a fight against the sea, the surf, the volcanic ash and the Japanese, all joined in one colossal alliance against us. We thanked God for that D-day calm before the ocean's storm.

The result of the first day's operation was satisfactory. On the right, the Fourth Division had suffered heavily and, although reserves were thrown in, the Division was unable to improve on the initial gains of the morning. It was held up on the right flank by resistance from a piece of high ground named Quarry Ridge, after a quarry gouged out of the cliff rising sharply from the water's edge, and strongly defended by the Japanese. One battalion was depleted 50 percent. One company lost all seven of its officers before dark fell. But we held the tip of Motoyama Airfield One, though the fire on our beachhead troops was murderous.

On the left, the Fifth Division, fighting on better terrain and against lighter fire, made greater progress. Striking across the 800-yard isthmus, the Fifth reached the western shore of Iwo Jima by noon and three hours later had crossed the southern end of the airfield. As a result, Suribachi was isolated and the Japanese forces were split. The road was clear for the capture of the volcano which, with its deep patriotic appeal, was to become the crowning episode of the Pacific war.

The story of Suribachi is too familiar to be repeated. The world knows how the Marine patrol scaled the mountain face and planted the Stars and Stripes on the summit, producing the greatest photograph of this war and, perhaps, of any war. It has inspired bond drives, tableaux and postage stamps. The men who raised the flag on Suribachi will be remembered in our history as long as patriotic American hearts beat warm and proud, although only a few are alive today.

But the capture of Mount Suribachi did not just happen. It was planned as early as December, when we started to study the problems of Iwo Jima. Suribachi was our first big target. The brown, knobby 556-foot rock at the southern end of this island of eight square miles commanded our landing beach. Long plumes of steam rose from its southern and seaward sides, heat and fumes permeated its recesses, but they did not prevent the Japanese tunnelling in and converting the "Hot Rock" into a powerful fortress. While the enemy held that position, his guns not only covered our landing beach but he had an observation post of great value to batteries in other parts of the island. The success of our entire assault depended upon the early capture of that grim, smoking rock.

For the job we selected the 28th Regiment, Fifth Division, commanded by Colonel Harry Liversedge—called "Harry the Horse" by his men. Perhaps other officers and other regiments could have done the Suribachi job, but both Harry Schmidt and Major General Keller E. Rockey felt that Harry Liversedge was the man and the 28th was the regiment. He had a good record in the South Pacific for tackling tough assignments and, although Iwo Jima was no tropical, jungle-covered island, this qualification was vital.

The attack on Suribachi started on the morning of February 20, the day after we landed, but it was four days before we gained the summit. The main defenses were a series of mutually supporting concrete pillboxes ringing the base. They were close enough together to make an almost complete wall and this was supported by guns in caves, machine gun pits, trenches, and other obstacles among the scrub growth and the rocks surrounding the base.

The main problem was to break through that ring of pillboxes and it was a Herculean task. Tanks, flame throwers, artillery, and demolition charges were used. From out at sea, warships dropped their shells, sometimes only a hundred yards ahead of the Marines. Gunboats came in as close as 200 yards and smashed at machine gun positions; air strikes and rocket attacks were all thrown into the task. The attacking troops met with heavy resistance from pillboxes, caves in the rock, and enemy artillery and mortars in the northern part of the island, which laid down terrific fire from a variety of weapons we had not experienced before. These latter included giant mortars, the largest of which fired a 320-mm. shell that "made a noise like a P-61 night fighter," as one Marine said. The big mortar shells flew right over the island and dropped into the sea, but smaller calibers caused us many casualties.

Still Liversedge's men continued their slow but definite advance, methodically reducing the fortifications at the base of Suribachi with flame throwers and demolitions, gradually working their way around until the volcano was completely surrounded and it was possible to make an attack up the north face, which Liversedge considered the feasible route. Other paths had been worn by the Japanese but shelling and bombing had completely obliterated them.

Once the base defenses had been destroyed, there was little opposition left in the garrison on the rock. On the morning of the fourth day, four men climbed to the summit and were followed by Lieutenant H. G. Schrier, leading a 40-man patrol from Company "E", 2nd Battalion, 28th Regiment, who reached the northeast rim. The only resistance came from across the rim, where they killed several Japanese. The flag was raised at 1037 on February 23 and this vision of triumph had an electrifying effect on all our forces ashore and afloat. We were in a mood for victory and this glorious spectacle was the spark.

The raising of the flag high atop Suribachi was one of the proud moments of my life. No American could view this symbol of heroism and suffering without a lump in his throat. By a happy circumstance, I was standing beside Secretary of the Navy Forrestal when the tiny speck of red, white and blue broke and fluttered on the gaunt crest of the volcano. Turning to me, the Secretary said gravely, "Holland, the raising of that flag on Suribachi means a Marine Corps for the next 500 years."

The night before Suribachi was taken, we were told by Liversedge of the final plans for its conquest. Secretary Forrestal said he would like to go ashore next morning and witness the last stage of the Suribachi battle. I was not pleased at the suggestion, in view of the dangers of the beach, but I acquiesced. Wearing a steel helmet and a life jacket, the Secretary boarded a boat with Vice Admiral Louis E. Denfeld and Rear Admiral Mills. I was accompanied by Mac Asbill. Before leaving the *Eldorado*, I extracted a promise from Mr. Forrestal that he would take orders from me. He vowed he wouldn't expose himself too prominently.

Our boat touched shore just after the flag was raised. The cry went up from all quarters, "There goes the flag!" I could see the tiny figures of the patrol on top of the volcano and more tiny, agile figures climbing up the side. The backs of the climbers glistened white in the morning sun. An officer explained to me that the men had painted fluorescent panels on their uniforms to distinguish them from the Japanese. I knew that the battle area at the base of Suribachi was so confined that we had to tape out lines as a guide to our planes but those glistening panels on the uniforms of the men climbing the volcano seemed even more resourceful.

The beach wreckage made it difficult to find a place to land.

Small boats, tanks, tractors, DUKW's, and other massed items of equipment which had been knocked out by Japanese fire or the satanic surf were strewn down to the water's edge, and under the battering of the waves were sinking deep into the ash. Great waves raced up the beach and boats strained at their hawsers. At first glance, it seemed that the beachhead was in a state of complete confusion with 60,000 men choked up in an area that could be measured in city blocks. But this was not so. Despite the litter, wreckage, and apparent chaos, a regular movement of supplies was going ashore, often sorely disrupted by enemy shelling.

Out of the boat, Mr. Forrestal began to walk around the beach, inspecting the unloading, watching our tanks and tractors coming and going, despite the yielding sand which offered so little traction. He asked questions of several men. His admiration of their magnificent work was unstinted.

At first, some of the Marines were skeptical of his identity. They didn't believe any Secretary of the Navy in his right mind would be there on the beach at Iwo Jima, where Japanese shells and mortars still fell. But soon the news spread around and men came from all over, flocking around the visitor, shaking him warmly by the hand.

This growing concentration of men caused me considerable concern. If the Japanese spotted us, they would assume it was an important troop movement and we would have the full force of their guns on our heads in a very short time. I cautioned the Secretary that he must not leave the immediate vicinity of the beach. It was too dangerous. Artillery was falling very close to us. In fact, 20 men were killed or wounded within a hundred yards of where we were standing, but the Secretary seemed utterly indifferent to danger. His *sang froid* impressed us all and, though I could not hide my qualms, I knew I could not deny the men an opportunity to see, hear and shake hands with the Secretary of the Navy.

After the anxious (for me) hour ashore, I persuaded him to return to the *Eldorado*. As we came over the side, I heaved a sigh of relief that he was back again unharmed. Pillars of smoke and loud crashes on the beach showed the Japanese were shelling again. Mr. Forrestal departed from Iwo Jima the next day, leaving Kelly Turner and me with an inspiring message: "The operation is in good hands."

Later, I went back to inspect Suribachi. Harry Liversedge had done a magnificent piece of work in the face of great difficulties. It cost us a thousand casualties, but now our beachhead no longer was threatened from the south and no longer could the enemy on the volcano tell the enemy on the other side of the island what we were up to.

Several hundred Japanese remained alive in the recesses of this smoking rock, necessitating mopping up throughout the campaign. As the details of the volcano's strength became known, the greater appeared the accomplishment of the 28th Regiment. Among the caves and tunnels that riddled the rock, we counted more than a thousand enemy strongpoints. Six hundred Japanese were dead and we estimated that another thousand were holed up in their caves. Suribachi was a gigantic warren and our engineers sealed nearly 200 caves and entrances as tombs for its garrison.

I found a young Marine on guard among the blasted pillboxes at the base of the volcano. He had a Japanese *samurai* sword at his belt.

"We flushed a Jap officer out of a cave over there," he told me, indicating a fire-blackened hole in the face of the cliff where a flame thrower had been used. "He came out waving his sword and we shot him. There were three of us and when we took his sword we couldn't decide which one had killed him and whose sword it was. So we decided to share." Drawing the blade from the scabbard, he added proudly, "It's my turn to wear it today, sir."

I wanted to climb Suribachi and look over Iwo Jima as I had looked over Saipan from Mount Tapotchau, but there was no motor road until later. Asbill went up. When he came back he shook his head and announced, "No, General, I can't let you climb that cliff. You're too old to make it." I accepted his decision. I have commanded hundreds of thousands of men in my life but for the first time I got ordered around by my aide.

I have jumped ahead to describe the heroic capture of Suribachi, because as an individual exploit of the Marines it occupies a special place in history, and now I return to the main battle of Iwo Jima.

In any operation, the first night ashore always is a nervous and often critical period. We believed the Japanese would make their strongest counterattacks against us on that first night, when our position was not too strong. We had 40,000 men ashore, holding an irregular line with a gap between the divisions, but no counterattack in force came. This surprised us, because it was so contrary to enemy tactics. As we advanced up the island, we learned it was part of Kuribayashi's well planned scheme of defense. His basic idea was to occupy a position and refuse to budge until we dug him out. He would waste no men on counterattacks, which would bring the Japanese under fire in force, and tactical withdrawal did not figure in his battle plan. He later altered his scheme to include minor counterattacks but no *banzai* charges.

The weather that favored us on D-day turned against us the following day and greatly complicated the beach situation. The wind whipped up a high surf, making it impossible to use small boats. All our supplies were brought in by LSM's and LST's, hawsered ashore to anchor them and keep their ramps down. This mass of shipping was an easy target for Japanese guns, but we allowed neither beach conditions nor enemy fire to halt the increasing flow of supplies and equipment. We got all our artillery ashore in the next two days and the supply situation, which for a time was serious, improved as beach parties wrestled successfully with sea and ships. Over the yielding, ashy terrain, only amphibious and tracked vehicles could make their way up the terraces, and inland routes had to be cleared of mines before vehicles could move with safety.

On the morning of the second day, during the assault on Suribachi, the Fourth and Fifth Divisions continued their advance and by nightfall we had secured Motoyama Airfield One and thus held a continuous line across the island. Motoyama Airfield Two, adjoining Airfield One on a slightly higher elevation, was our next objective.

The fight for the second airfield, and the third which was under construction beyond, brought us up against the enemy's main line of resistance. This was a broad, deep belt of fortifications running from coast to coast, a mass of mutually supporting pillboxes and concrete bunkers, many of them almost buried underground. Behind were thousands of caves and subterranean positions, in the rocky fastness of the north. This was the "masterpiece of impregnability" produced by the specialists from Japan, who utilized natural caves and dug hundreds more, all interconnected with tunnels, and linked them to underground fortresses 30 to 40 feet below ground, hiding guns and mortars. Beyond the first line of pillboxes, protected by mine fields and accurately placed overlapping fire from hidden guns, the island was a huge warren of holes, caves and passages in rocky ridges and cliff faces. Every day of our advance on Iwo Jima showed us another marvel of defensive construction.

Motoyama Airfield Two again left us with no choice but frontal attack. Only direct hits by large caliber guns had any effect on the blockhouses. In the runways we found pillboxes almost buried in the sand, with machine gun slots protruding a foot or so above ground. On the flat, sandy stretches of the airfield we were exposed not only to fire from the first line of defenses but also from guns in the rear. Bitter fighting, which cost us heavily, measured our gains only in yards. The first two days of the assault on this airfield were the most costly in the entire Iwo Jima operation.

The third day after our landing on the island I released the 21st Regiment, Third Division, which was in floating reserve. This regiment Schmidt attached initially to the Fourth Division, which was in difficulties at the shore end of the ridge. This ridge disappeared into a hollow, oval rise in the ground and the attacking Marines promptly named it the Amphitheater. The enemy had burrowed inside the hollow bowl and fortified it. Our attacks seemed to leave no impression on the Amphitheater, because the

Japanese could get reinforcements through tunnels connecting with their main positions in the formerly wooded area beyond.

Before we reached the southern end of the second airfield, we ran into a solid wall of fire from pillboxes, heavy artillery, mortars of all sizes, and flat trajectory weapons, and, although our attacks were supported by our own artillery, heavy naval gunfire and air strikes, we made little progress. We were in the very heart of the defense belt Kuribayashi had prepared against us for more than a year.

From our heavy casualties and the fact that we were scarcely moving, it was evident to me that another regiment of the Third Division was necessary to relieve the battle-weary troops in the line and provide the additional push that would dislodge the Japanese. Although we appeared to have reached a stalemate, the enemy was ready for a swift punch in the belly. Then we could break through into the northern part of the island, where we thought we would have things all our own way.

I put in the entire Third Division, less the 3rd Regiment, which I kept in reserve. The 21st Regiment reverted to its original divisional control. I doubt if Major General Erskine, commanding the Third Division, his officers or his men ever expected such a dramatic change in their role on Iwo Jima. They had been held in floating reserve and instead of playing the spectator part in the battle they were ordered to spearhead the attack down the center of the island.

I was convinced that Bobby Erskine and his able division would be able to handle the zone assigned to them, and I knew that in the field he would practice the essentials of drive and action he preached to divisional commanders when he was my Chief of Staff. The sector was perhaps the most difficult on the island but I predicted that if we ever got through this defense belt we could go on to complete the capture of Iwo Jima.

Erskine—or the "Big E," as he was known to his men— did punch his way to the sea, driving clear through the enemy's defenses, crossing two fire-swept airfields, and cutting the garrison in two. But this required another 20 days of bitter fighting during which, at one stage, we were forced to call a halt and dig in for a short period to rest the men, who had been fighting under unbelievable pressure.

I went ashore every second day, calling on Harry Schmidt at V Corps Headquarters, or on Rockey, Cates, and Erskine at their Command Posts, and going forward to watch the progress of the fighting. None of these Command Posts was the Hotel Splendide the invading general seizes for himself and his staff in fictional war. Cates' post, overlooking the sea near the fortified quarry, was a knocked-out Japanese pillbox, where the smell of decomposing enemy dead, buried in the ruins, grew more loathesome every day. Erskine, just south of Motoyama Airfield Two, occupied an abandoned Japanese gun emplacement, with a tarpaulin slung over a 4.7-inch dual purpose gun. Over on the left, Rockey had a ramshackle place up against a cliff, where the Japanese had been flushed out recently.

After we captured Suribachi, we began using the western beach for unloading. This was necessary because the eastern beach, where we landed on D-day, was almost choked with wreckage and debris, and conditions were getting worse with every tide. But even on the new western beach prodigious feats of seamanship, stevedoring, and engineering had to be performed to get supplies ashore because the surf was higher and more treacherous than on the east coast. Nevertheless, a direct transport route was opened and through it the front line was fed and supplied.

Corps Headquarters was a group of sandbagged tents near the beach, overlooked by Suribachi, by no means a nice, sheltered rear position. As long as Japanese artillery and mortars remained unsilenced, the front line was everywhere on Iwo Jima—among the pillboxes, in the hills, on the beach, in the rear. Corps Headquarters took a score of shells one night, fortunately without much damage. Since our artillery positions were near Headquarters, it was almost impossible to distinguish the sending from the receiving when Americans and Japanese exchanged fire.

On one trip ashore, I was talking with Harry Schmidt outside his tent. An AKA, a transport loaded with ammunition, anchored off the beach not far from Corps Headquarters. The Japanese spotted the ship's arrival and opened fire with all the artillery they could bring to bear.

The first two salvos fell in rear of the ship but close enough to wound a man on the stern. The captain put on full speed to get away. But the second salvo fell ahead of the ship. Harry and I watched with our hearts in our mouths. (At least mine was.) The enemy had bracketed the ship; would the next shells hit the target? If so, it would be curtains for us, Corps Headquarters and the beach working parties. The explosion of several thousand tons of ammunition would have devastated the lower part of the island.

But the next salvo fell astern of the ship, which had picked up speed and was out of the danger zone. I shall never forget the look on Harry's face when those last shells dropped harmlessly in the sea, but I suppose it was the same look I gave him. It said: The age of miracles hasn't passed, thank God.

After two weeks of terrific fighting, during which each day seemed worse than the last, two-thirds of Iwo Jima was in our possession. We had broken through the main belt of defenses and captured the two operable airfields and the third embryo field. Army P-51 Mustangs and P-61 Black Widows were operating from Motoyama Airfield One, B-29's were using the island's emergency facilities. We were evacuating hundreds of wounded Marines by plane, which greatly eased our hospitalization problem. But there was still bitter fighting ahead. On Iwo the bitter fighting seemed never to end.

Before we reached the wide area of crags and rocky ridges leading to the sheer cliffs at the northern end of the island, we had to pass through the Japanese sulphur wells—a valley of foul emanations that looked like something left over when they finished building Hell. Iwo Jima was a queer contrast. At the lower end of the island and around the airfields, Marines who had fought their way across the Pacific in the tropical heat of coral atolls and jungle islands shivered under blankets in foxholes at night. In the sulphur valley, the ground heat was hot house temperature. Scratching below the surface of this gnarled, misshapen earth, stained deathly white and pestilential yellow by chemical mists, you couldn't dig a foxhole without starting a sulphur steam bath. And you could cook a can of "C" rations by burying it in the ground for 15 minutes.

Beyond this hellish valley lay the road to the sea, but it was a hard road. Kuribayashi had wedded modern fortification science to stubborn rock and earth and built his last line of defense, which ended at Kitano Point and the sea. We had to capture three high hills before we got to grips with him. He had every advantage of shelter and concealment. Crevices and ridges were honeycombed with caves and tunnels. Some of his concrete bunkers had four-foot walls and his artillery, his mortars and rocket launchers were cleverly hidden. We learned about them the hard way—through our sickeningly heavy casualties.

His ground organization was far superior to any I had seen in France during World War I and observers said it excelled German ground organization in World War II. The only way we could move was behind rolling artillery barrages and concentrations of fire that pulverized the area. Then we went in and reduced each position, using flame throwers, grenades, and demolitions. Every cave, every pillbox, every bunker was an individual battle, where Japanese and Marine fought hand to hand to the death.

We had prepared for tank battles, but they did not materialize. The Japanese never moved a tank on Iwo Jima. They used their tanks as additional pillboxes, emplacing them in crevices and behind revetments, using tank guns to cover approaches to strategic points. We employed our tanks in a manner never contemplated in training, over terrain we never believed tanks could cross. Our tanks suffered heavily from mines and the enemy's very effective 47-mm. anti-tank guns but they performed well under totally unexpected circumstances.

What the Japanese most feared was the tank bulldozer (tankdozer), a heavily armored vehicle that pushed a blade in front and could withstand much fire. In this war among caves and human burrows, our tank flame throwers, shooting out a long stream of fire, were invincible against the Japanese— if they got close enough. But they were helpless without the dozers, which had to cut roads through otherwise impassable terrain for the flame tank to advance and burn up the area. This pattern of attack was repeated hundreds of times on Iwo Jima.

Then the Japanese got wise and started to concentrate on the devastating dozer. We had to take special measures to protect them from suicide attacks by the enemy, who always singled them out. We organized armored tank patrols as convoys, but unsuspected electric mines laid on the roads wrecked all our blades before the campaign ended. In the dozers, the Japanese saw death by fire, or entombment, staring them in the face, and our few dozers suffered.

I paid particular attention to the Third Division because I felt that Erskine's drive through the center would be a short cut to victory. Therefore, I made frequent visits to his Command Post and during one visit an orderly brought in Bobby's mail.

One of the great achievements of the Pacific war was the regular delivery of mail in the forward areas. Men up front got letters from home with amazing promptness. Undazzled by brass, the American public regarded a general at the front almost as a member of the family, to be praised, criticized, and appealed to for help in time of trouble. A general's job is not all fighting. The men and women who wrote those letters expected a reply—promptly. And they usually got it.

Bobby's mail that day included a letter from a father asking that his son be sent home to North Dakota on emergency leave, because his mother was seriously ill and wanted to see her boy. A man in New York congratulated the Third Division on its excellent work in Iwo Jima and a mother, writing from a little town in Iowa, wanted the General to tell her son that his favorite sister had died and that his buddy had been killed in France.

It was a saddening letter and I wondered how that boy, fighting the toughest battle of the Pacific war, would react when he learned of the double tragedy. I wondered if I could help soften the blow—even a little—by telling him myself, but I discarded the idea. That was the Chaplain's job and I knew that the man of God would do a better job than the soldier. Erskine agreed and promised me, "We'll find that boy—if he's alive—and the Chaplain will tell him."

Directly in front of Erskine's Third Division, Kuribayashi's interlocking subterranean defense system reached its zenith in the center of our line. In an area of one square mile, a thousand caves and fortified points were counted and going was slow. The Fourth Division, on the right, also was having a hard time. After finally taking the Amphitheater and the commanding hill, the Division surmounted the ridge and faced what seemed a continuation of the ground just covered. On the left, the Fifth Division was having trouble in equally rugged terrain, with heavy resistance coming from a gorge which was reputed to be the headquarters of Kuribayashi himself.

On March 6 we decided a coordinated attack by the whole Corps might break through. The previous day was devoted to resting our tired men and reorganizing. To prepare for the attack we employed artillery on a scale exceeding any previous effort. We laid down a devastating barrage, using all Corps and divisional artillery and heavy guns from supporting warships. After the barrage was lifted, the assault forces ran into unusually heavy resistance. Although most of the enemy's large caliber guns in the immediate front had been destroyed, enough were left in the northeastern part of the island to resist our advances. Moreover, the rocky country made close tank support difficult and reduced the effectiveness of our shelling. As a result, the initial assault bogged down. We made slight gains and could count only a number of destroyed installations and sealed-off caves in our favor. Later in the day we attacked again, supported by a heavy barrage, and did a little better. But by nightfall we had consolidated our line and were in a far stronger position for continued assault.

The next day we tried something we had never attempted in the entire Pacific war. As the preliminary artillery attack of the previous day had little effect, we tried a night attack. The Third Division, in the center, moved off before dawn and took the enemy by surprise. The main objective was Hill 362 C, an anchor of Kuribayashi's defense line. Another purpose was to circumvent enemy artillery fire. Our artillery drove the Japanese into their pillboxes, but when we advanced, their artillery, registered on their own pillboxes, came down upon our attacking troops and inflicted many casualties. By making a night attack we hoped to catch the enemy off guard and reach our objective before he brought his artillery into use.

Although the Third Division did take the Japanese by surprise, the plan was only partially successful. Before the enemy was aware of the Marines, the 3rd Battalion, 9th Marines, had made a fair advance, but when daylight came we discovered that, in the darkness, part of the attacking force had overrun a smaller and less important hill, not the objective hill. The Japanese immediately guessed our objective and fierce fighting ensued. The Marines were called upon to fight as they had never fought before. Two companies were cut off and could not be rescued for 30 hours. Another company was virtually cut to pieces. Doggedly the attack continued, with tanks doing the impossible on impossible terrain, and at the end of the day we had taken that vitally important hill.

Possession of this objective made a great change in the situation, a change reflected immediately in easier progress. On the night of March 8, Kuribayashi made a determined counterattack in the Fourth Marine sector. This was the one attack in force he made on Iwo Jima. It was preceded by heavy mortar, rocket and machine gun fire. The advance started just before midnight.

As soon as the Fourth Division received the first impact of the attack, we started to pour intense artillery fire into this area, which scattered the main body of the enemy. A number of Japanese did get through our lines and reached the Command Post areas, where they were killed. They carried demolition charges. We learned later the object of the attack was a break-through to Motoyama Airfield One to wreck our planes and installations. The advance troops, having found a weak spot in our line, were to be followed by a much larger force. Thus the only counterattack on Iwo Jima that promised the Japanese any results was checked, with heavy losses for them.

On the morning of March 9, we re-opened the attack in the other sectors and, while the Fifth Division recorded a slight gain, the Third Division continued to punch through the center and a six-man patrol from the 21st Regiment clambered over the last ridge dividing us from the northeast coast. To celebrate the event, they splashed in the sea in plain sight of the dumfounded Japanese manning caves on the east side of the ridge but outside the range of their guns—by now they only had small calibers left.

"We wanted to wash off the Jap dirt," one Marine explained. They also scooped up a canteen of sea water and sent it back to Erskine with the famous admonition: "For inspection, not consumption."

Now the Japanese were split in two. The Third Division advanced in the footsteps of the patrol and seized the ridge overlooking the beach. Severance of the two Japanese forces was complete. One was contained in the Fourth Division sector, but the main body of survivors held the rocky area around Kitano Point in the northwest, hemmed in by the Third and Fifth Divisions. The capture of Iwo Jima was in sight.

With the reduction of enemy-held territory to two small areas occupied by only a fraction of the original garrison, resistance decreased, but we did not relax pressure. Artillery barrages, poundings by naval guns, and air strikes were maintained as a matter of routine, although shrinking enemy terrain made these assaults somewhat unmanageable. Kuribayashi was reported still alive, commanding the group in the caves at Kitano Point. He gave no indication that he would surrender, which did not surprise us overmuch.

The last enemy artillery fire fell in our lines on the morning of March 11, a few hours before we launched our final attack. The Fourth Division, with elements of the Third, jumped off in the eastern sector without any artillery preparation and by mid-afternoon reported all organized resistance had been eliminated. The Japanese in this pocket were well dug in among deep crevices connected with caves and tunnels, and fought desperately as their lines shrank around them. It took us five days to wipe out that pocket.

For the Kitano Point assault, the fire power of all three

regiments of artillery, plus the Corps artillery, was brought to bear on that stubborn corner in a rolling barrage of exceptional intensity. This was augmented by warship fire and air attack. For nearly an hour, the rocky area was blasted, with apparently little result. The only direct route to the main enemy fortifications was a rocky gorge, 200 yards wide and 700 yards long. Entrance to the gorge was denied us by covering machine gun and rifle fire.

This was Kuribayashi's last stand. Undoubtedly he was in command and his personality was apparent in the tenacity of the defense. Although his forces had been reduced to a shadow, he suffered no lack of small arms and supplies. There was nothing to do but proceed methodically against cave after cave, pillbox after pillbox, advancing by the yard, until the enemy was wiped out.

The Third Division, on the right at Kitano Point, quickly cleared its sector, but two weeks elapsed before we finally cleaned out the area. This task fully occupied the attention of the Fifth Division after the island was declared secured and the fifth suffered heavily. There were no suicide leaps on Iwo Jima. The Japanese fought to the end and made mopping up expensive. Kuribayashi was determined to take every last American with him.

On March 26, the Japanese made a carefully prepared sortie from their caves. This was their last counterattack, and it caused much confusion and many casualties before they were annihilated. A prisoner said that Kuribayashi was among the officers who came out, swords at their sides, to make this final demonstration, but an examination of the bodies, swords, and personal papers revealed no trace of him. Perhaps he was killed at that time; perhaps he died in one of the thousands of caves sealed by the Marines. I do not know.

The official flag raising on Iwo Jima was held at V Corps Headquarters on the morning of March 14, two days before the island was declared secured. The ceremony was attended by flag and general officers of the fleet and landing force, and Military Government Proclamation Number I, proclaiming United States sovereignty over the Volcano Islands, was published. The original flag, which had flown on Suribachi, was removed.

Tears filled my eyes when I stood at attention and saluted the flag. The ceremony marked the capture of Iwo Jima and the end of the most terrific battle in the history of the Marine Corps. The mission to take the island had been carried out successfully and I was proud, although this pride was saddened by the realization that so many brave men had given their lives to perform that mission. On a personal note, too, the ceremony was saddening, because Iwo Jima was my last combat command.

This momentous event gave pause for reflection. The amount of effort that had gone into the capture of the barren island was staggering. The Navy had put more ammunition on Iwo Jima than anywhere else in the Pacific. Marine artillery expended 450,000 shells and we used huge quantities of mortar shells, grenades, and rockets. Our air force made it the principal target this side of Japan proper. Yet, in the final analysis, it was the man on the beach with his rifle who completed the job.

Our casualties were extremely heavy among both officers and men. The average battalion, landing with 36 officers and 885 enlisted men, was reduced to approximately 16 officers and 300 men at the end of the campaign. Many company commanders, platoon leaders, and squad leaders were casualties. Pfc's found themselves platoon leaders and junior officers became company commanders. One Fourth Division captain commanded a battalion throughout all but the first few days of the battle. Iwo Jima proved the falsity of the theory that regiments or battalions which are decimated can never win battles. Our regiments and battalions were down to a record low in combat efficiency, owing to losses, but morale remained at an inspiring high, and morale is the decisive factor in a battle of such intensity.

No single chapter, no single book could describe that battle. To tell the story of Iwo Jima, I would have to tell the individual story of every man in the assault force. As Admiral Nimitz said: "Among the Americans who served on Iwo Island, uncommon valor was a common virtue."

I have been criticized for my conduct of the Iwo Jima operation. "Why didn't you use gas?" has been the most frequent question. During the first week in March, 1945, a Washington newspaper came out boldly with the challenge: "Give Our Boys a Break—Gas the Japs."

I am not prepared to argue this question. Certainly, gas shells smothering the island, or gas introduced into caves and tunnels would have simplified our task, but naturally the use of this prohibited weapon was not within the power of a field commander. The decision was on a higher level. It was in the hands of the Allied Powers, who alone could authorize its use in a war which would have assumed even more frightful proportions had gas been allowed.

Another suggestion, made later, was that we should have used the atom bomb. It is true that atomic bombing would have destroyed Iwo Jima but, as far as I know, we did not possess the bomb at that time. The final successful test was made four months later, in New Mexico. Therefore we took the island the only way possible, the way I have described.

I left Iwo Jima on March 17 for Guam and after a few days there returned to Headquarters of the Fleet Marine Corps, Pacific, at Pearl Harbor. On July 3, I handed over that command to Lieutenant General Geiger and returned to the United States.

I found it hard to tear myself away from the force I had commanded throughout the Central Pacific campaign, but the time had come for me to go. I said my farewell at a ceremony held at Camp Catlin. Captain John A. De Chant, USMCR, described it as I like to remember it:

He stood there, proudly, tears rolling unchecked and unashamed down his cheeks.

"Au revoir, God bless you . . . and I believe in you." With that Howlin' Mad Smith took leave of his Pacific Marines. He stepped down from the little bandstand and his fingers pushed underneath his horn-rimmed glasses to brush away the tears.

He wasn't the only one. Next to me stood a young Raider colonel. He had been crying, just as unashamed, from the moment the Old Man had stopped up to make his last impromptu speech to the command. And there were dozens like him all over the room. The leather-faced old men who'd come up through the ranks with him and the kid majors and the young lieutenants who loved him. They had gathered in the low-ceilinged officers' club at Camp Catlin—the flyers and the line alike—in their last little tribute to the man from Alabama who had inspired them across the Pacific.

General Roy Geiger had said the Old Man wasn't going home because he was tired. And when you looked at him there, with the field musics grouped behind him, you were sure of that.

"When I was a first lieutenant, which was before most of you were born (and the grin wrinkled his face) I made a promise to the Great God that, if I was ever in a position to do so, I would see to it that Marines were treated with the decency and respect that are due to them. I started back in 1938. I advise you not to try it—unless you are lucky, damned lucky—because you may not be as lucky as I was."

Then he told of the Marines who had "marched across the Pacific" and of Geiger, now his successor, who took the southern prong . . . Guadalcanal . . . Bougainville . . . Peleliu . . . and turned north to Okinawa . . . while "we in the the Central Pacific," and he tolled off the bloody stepping stones from Tarawa to Iwo Jima which the men under his personal command had taken.

"They went to the front door of Japan," he said, "and nothing stopped them. Nothing will!"

He had talked brilliantly and easily until then. Bushy browed, clean and smart-looking, the Old Man was telling the story that he had lived and was now his whole heart.

"Out there are the bodies of 15,000 Marines (and he choked a hurt sob) that lie buried under the burning tropical sun. Remember them."

He tried to gruff himself back into line with "I shouldn't say any more. I'm getting too damned sentimental."

And the young colonel cried silently, not even bothering with the crumpled handkerchief in his hand. Like the other hundreds in the room, this was hurting him as deeply as the Old Man himself.

At the end, he joked a little about fishing. "I'm going to try that," he said, "they tell me it's good for *old men*." And we laughed with him at that.

Roy Geiger had paid him the adequate compliment. "He fought enemies—and friends—for what he believed in. And that was you." And no one knew it better than the living who stood there or the 15,000 Marines who died violently with their faces to the enemy. He had lived on their courage and devotion . . . and they on his.

His staff of the Fleet Marine Force went out there to the airfield in the gathering dusk to see him off from his last mission. He said a few words to each one of them. Nothing trite or hasty nor in bravado because he couldn't. That wasn't his way. What little he said hit the men around him below the belt. And the cold-blooded beachhead veterans cried again because this was finality. The lovable and brilliant Old Man was going home from his last war.

Somewhere in history—or tomorrow—other generals may have more stars, or better profiles, or more headlines, or more on the political ball. But Howlin' Mad Smith was like a military Franklin Roosevelt; when he left, something of you went with him. He had bulldog courage . . . to beat and beller down all who stood in the way of his Marines. He is the unchallenged master of amphibious warfare . . . a brilliant tactician . . . and unbested field general. But it was his heart that made him truly great. A big kindly heart . . . even bigger it seemed, at times, than his own body. For this great and grand Old Man had inside him the hearts of all his Pacific Marines . . . living and dead . . . as they had his. Tonight, he cried and they cried . . . in simple, unaffected proof.

My last assignment was as Commanding General of the Marine Training and Replacement Command at San Diego. I retired from the Marine Corps on May 15, 1946, at the age of 64.

Today I live in a little white house by the side of the road, strive to be a friend to my fellow man, and raise flowers, vegetables, and grandchildren.

INDEX

5000